Ohio
Atlas & Gazetteer™

D1561232

1 inch equals 23 miles

Grid numbers refer to detailed map pages

© DeLorme

SEVENTH EDITION. Copyright © 2004 DeLorme. All rights reserved.
P.O. Box 298, Yarmouth, Maine 04096   (207) 846-7000   www.delorme.com

Table of Contents

THE ATLAS

THE GAZETTEER

Index

4

5

Louisville 52 B1
Louisville 84 A1
Loveland 75 B5
Loveland Park 75 B5
Lovell 47 A6
Lowdon 51 D6
Lowell 38 C1
Lowell 71 D6
Lowellville 43 D7
Lower Newport 73 D5
Lower Salem 71 D7
Lucas 49 C6
Lucasburg 71 A6
Lucasville 85 A5
Lucerne 59 A4
Luckey 37 A5
Ludington 70 D1
Ludlow Falls 65 A5
Luhrig 80 B1
Lumberton 66 D2
Lunda 57 B4
Luray 67 D4
Luray 69 A5
Luttrell 66 D3
Lybrand 57 B7
Lykens 48 A1
Lynchburg 52 C4
Lynchburg 76 C2
Lyndhurst 31 D7
Lyndon 77 B6
Lynn 58 A1
Lynns Corners 43 D6
Lynx 84 B1
Lyons 25 C7
Lyra 85 C7
Lysander 80 B2
Lytle 65 D6
Lytton 26 C1

M

Mabee Corner 85 A7
Macedon 54 A1
Macedonia 41 B6
Macedonia 74 B1
Mack 74 C2
Macksburg 71 C7
Mackstown 58 C2
Macon 83 A6
Madden Corners 43 C6
Madeira 75 C5
Madison 32 B3
Madison Hill 50 B3
Madison Lake 67 B5
Madison Mills 67 C6
Madison on the Lake 32 B3
Madisonburg 50 B3
Madisonville 75 C4
Magnetic Springs 57 B6
Magnolia 52 C1
Mahoning 42 B3
Maineville 75 B6
Mainsville 70 C1
Malaga 72 B2
Malinta 35 B7
Mallet Creek 40 C3
Malta 70 C4
Malvern 52 C2
Manara 67 D6
Manchester 51 A6
Manchester 83 C6
Mandale 35 D5
Manker 86 D1
Mansfield 49 B5
Mantua 42 B2
Mantua 61 D5
Mantua Center 42 B2
Mantua Corners 42 B2
Maple 82 A3
Maple Corner 66 D1
Maple Grove 37 C7
Maple Grove 42 B3
Maple Grove 78 A1
Maple Heights 41 A6
Maple Ridge 52 A3
Maple Valley 41 D6
Mapleton 52 C1
Maplewood 55 A7
Marathon 75 C7
Marble Cliff 68 A1
Marble Furnace 84 A1
Marblehead 28 D4
Marchand 51 A7
Marcy 68 B3
Marengo 58 A3
Maria Stein 54 A4
Mariemont 75 C4
Marietta 81 A7
Marion 48 D1
Mark Center 34 B2
Marl City 56 A3
Marlboro 52 A2
Marne 59 D7
Marquand Mills 61 C4
Marquis 53 A5
Marr 72 C2
Marseilles 47 C5
Marshall 77 C5
Marshallville 51 A5
Martel 48 C2
Martin 27 D6
Martins Ferry 63 D5
Martinsburg 59 B7
Martinsville 50 D4
Martinsville 76 B2
Marysville 57 C5
Mason 75 B5
Massieville 78 B2
Massillion 51 B6
Masury 43 C7
Mathers Mill 75 A7
Matville 68 B1
Maud 75 B4
Maumee 26 D3
Maustown 74 A4
Maximo 52 A2
Maxville 69 D7
May Hill 77 D4
Maybee 49 B5
Mayburn Corners 43 A7
Mayfield 31 D7
Mayfield Heights 31 D7
Maynard 63 D5
Maysville 46 C1
Maysville 51 C4
Maysville 61 C4
Maysville 70 A2
McArthur 79 C6
McAvan 81 A6
McCance 50 C3
McCartyville 55 A5
McClainville 63 D5
McClimansville 67 C6
McClure 36 B1
McComb 36 D2
McConnelsville 70 C4
McCoppin Mill 77 C5
McCracken Corners 53 B5
McCuneville 70 C1
McCutchenville 47 A6
McDaniel Crossroad 86 B2
McDermott 84 B4
McDonald 43 C6
McDonald 70 B4
McDonaldsville 51 A7
McFarlands Corners 42 A1
McGaw 84 C3
McGill 34 D1
McGonigle 74 A2
McGuffey 46 C2
McGuffey Heights 43 C7
McIntyre 63 B5
McKay 50 C1
McKays Corners 43 D6
McKendree 67 B6
McKinley Heights 43 C6
McLean 77 A6
McLeish 70 D2
McLuney 70 C2
McMorran 56 A2
McVitty 47 B4
McZena 50 C1
Meacham Corners 43 A5
Mead Corners 58 A4
Meade 68 D2
Meadowbrook 70 A2
Mecca 43 A6
Mechanicsburg 48 A3
Mechanicsburg 50 B3
Mechanicsburg 57 D4
Mechanicstown 52 D4
Mechanicsville 33 B4
Mechanicsville 72 C3
Medina 40 C3
Medway 65 A7
Meeker 47 C6
Meeker 54 C2
Meigs 71 C4
Meigs 80 C3
Melbern 34 A2
Melco 49 C7
Melmore 38 D1
Melrose 35 D4
Melvin 76 A3
Memphis 76 A4
Mendon 44 C3
Mentor 32 C1
Mentor Headlands 32 C1
Mentor on the Lake 31 C7, 32 C1
Mentzer 46 D4
Mercer 44 C3
Mercerville 86 C3
Meredith 57 A7
Mermill 36 B3
Merriam 70 B3
Merritt 80 D4
Merwin 75 D5
Mesopotamia 42 A4
Metamora 26 C1
Metham 60 B3
Metzger 78 A2
Mexico 47 A7
Meyers Lake 51 B7
Miami Heights 74 C2
Miami Villa 65 B6
Miamisburg 65 C5
Miamitown 74 C2
Miamiville 75 C5
Middle Corners 43 A5
Middle Point 44 B4
Middleboro 75 B7
Middlebourne 62 D1
Middlebranch 52 A1
Middleburg 56 B4
Middleburg 63 A4
Middleburg 71 C7
Middleburg Heights 41 B4
Middlebury 44 B2
Middlefield 42 A3
Middleport 80 D2, 87 A5
Middleton 53 B6
Middleton 79 D6
Middleton Corner 66 D2
Middletown 48 B3
Middletown 56 C4
Middletown 65 D4, 75 A4
Middletown Junction 75 B6
Midland 76 B1
Midvale 61 A7
Midway 26 D2
Midway 55 D6
Midway 63 C4
Midway 64 A4
Midway 67 C5
Midway 80 D2
Mifflin 49 B7
Mifflinville 58 D2
Milan 39 B5
Miley Crossroads 50 D2
Milford 75 C5
Milford Center 57 C5
Milfordton 59 B5
Mill Grove 71 D5
Mill Rock 53 B7
Millbrook 50 C2
Millbury 27 D5
Milledgeville 66 D4
Miller 86 D3
Miller City 35 D6
Miller Grove 54 D4
Miller Station 63 B4
Millers Corners 51 D4
Millers Corners 58 D4
Millersburg 50 D3
Millersport 69 A5
Millerstown 56 C1
Millersville 37 B6
Millertown 70 D2
Millfield 80 A2
Milligan 70 C2
Millport 53 C4
Millport 68 C2
Mills 85 C6
Mills 86 B4
Millsboro 49 C4
Millville 53 A5
Millville 74 A2
Millwood 59 A7
Milton Center 36 B2
Miltonsburg 72 B2
Miltonville 64 D4
Mina 34 A2
Mineral 79 B7
Mineral City 52 D1
Mineral Ridge 43 C5
Mineral Springs 84 A2
Minersville 80 D3
Minerton 79 D6
Minerva 52 C2
Minerva Junction 52 C2
Minerva Park 58 D2
Mineyahta on the Bay 28 D4
Minford 85 B6
Mingo 56 C3
Mingo Junction 63 B6
Minster 55 A5
Misco 70 C2
Mishler 52 A1
Misner Corners 43 D5
Mitchaw 26 C2
Mitchells Mill 32 D1
Mitiwanga 39 A6
Moats 34 B3
Modest 75 C7
Modoc 80 A1
Moffitt 36 D2
Moffitt Heights 51 B6
Mogadore 41 D7
Mohawk Village 60 B2
Mohicanville 50 C1
Moline 27 D4
Momeneetown 27 C5
Monclova 26 D3
Monday 80 A1
Monday Circle 69 D7
Monfort Heights 74 C3
Monnett 48 C1
Mononcue 47 B6
Monroe 66 C2
Monroe 75 A5
Monroe 86 B1
Monroe Center 33 B7
Monroe Mills 59 A7
Monroe Station 85 B7
Monroefield 72 B2
Monroeville 38 C4
Monroeville 53 D5
Monterey 54 A1
Monterey 75 C7
Montezuma 54 A3
Montgomery 75 C5
Monticello 45 C4
Montpelier 24 D3
Montra 55 A7
Montrose 41 C5
Montville 32 D3
Moonville 79 B7
Moore Junction 81 A6
Moorefield 62 C2
Moores Fork 75 C7
Moores Junction 70 C2
Mooresville 78 B3
Moraine 65 C6
Moran 41 B7
Moreland 50 C3
Moreland Corners 58 D4
Moreland Hills 41 A7
Morgan Center 59 B6
Morgan Center 86 A3
Morgan Place 65 B5
Morgan Run 61 B4
Morgandale 43 B5
Morgantown 53 A6
Morgantown 77 C7
Morganville 70 C3
Morges 52 C2
Morning Sun 64 D2
Morningview 63 C5
Morral 47 C7
Morristown 62 D3
Morristown 80 A1
Morrisville 76 B2
Morrow 75 B7
Mortimer (North Findlay) 36 D3
Morton 72 C4
Moscow 82 B2
Moscow Mills 71 C6
Moss Run 73 C5
Moulton 45 D5
Moultrie 52 B3
Mound 60 A4
Mound Crossing 69 D4
Mountain Lake Camp 56 A3
Mountville 70 D3
Mowrystown 76 D2
Moxahala 70 C1
Moxahala Park 70 A2
Mt Adams 74 D3
Mt Air 58 C1
Mt Airy 74 C3
Mt Auburn 74 C3
Mt Blanchard 47 A4
Mt Blanco 79 C7
Mt Carmel 38 B2
Mt Carmel 75 D5
Mt Carmel Heights 75 D5
Mt Carrick 72 B3
Mt Cory 46 A2
Mt Eaton 51 C5
Mt Ephraim 71 B7
Mt Gilead 48 D3
Mt Healthy 74 C3
Mt Heron 54 C2
Mt Holly 65 D7
Mt Holly 75 D6
Mt Hope 51 C4
Mt Jefferson 55 C5
Mt Joy 84 A3
Mt Liberty 59 B4
Mt Lookout 75 C4
Mt Nebo 80 A2
Mt Olive 82 A3
Mt Orab 76 D1
Mt Perry 70 A1
Mt Pisgah 82 A2
Mt Pleasant 51 A7
Mt Pleasant 63 C5
Mt Pleasant 66 D2
Mt Pleasant 79 A6
Mt Repose 75 C6
Mt Sinai 78 C3
Mt Sterling 67 C6
Mt Sterling 70 A1
Mt Summit 75 D5
Mt Vernon 59 A6
Mt Victory 47 D4
Mt Washington 75 D4
Mt Zion 71 B6
Muddy Corners 55 D4
Mudsock 57 D7
Mulberry 75 C5
Mulberry Corners 32 D1
Mulberry Grove 55 D5
Mule Town 85 B6
Mulga 79 D6
Muncie Hollow 38 A1
Mungen 36 B3
Munks Corners 68 A2
Munroe Falls 41 C7
Munson Hill 33 B5
Muntanna 45 A5
Murdock 75 B6
Murlin Heights 65 B6
Murphy 73 D6
Murray City 70 D1
Museville 71 B4
Muskingum 72 D2
Musselman 77 B7
Muttonville 64 C2
Mutual 56 D3
Myers 52 B2
Myers Corners 59 B4
Myersville 51 A7

N

Nace Corner (Naceville) 77 D6
Naceville, see Nace Corner
Nankin 49 A7
Naomi 35 A6
Napier 81 B5
Napoleon 35 A6
Narva 62 B4
Nashport 60 D1
Nashport Station 60 D1
Nashville 50 D2
Nashville 54 D1
Nashville 65 A5
Navarre 51 C6
Naylor 52 A4
Neals Corner 82 A4
Neapolis 36 A2
Nebraska 68 C2
Needfull 76 D2
Needmore 45 B5
Needmore 54 C3
Neel 83 B6
Neelysville 71 C4
Neffs 63 D5
Negley 53 B7
Nellie 60 B2
Nelson 42 B3
Nelsonville 80 A1
Neptune 44 D4
Netop 81 A7
Nettle Lake 24 C2
Nevada 47 B7
Neville 82 B2
New Albany 53 A5
New Albany 58 D3
New Alexander 52 B3
New Alexandria 63 B6
New Antioch 76 A3
New Athens 62 C4
New Baltimore 52 A1
New Baltimore 74 B2
New Bavaria 35 C6
New Bedford 61 A4
New Bloomington 47 D6
New Boston 85 B5
New Bremen 55 A5
New Buffalo 53 A6
New Burlington 66 D1
New Burlington 74 B3
New California 57 C7
New Carlisle 65 A7
New Castle 72 A3
New Castle 85 D7
New Chicago 65 C5
New Concord 61 D5, 71 A5
New Cumberland 52 D1
New Dover 57 C6
New England 80 B3
New Floodwood 80 A1
New Franklin 52 B3
New Garden 53 B4
New Germany 65 B7
New Gottingen 71 A7
New Guilford 60 B1
New Hagerstown 62 A2
New Hampshire 46 D1
New Harmony 75 D7
New Harrisburg 52 D2
New Harrison 54 D3
New Haven 39 D4
New Haven 74 B1
New Holland 67 D6
New Hope 64 B2
New Hope 83 A4
New Hope Station 64 B2
New Jasper 66 C2
New Jasper Station 66 C2
New Jerusalem 56 B3
New Knoxville 55 A5
New Lebanon 65 C4
New Lexington 64 B3
New Lexington 70 C1
New London 39 D6
New Lyme 33 D5
New Lyme Station 33 D5
New Madison 64 A2
New Market 76 C3
New Marshfield 80 B1
New Martinsburg 77 A5
New Matamoras 72 D3
New Miami 74 A3
New Middleton 53 B4
New Middletown 53 A7
New Milford 42 D2
New Moorefield 66 A3
New Moscow 60 C3
New Palestine 75 D5
New Paris 64 B1
New Petersburg 77 B5
New Philadelphia 51 D7, 61 A7
New Pittsburg 50 B2
New Pittsburg 70 D1
New Pittsburgh 48 A4
New Plymouth 79 A6
New Princeton 60 A2
New Reading 69 B7
New Richland 56 A2
New Richmond 82 A1
New Riegel 37 D6
New Rochester 34 C3
New Rochester 37 B4
New Rome 67 A7
New Rumley 62 A3
New Salem 69 B6
New Salisbury 53 D6
New Somerset 53 D6
New Springfield 53 A7
New Stark 46 B3
New Straitsville 70 D1
New Strasburg 68 C3
New Town 70 D1
New Vienna 76 B3
New Washington 48 A3
New Waterford 53 B6
New Way 59 C5
New Weston 54 B2
New Westville 64 B1
New Winchester 48 C2
Newark 59 D6
Newbern 55 B6
Newburgh Heights 41 A5
Newbury Center 42 A2
Newcastle 60 B1
Newcomerstown 61 B6
Newell 63 B5
Newell Run 73 D6
Newfain 77 D6
Newkirk 74 A1
Newman 51 B6
Newmans 57 A7
Newport 55 B5
Newport 62 B1
Newport 67 B5
Newport 73 D6
Newton Falls 42 C4
Newtonsville 75 C7
Newtown 63 C5
Newtown 75 D5
Newville 49 C6
Ney 34 A3
Nicholsville 82 A2
Niles 43 C5
Niles Beach 27 C6
Niles Junction 43 C5
Nineveh 54 D3
Nipgen 77 C7
No Name 78 D1
Norristown 52 C4
North Auburn 48 A3
North Baltimore 36 C3
North Bend 74 C2
North Benton 52 A3
North Benton Station 52 A3
North Berne 69 C5
North Brewster 51 C6
North Bristol 43 A5
North Canton 51 A7
North College Hill 74 C3
North Condit 58 B3
North Creek 35 C6
North Dayton 54 B1
North Eaton 40 B3
North Fairfield 39 D5
North Findlay, see Mortimer
North Fork Village 78 B1
North Georgetown 52 B4
North Greenfield 56 A4
North Hampton 66 A1
North Hill 41 D6
North Industry 52 C1
North Jackson 43 D5
North Kingman 66 D1
North Kingsville 33 A6
North Lawrence 51 B5
North Lewisburg 57 C4
North Liberty 49 D6
North Lima 53 A6
North Madison 32 B3
North Monroeville 38 B4
North Moreland 85 B5
North Olmsted 40 A3
North Perry 32 B2
North Randall 41 A6
North Richmond 33 C7
North Ridgeville 40 A2
North Robinson 48 B3
North Royalton 41 B4
North Salem 61 C6
North Star 54 B3
North Uniontown 77 D5
North Woodbury 49 D4
North Zanesville 70 A2
Northbrook 74 C3
Northfield 41 B6
Northfield Center 41 B6
Northhampton Center 41 C6
Northridge 65 B6
Northridge 66 A2
Northup 86 B3
Northville 56 C2
Northwood 27 D5
Northwood 56 A3
Norton 41 D5
Norton 58 A1
Norwalk 39 C5
Norwich 71 A4
Norwood 74 C4
Norwood 81 A7
Nova 39 D7
Novelty 42 A1
Nunda 49 D7
Nutwood 43 B6

O

O'Connor Point 56 A2
Oak Grove 81 A7
Oak Harbor 27 D7
Oak Hill 60 A1
Oak Hill 86 A1
Oak Knoll 47 D7
Oak Park 62 B4
Oak Ridge 51 B6
Oakdale 70 D2
Oakfield 43 A5
Oakfield 70 C2
Oakgrove 62 C2
Oakland 68 D3
Oakland 76 A1
Oakland 78 D4
Oakley 75 C4
Oakshade 25 C6
Oakthorpe 69 B6
Oakview 45 C6
Oakwood 35 D4
Oakwood 41 B6
Oakwood 65 C6
Oberlin 40 B1
Oberlin Beach 39 A5
Obetz 68 A2
Oceola 48 B1
Oco 62 D4
Octa 66 D4
Odell 61 C7
Ogden 76 A1
Ogontz 39 B6
Ohio City 44 B2
Ohio Furnace 85 D6
Okeana 74 B1
Okey 86 D2
Oklahoma 64 B2
Okolona 35 B6
Olbers 80 A2
Old Fort 37 C7
Old Washington 61 D7
Oldham 61 D6
Oldtown 66 C1
Olena 39 C5
Olentangy 48 B3
Olive Branch 75 D6
Olive Furnace 85 B7
Olive Green 58 B3
Olive Green 71 C6
Olivesburg 49 A6
Olivett 62 D2
Olmsted Falls 40 A3
Omar 38 C3
Omega 78 C2
Oneida 52 C2
Oneida 75 A4
Ontario 49 B5
Opperman 71 A6
Oran 55 B5
Orange 41 A7
Orange 58 C1
Orange 61 B5
Orangeburg 64 B1
Orangeville 43 B7
Orbiston 80 A1
Orchard Beach 39 A6
Orchard Island 56 A1
Oregon 27 C5
Oregonia 75 A7
Oreton 79 C6
Oreville 69 D7
Orient 67 B7
Orland 79 A6
Orpheus 86 A2
Orrville 51 B4
Orwell 33 D5
Osage 63 A6
Osborn Corners 41 C5
Osceola 75 B7
Osgood 54 B3
Ostrander 57 B7
Otsego 36 A2
Otsego 61 D4
Ottawa 35 D7
Ottawa Hills 26 C3
Otter 57 B5
Otterbein 64 A2
Otterbein 75 A5
Ottokee 25 D6
Ottoville 45 A5
Otway 84 B3
Outville 69 A5
Overlook Hills 63 A6
Overpeck 74 A3
Overton 50 B2
Owens 47 D7
Owens Hills 70 A2
Owensville 75 D6
Owensville 85 B4
Oxford 64 D2, 74 A1
Ozark 72 B3

P

Padanaram 33 C7
Padua 44 D1
Page Manor 65 B7
Paget 58 B1
Pagetown 58 B3
Pageville 80 C1
Painesville 32 C1
Painesville on the Lake 32 B2
Paint Valley 50 D2

continued on next page

State Road 43 B4
Station 15 62 A1
Staunton 55 D6
Staunton 77 A5
Steam Corners 49 C4
Steamburg 33 C6
Steel Point 54 D3
Steel Run 73 C6
Steinersville 73 B5
Stella 79 B5
Stelvideo 54 C3
Stemple 52 D3
Sterling 50 A4
Steuben 39 D4
Steubenville 63 B6
Stewart 80 B3
Stewartsville 63 D5
Stillwater 62 B1
Stillwater Junction 65 B5
Stillwell 60 A2
Stiversville 81 D4
Stockdale 85 A6
Stockdale Siding 85 A5
Stockham 85 C4
Stockport 71 D4
Stockton 74 B3
Stone 70 B3
Stone Creek 61 A6
Stonelick 75 D6
Stoneville 32 D4
Stoney Hill 41 C5
Stony Ridge 27 C4
Stony Ridge 43 D5
Storms 77 C7
Stoudertown 68 B4
Stoutsville 68 D3
Stovertown 70 B3
Stow 41 C7
Straitsville 70 D1
Strasburg 51 D6
Stratford 58 B1
Stratton 53 D6
Streetsboro 42 C1
Stringtown 50 C3
Stringtown 60 D2
Stringtown 65 B5
Stringtown 68 D3
Stringtown 70 C2
Stringtown 76 D1
Stringtown 77 C5
Stringtown 80 B3
Stringtown 82 B3
Stringtown 83 B5
Strongs Ridge 38 B3
Strongsville 40 B4
Stroups 43 B4
Struthers 43 D7
Stryker 25 D4, 35 A4
Stubbs Mills 75 B6
Success 80 C4
Suffield 42 D1
Suffield Station 42 D1
Sugar Bush Knolls 42 C1
Sugar Creek 80 A2
Sugar Grove 53 D6
Sugar Grove 55 D5
Sugar Grove 69 C5
Sugar Grove 85 C4
Sugar Ridge 36 A4
Sugar Tree Ridge 76 D3
Sugar Valley 64 C2
Sugarcreek 51 D5, 61 A5
Suiter 86 D2
Sullivan 40 D1
Sulphur Grove 65 B7
Sulphur Lick 78 B1
Sulphur Springs 48 B3
Sulphur Springs 70 D1
Summerford 72 B1
Summerford 67 A5
Summerside 75 D5
Summerside Estates 75 C5
Summit Corners 43 C6
Summit Station 68 A3
Summithill 78 C1
Summitville 54 C4
Sumner 80 C3
Sunaire 74 D2
Sunbury 58 C3
Sunbury 65 D4
Sundale 71 A4
Sundale 75 C5
Sunnyland 66 A2
Sunnyside 39 A4
Sunray 70 A3
Sunset Beach 42 D4
Sunset Harbor 38 A2
Sunset Heights 63 D5
Sunshine 84 C2
Superior 85 C7
Swan Creek 86 D4
Swander, see Ink
Swanders 55 B6
Swanktown 65 B4
Swans 59 D7
Swanson 63 A4
Swanton 26 D1
Swartz Mill 69 C5
Swazey 72 B1
Sweetwine 75 D4
Swift 71 D5
Switzer 73 B4
Sybene 87 D6
Sycamore 47 A7
Sycamore 75 B5
Sycamore Valley 72 C2

T

Tabor 52 D2
Taborville 42 B1
Tacoma 72 A2
Talawanda Springs 64 D1
Tallmadge 41 D7
Tallmans 81 C5
Tama 44 D3
Tampico 54 D1
Tappan 62 B2
Tarlton 68 D3
Tawawa 55 C7
Taylor Corners 43 D5
Taylor Station 68 A3
Taylors Creek 74 C2
Taylorsburg 65 B5
Taylorsville 65 B6
Taylorsville 76 D3
Taylortown 49 B5
Taylortown 63 A6
Tedrow 25 D6
Teegarden 53 B5
Temperanceville 72 A2
Tennyson 78 D1
Terrace Park 75 C5
Terre Haute 56 D2
Texas 36 A1
Thacher 68 D2
Thackery 56 D1
The Bend 34 B3
The Eastern 63 A4
The Pines 74 D2
The Plains 80 B1
The Point 77 C6
The Village of Indian Hill 75 C5
Thelma 25 C6
Thivener 86 C4
Thomas 80 D2
Thomastown 41 D7
Thompson 32 C3
Thornport 69 A6
Thornville 69 A6
Thorps 66 A3
Three Forks 71 C6
Three Locks 78 B2
Thrifton 77 B6
Thurman 86 A2
Thurston 69 B5
Tibbetts Corners 43 C6
Tick Ridge 81 B5
Tiffin 37 D7
Tilton Crossroads 60 C1
Tiltonsville 63 C6
Tim Corners 59 A4
Timberlake 31 C7
Tinney 37 B6
Tipp City 65 A6
Tippecanoe 62 B1
Tipton 34 D2
Tiro 47 A7
Tiverton Center 60 A1
Tobasco 75 D5
Tobias 48 C1
Toboso 60 D1
Todds 70 D4
Toledo 26 C4
Toledo Junction 49 B5
Tom Corwin 79 D5
Tomlison Addition 85 A5
Tontogany 36 A3
Toots Corners 53 A5
Toots Crossroads 52 D3
Top of the Ridge 75 C5
Torch 81 C4
Toronto 63 A7
Townwood 36 D1
Tradersville 57 D4, 67 A5
Trail 51 D5
Trail Run 72 D3
Tranquility 83 A7
Trebein 66 C1
Tremont City 56 D2
Trenton 74 A4
Triadelphia 70 C3
Trimble 80 A2
Trinway 69 C2
Triumph Corners 43 A5
Trombley 36 B3
Trotwood 65 B5
Trowbridge 27 D6

Troy 55 D6
Troyton 58 A1
Truetown 80 A2
Trumbull 32 C4
Tucson 78 B3
Tulip 84 C1
Tunnel 81 A6
Tunnel Hill 60 B2
Tuppers Plains 80 C4
Turkey Foot Corner 33 C5
Turpin Hills 75 D5
Tuscarawas 61 A7
Twelve Corners 58 C4
Twenty Mile Stand 75 B5
Twightwee 75 B5
Twin Bridges 81 B5
Twin Valley 85 B5
Twinsburg 41 B7
210 Row 80 B2
Tylers Corners 59 D4
Tylersville 75 B4
Tymochtee 47 A6
Tyndall 60 C3
Tyner 61 D6
Tyrone 60 B3
Tyrrell 43 B6

U

Uhrichsville 62 A1
Ulric 87 A7
Union 65 A3
Union City 54 C1
Union Corners 54 D4
Union Furnace 79 A7
Union Ridge 53 B7
Union Station 59 D5
Unionport 63 B5
Uniontown 51 A7
Uniontown 62 C4
Unionvale 63 B4
Unionville 32 B3
Unionville 53 B6
Unionville 71 C5
Unionville 81 A7
Unionville Center 57 C6
Uniopolis 45 D7
Unity 53 B7
Unity 83 A7
University Heights 41 A6
Uno 55 B5
Upland Heights 63 C6
Upper Arlington 58 D1
Upper Fivemile 76 D1
Upper Sandusky 47 B6
Upton 38 A1
Urban Hill 51 B6
Urbana 56 D3
Urbancrest 68 A1
Utica 59 C6
Utica 75 A6
Utley 80 A3
Utopia 82 B3

V

Vadis 73 A5
Vails Corners 58 B3
Vales Mills 79 C7
Valley 52 B4
Valley City 40 C3
Valley City Station 40 C3
Valley Crossing 68 A2
Valley Ford 80 C1
Valley Glen 63 B6
Valley Hi 56 B3

Valley Junction 74 C1
Valley View 41 A6
Valley View 63 B5
Valley View 68 A1
Valley View 85 B4
Valleywood 65 C7
Vallonia 73 A5
Van 46 D4
Van Buren 36 C3
Van Meter 78 D1
Van Wert 44 B3
Vanatta 59 C6
Vandalia 65 A6
Vanderhoof 80 C4
Vandervorts Corners 76 A1
Vanlue 47 A5
Vauces 78 B2
Vaughnsville 45 A6
Vega 86 A2
Venedocia 44 B4
Venice 38 A3
Venice Heights 43 B6
Venice, see Ross
Vera Cruz 76 C1
Vermilion 39 A7
Vermilion on the Lake 39 A7
Vernon 85 C7
Vernon Center 43 A7
Vernon Junction 49 B4
Verona 64 A4
Versailles 54 C4
Vesuvius 85 D7
Veto 81 B5
Vickery 38 A2
Vicksville 70 D2
Victoria, see St Joseph
Victory Camp 58 C2
Vienna Center 43 C6
Vigo 78 C3
Viking Village 75 D5
Villa 66 A2
Villa Nova 44 D4
Vincent 81 A5
Vinton 79 C6
Vinton 86 A3
Volunteer Bay 39 A6

W

Wabash 44 D1
Waco 52 B1
Wade 73 D7
Wadsworth 41 D5
Wagram 68 A4
Wahlsburg 83 A4
Wainwright 61 A7
Wainwright 79 D6
Waite Hill 31 D7, 32 N1
Wakatomika 60 C2
Wakefield 54 C2
Wakefield 85 A4
Wakeman 39 B6
Walbridge 27 D5
Waldo 58 A1
Wales Corners 38 B2
Walhonding 60 B1
Walhonding 71 A6
Wallace Heights 63 A6
Wallace Mills 85 B6
Walnut Creek 51 D5
Walnut Grove 46 C3
Walnut Grove 56 A4
Walnut Hills 74 C4
Walton 46 C2
Walton Hills 41 B6
Wamsley 84 B2
Wananaker 72 D3
Wapakoneta 45 D6
Ward 21 D1
Warner 71 D7
Warnock 62 D4
Warren 43 C5
Warrensburg 57 B7
Warrensville Heights 41 A6
Warrenton 63 C3
Warrentown 61 D7
Warsaw 60 B2
Warsaw Junction 60 B2
Washingtonville 53 A5
Washington Court House 67 D5
Washington Hall 52 D3
Washington Mills 65 C7
Waterford 49 D5
Waterford 71 D5
Waterloo 52 D3
Waterloo 68 B3

Waterloo 86 C2
Watertown 81 A5
Waterville 26 D3, 36 A3
Watheys 52 C3
Watkins 57 C6
Watson 38 C1
Wattsville 53 D4
Waverly 78 C2
Waverly Gables 78 D1
Way 72 C2
Wayland 42 C3
Wayne 33 D6
Wayne 37 B5
Wayne Lakes Park 54 D2
Waynesburg 48 A3
Waynesburg 52 C2
Waynesfield 46 D1
Waynesville 65 D7
Weavers 54 D2
Weavers Corners 38 C3
Webb 73 A5
Webb Summit 69 D7
Webertown 76 C2
Webster 54 C1
Weems (Smithfield Station) 63 B5
Wegee 73 A5
Weiersville 50 B4
Weimers Mills 54 C2
Welcome 50 D2
Weldon 43 B7
Wellington 40 C1
Wellman 75 A7
Wellston 79 B5
Wellsville 53 D6
Welsh 80 C1
Welshfield 42 A2
Welshtown 80 D3
Wendelin 54 A2
Wengerlawn 64 B4
Wesley 70 A1
West Alexandria 64 C3
West Andover 33 D7
West Austintown 43 D5
West Bass Lake 32 C4
West Bedford 60 B2
West Berlin (Pershing Station) 58 B1
West Canaan 50 A3
West Carlisle 60 C2
West Carrollton City 65 C6
West Charleston 65 A6
West Chester 62 C1
West Chester 75 B4
West Clarksfield 39 C6
West Covington 55 D5
West Delta 25 D7
West Elkton 64 D3
West Farmington 42 A4
West Florence 64 C1
West Hartland 39 C5
West Independence 37 D5
West Jackson 57 A5
West Jefferson 24 D3
West Jefferson 67 A6
West Junction 78 C3
West Lafayette 61 B5
West Lancaster 66 C4
West Lebanon 51 C5
West Leipsic 35 D7
West Liberty 48 B3
West Liberty 56 B3
West Liberty 58 A2
West Lodi 38 C2
West Logan 69 D6
West Manchester 64 A3
West Mansfield 57 A4
West Mecca 43 A5
West Middletown 65 D4
West Millgrove 37 C5
West Milton 65 A5
West Newton 46 C1
West Park 36 D3
West Point 48 C3
West Point 53 D6
West Portsmouth 85 B4
West Richfield 41 D7
West Rushville 69 B6
West Salem 50 A2
West Sonora 64 A3
West Steels Corners 41 C6
West Union 83 B7
West Unity 25 D4
West View 40 B3
West Wheeling 63 D5
West Williamsfield 33 D7

Wetsel 45 A4
Weyers 38 B3
Weymouth 41 C4
Wharton 47 B5
Wheat Ridge 83 A7
Wheatville 64 C3
Wheelers Mill 85 B6
Wheelersburg 85 C6
Wheeling Creek 63 D5
Wherrys Crossroads 52 B3
Whigville 72 B1
Whipple 71 D7
Whipple Heights 51 B7
Whisler 78 A3
White Cottage 70 B2
White Oak 67 C6
White Oak 74 C2
White Oak 76 D1
White Oak Valley 83 A4
White Sulphur 57 B7
Whitehall 68 A2
Whitehouse 26 D2
Whites Corner 65 C7
Whites Landing 38 A2
Whiteville 26 C1
Whitfield 65 C5
Whitney 63 D4
Whittlesey, see Lafayette
Wick 33 D6
Wickliffe 31 D7
Widowville 49 C7
Wiggonsville 82 A3
Wightmans Grove 38 A1
Wilberforce 66 C1
Wilbren 70 C1
Wildare 43 B5
Wilgus 86 C2
Wilhelm Corners 43 B5
Wilkesville 79 D7
Wilkins 26 B2
Wilkins Corners 59 C7
Wilkshire Hills 51 C7
Willard 38 C1
Willettsville 76 B3
Williams Center 34 A3
Williams Corners 75 C6
Williamsburg 75 D7
Williamsdale 74 A3
Williamsfield 33 D7
Williamsport 48 B4
Williamsport 53 C6
Williamsport 68 D1
Williamstown 46 B3
Williston 27 D6
Willoughby 31 C7
Willoughby Hills 31 D7
Willow Crest 53 A6
Willow Farm 81 A7
Willow Grove 53 A4
Willow Wood 86 D2
Willowbrook 60 C3
Willowdell 54 B4
Willowick 31 C7
Willowville 75 D6
Wills Creek 60 C4
Willshire 44 C1
Wilmer 38 A4
Wilmington 76 A2
Wilmot 51 B5
Wilna 34 A4
Wilson 72 B5
Winameg 25 C7
Winchester 33 A6
Winchester 86 A1
Windfall 41 C4
Windham 42 C3
Windsor 33 D4
Windsor 49 B6
Windsor 75 B7
Windsor Corners 58 A1
Windsor Mills 32 C4
Winesburg 51 D5
Winfield 51 D6
Wingett Run 72 D1
Wingston 36 B3
Winklers Mills 73 C4
Winona 53 34
Winterset 41 D7
Wintersville 63 A6
Winton Place 74 C3
Wisterman 35 C6
Withamsville 75 D5
Wolf 61 B6
Wolf Corners 42 D4
Wolf Creek 81 A5
Wolf Run 63 A4
Wolfcale 44 A1
Wolfhurst 63 D5
Wolfpen 80 D2
Woodbourne 65 C6
Woodington 54 C2
Woodland 57 A6
Woodland Park 75 C7
Woodlawn 74 B4
Woodlyn 68 D1
Woodmere 41 A7
Woods 74 A2
Woods Mill 86 A3
Woodsdale 74 A4
Woodsfield 72 B3
Woodside 37 B5
Woodstock 57 C4
Woodview Park 57 B6
Woodville 37 A6
Woodville 75 B7
Woodville Gardens 27 D5
Woodworth 53 A6

Woodworth Corners 43 C6
Woodyards 80 C1
Wooster 50 B3
Wooster Heights 49 B6
Worstville 34 D2
Worthington 58 D1
Wortley 70 A3
Wren 44 B1
Wrightstown 80 A3
Wrightsville 67 B6
Wyandot 48 C1
Wyandotte 68 C3
Wyoming 74 C4

X

Xenia 66 C1

Y

Yale 27 D6
Yale 42 D3
Yankee Crossing 53 A4
Yankee Hills 43 C7
Yankee Lake 43 B7
Yankeeburg 73 D5
Yankeetown 64 A2
Yankeetown 67 C6
Yankeetown 82 A3
Yarico 86 C2
Yates Corners 42 A1
Yatesville 67 C5
Yellow Creek 53 D6
Yellow House 72 D3
Yellow Springs 66 B1
Yellowbud 68 C5
Yellowtown 70 C2
Yelverton 46 B3
Yoder 45 C7
Yondota 27 C6
York 63 B5
York Center 57 A5
Yorkshire 54 B3
Yorktown 61 A6
Yorkville 63 C6
Youba 81 C4
Young Hickory 71 B4
Youngs 84 A3
Youngs Corners 41 C5
Youngstown 43 D6
Youngsville 83 A7

Z

Zahns Corners 78 D2
Zaleski 79 B6
Zanesfield 56 B3
Zanesville 70 A2
Zeno 71 B5
Zenz City, see Sharpsburg
Zimmerman 65 C7
Ziontown 69 B7
Zoar 51 D7
Zoar 75 B6
Zoarville 51 D7
Zone 25 D5
Zuck 60 A1
Zumbrum Corners 54 C2

Parks

NAME, TOWN, PHONE	CAMPSITES	FISHING	HUNTING	HIKING	SWIMMING	BOATING	SNOWMOBILING	X-C SKIING	COMMENTS	ATLAS LOCATION
A. W. Marion State Park, Circleville, (740) 869-3124	60	●	●	●		●			Electric motors only.	Page 68, C-2
Adams Lake State Park, West Union, (740) 858-6652		●		●		●			Electric motors only. Adjacent to nature preserve.	Page 83, B-7
Alum Creek State Park, Delaware, (740) 548-4631	297	●	●	●	●	●	●	●	Bridle trails.	Page 58, C-2
Atwood Lake, 1.5 mi. SE of New Cumberland, (330) 343-6780	500	●	●	●	●	●			Nature center. Waterslide. 25-horsepower limit.	Page 52, D-1
Barkcamp State Park, Belmont, (740) 484-4064	151	●	●	●	●	●		●	Bridle trail. Universally accessible fishing pier. Electric motors only.	Page 62, D-3
Beaver Creek State Park, East Liverpool, (330) 385-3091	55	●	●	●				●	Restored mill and pioneer village. Bridle trail.	Page 53, C-7
Bedford Reservation, Bedford, (216) 351-6300				●			●	●	Tinkers Creek (see Unique Natural Features). Bridal Veil falls.	Page 41, A-6
Big Creek Reservation, Brooklyn, (216) 351-6300				●				●	Waterfowl refuge on Pothole Lake.	Page 41, A-4
Blue Rock State Park, Blue Rock, (740) 674-4794	101	●		●	●	●			Scenic views. Electric motors only.	Page 70, B-4
Bradley Woods Reservation, North Olmstead, (216) 351-6300				●					Ice skating. Birdwatching.	Page 40, A-3
Brecksville Reservation, Brecksville, (216) 351-6300				●			●	●	Golf course. Nature center. Seven separate gorges.	Page 41, A-6
Buck Creek State Park, Springfield, (937) 322-5284	101	●	●	●	●	●		●	Marina. Scuba diving. Historic Crabill House.	Page 66, A-3
Buckeye Lake State Park, Millersport, (740) 467-2690		●		●	●	●			Cranberry Bog (see Unique Natural Features).	Page 69, A-5
Burr Oak State Park, Glouster, (740) 767-3570	100	●	●	●	●	●			Lodge. 10-horsepower limit. Backpacking trail.	Page 70, D-2
Caesar Creek State Park, Waynesville, (513) 897-3055	287	●	●	●	●	●		●	Bridle trails and horsemen's camp. Restored pioneer village.	Page 75, A-7
Catawba Island State Park, Catawba Island, (419) 797-4530		●				●			Fishing pier on Lake Erie.	Page 28, D-3
Charles Mill Lake, Mifflin, (419) 368-6885	500	●	●	●	●	●			Marina. 10-horsepower limit.	Page 49, B-7
Clendening Lake, 3 mi. NE of Freeport, (740) 658-3691	70	●	●	●		●			Marina. 10-horsepower limit. Undeveloped natural area.	Page 62, C-2
Cleveland Lakefront State Park, Cleveland, (216) 881-8141		●		●	●	●			Marina. Four separate park areas.	Page 31, D-5
Cowan Lake State Park, Wilmington, (937) 382-1096	237	●	●	●	●	●		●	10-horsepower limit. Unique water lily colony.	Page 76, A-1
Crane Creek State Park, Oak Harbor, (419) 898-7758		●		●	●		●		Birdwatching. Adjacent to Wildlife Area.	Page 27, C-7
Cuyahoga Valley National Recreation Area, Peninsula, (330) 650-4636		●		●				●	Golf course. Blossom Music Center. Bridle and bicycle trails	Page 41, C-6
Deer Creek State Park, Mt. Sterling, (740) 869-3124	232	●	●	●	●	●		●	Lodge. Golf course. Bridle and bicycle trails.	Page 67, C-7
Delaware State Park, Delaware, (740) 369-2761	214	●	●	●	●	●		●	Abundant wildlife and wildflowers.	Page 58, A-1
Dillon State Park, Nashport, (740) 453-4377	195	●	●	●	●	●		●	Shooting ranges, trap and skeet fields.	Page 60, D-2
East Fork State Park, Bethel, (513) 734-4323	416	●	●	●	●	●		●	Backcountry trail for hikers and horsemen (see Hiking).	Page 75, D-6
East Harbor State Park, Lakeside-Marblehead, (419) 734-4424	570	●	●	●	●	●		●	Wildlife sanctuary.	Page 28, A-3
Euclid Creek Reservation, Euclid, (216) 351-6300				●				●	Physical fitness trail.	Page 31, D-6
Findley State Park, Wellington, (440) 647-4490	283	●	●	●	●	●		●	Electric motors only. Wildflower and wildlife sanctuary.	Page 40, D-1
Forked Run State Park, Reedsville, (740) 378-6206	198	●	●	●	●	●			10-horsepower limit. Rugged, forest terrain.	Page 81, D-4
Garfield Park Reservation, Garfield Heights, (440) 341-3161				●					Picnicking. Nature center.	Page 41, A-6
Geneva State Park, Geneva, (440) 466-8400	91	●	●	●	●	●	●	●	2.5-mile beach on Lake Erie.	Page 32, B-4
Grand Lake St. Marys State Park, St. Marys, (419) 394-3611	206	●	●	●	●	●			Waterskiing on large man-made lake.	Page 44, D-4
Great Seal State Park, Chillicothe, (740) 663-2125	15		●	●					Hilly terrain. Bridle trails and horsemen's camp.	Page 78, A-2
Guilford Lake State Park, Lisbon, (330) 222-1712	42	●		●	●	●			10-horsepower limit.	Page 53, B-5
Harrison Lake State Park, Fayette, (419) 237-2593	178	●		●	●	●			Electric motors only.	Page 25, C-5
Headlands Beach State Park, Mentor, (216) 881-8141		●		●	●				Mile-long natural beach.	Page 32, B-1
Hinckley Reservation, Hinckley, (216) 351-6300		●		●	●	●	●	●	350-foot ledges rise above lake.	Page 41, C-5
Hocking Hills State Park, Logan, (740) 385-6842	170	●		●					Varied geological features (see Unique Natural Features: Ash Cave, Cantwell Cliffs, Cedar Falls, Old Man's Cave, Rock House).	Page 79, A-5
Hueston Woods State Park, College Corner, (513) 523-6347	490	●	●	●	●	●		●	Lodge. Golf course. Nature preserve (see Unique Natural Features). 10-horsepower limit.	Page 64, D-1
Huntington Reservation, Bay Village, (216) 351-6300		●		●	●	●		●	Nature center.	Page 40, A-3
Independence Dam State Park, Defiance, (419) 237-1503	40	●	●	●		●			Marina. Trail along former canal towpath.	Page 35, B-5
Indian Lake State Park, Huntsville, (937) 843-2717	443	●	●	●	●	●			Four marinas. Waterskiing. Lighted buoy systems.	Page 46, D-1
Jackson Lake State Park, Oak Hill, (740) 682-6197	36	●		●	●	●			10-horsepower limit. Remains of iron-smelting furnace.	Page 86, A-1
Jefferson Lake State Park, Richmond, (740) 765-4459	100	●	●	●	●	●			Scenic, rugged hiking trails. Electric motors only.	Page 63, A-5
John Bryan State Park, Yellow Springs, (937) 767-1274	100	●	●	●				●	Scenic limestone gorge along Little Miami River.	Page 66, B-2
Kelleys Island State Park, Kelleys Island, (419) 746-2546	129	●	●	●	●	●		●	Glacial Grooves (see Unique Natural Features). Indian pictographs.	Page 28, D-4
Kiser Lake State Park, St. Paris, (937) 362-3822	140	●	●	●	●	●		●	No motors permitted.	Page 56, C-1
Lake Alma State Park, Wellston, (740) 384-4474	60	●		●	●	●			Paved bicycle path. Electric motors only.	Page 79, C-5
Lake Hope State Park, Zaleski, (740) 596-5253	223	●	●	●	●	●			Nature program. Electric motors only.	Page 79, B-7
Lake Logan State Park, Logan, (740) 385-6842		●	●	●	●	●			Day-use park. 10-horsepower limit.	Page 69, D-6
Lake Loramie State Park, Minster, (937) 295-2011	184	●	●	●	●	●		●	High-speed boating area.	Page 55, B-5
Lake Milton State Park, Lake Milton, (330) 654-4989		●		●	●	●			Universally accessible fishing pier. Nature program.	Page 42, D-4
Lake Vesuvius Recreation Area, Ellisonville, (740) 532-0151	65	●		●	●	●			Restored iron furnace. Nature center and Museum. Bridle trails. In Wayne National Forest (see Forests).	Page 85, D-7
Lake White State Park, Waverly, (740) 947-5049	38	●		●	●	●			Waterskiing.	Page 78, D-1
Leesville Lake, Leesville, (330) 343-6647	200	●	●	●		●			Two marinas. 10-horsepower limit.	Page 62, A-2
Little Miami State Park, Milford, (513) 897-3055		●		●				●	Abandoned railroad right-of-way along river. Multi-use trail.	Page 75, B-5
Madison Lake State Park, London, (740) 869-3124		●		●	●	●			Day-use park. Electric motors only.	Page 67, B-5
Malabar Farm State Park, Lucas, (419) 892-2784	15	●		●				●	Historic working farm (see Historic Sites/Museums). Bridle trails.	Page 49, C-6
Mary Jane Thurston State Park, Grand Rapids, (419) 832-7662		●		●	●	●		●	Marina.	Page 36, A-1
Maumee Bay State Park, Oregon, (419) 836-7758	256	●	●	●	●	●		●	Lodge. Golf course. Wildlife haven. Birdwatching.	Page 27, C-5
Mill Stream Run Reservation, Strongsville, (216) 351-6300				●			●	●	Abundant wildlife. Unusual ferns and wildflowers.	Page 40, B-4
Mohican State Park, Loudonville, (419) 994-5125	177	●		●	●				Unique natural area. Waterfalls and rock formation in Clearfork Gorge (see Unique Natural Features).	Page 49, D-7
Mosquito Lake State Park, Cortland, (330) 637-2856	234	●	●	●	●	●	●	●	Abundant waterfowl.	Page 43, B-5
Mount Gilead State Park, Mount Gilead, (419) 946-1961	60	●		●		●			Electric motors only.	Page 48, D-3
Muskingum River Parkway, Zanesville, (740) 452-3820	20	●		●		●			10 hand-operated locks along river.	Page 70, A-2
Nelson–Kennedy Ledges State Park, Nelson, (440) 564-2279				●					Rugged cliffs in day-use park. Picnicking.	Page 42, B-3
North Chagrin Reservation, Mayfield, (216) 351-6300		●		●			●	●	Golf course. Historic Squire's Castle. Wildlife refuge (see Wildlife).	Page 31, D-7
Oak Point State Park, South Bass Island, (419) 285-2112		●				●			Small picnicking area on Lake Erie.	Page 28, C-3
Paint Creek State Park, Bainbridge, (937) 365-1401	199	●	●	●	●	●		●	Marina. Bridle trails. Pioneer Village.	Page 77, C-6
Piedmont Lake, Smyrna, (740) 658-3735	66	●	●	●		●			Marina. 10-horsepower limit.	Page 62, C-2
Pike Lake State Park, Bainbridge, (740) 493-2212	112	●	●	●	●	●			Electric motors only. Wildlife display.	Page 77, C-7
Pleasant Hill Lake, 2 mi. W of Perrysville, (419) 938-7884	380	●	●	●	●	●			Marina. Nature program.	Page 49, C-7
Portage Lakes State Park, Akron, (330) 644-2220	104	●	●	●	●	●			Waterskiing.	Page 51, A-6
Punderson State Park, Newbury, (440) 564-2279	201	●	●	●	●	●	●	●	Winter sports park. Electric motors only.	Page 42, A-2
Pymatuning State Park, Andover, (440) 293-6030	373	●	●	●	●	●	●	●	10-horsepower limit.	Page 33, D-7
Quail Hollow State Park, Hartville, (330) 877-1528			●	●				●	Golf course. Visitor and natural history center.	Page 52, A-1

10

PARKS, *continued*

NAME, TOWN, PHONE	CAMPSITES	FISHING	HUNTING	HIKING	SWIMMING	BOATING	SNOWMOBILING	X-C SKIING	COMMENTS	ATLAS LOCATION
Rocky Fork State Park, Hillsboro, (740) 393-4284	220	●	●	●	●	●			Waterskiing. Birdwatching.	Page 77, C-4
Rocky River Reservation, Rocky River, (216) 351-6300		●		●		●	●	●	Along river gorge with massive shale cliffs.	Page 40, A-4
Salt Fork State Park, Cambridge, (740) 439-3521	212	●	●	●	●	●	●	●	Golf course. Bridle trails. Waterskiing. Universally accessible facilities.	Page 61, D-7
Scioto Trail State Park, Chillicothe, (740) 663-2125	58	●	●	●	●	●		●	Bridle trail. Scenic views. Electric motors only.	Page 78, C-2
Seneca Lake Park, 3 mi. NE of Chaseville, (740) 685-6013	250	●	●	●	●	●			Marina. Nature program.	Page 71, A-7
Shawnee State Park, Portsmouth, (740) 858-6652	107	●	●	●	●	●			Lodge. Golf course. Marina. Electric motors only.	Page 84, C-3
South Bass Island State Park, South Bass Island, (419) 285-2112	135	●			●	●			Glacial grooves. Fishing pier.	Page 28, C-3
South Chagrin Reservation, Bentleyville, (216) 351-6300		●		●			●	●	Polo field. 19th-century carvings in sandstone boulder.	Page 41, A-7
Stonelick State Park, Pleasant Plain, (513) 625-7544	153	●	●	●	●	●		●	Electric motors only.	Page 75, C-7
Strouds Run State Park, Athens, (740) 592-2302	80	●	●	●	●	●		●	Bridle trail. 10-horsepower limit.	Page 80, B-2
Sycamore State Park, Trotwood, (513) 523-6347		●	●	●			●	●	Bridle trail.	Page 65, B-5
Tappan Lake Park, Deersville, (740) 922-3649	500	●	●	●	●	●			Amphitheater.	Page 62, B-2
Tar Hollow State Park, Laurelville, (740) 887-4818	96	●	●	●	●	●			Bridle and backpacking trails. Electric motors only.	Page 78, A-4
Tinkers Creek State Park, Streetsboro, (330) 296-3239		●		●				●	Adjacent to Tinkers Creek *(see Unique Natural Features).*	Page 42, B-1
Van Buren State Park, Van Buren, (419) 832-7662	48	●	●	●		●		●	Electric motors only.	Page 36, C-3
West Branch State Park, Ravenna, (330) 296-3239	103	●	●	●	●	●	●	●	Abundant wildlife.	Page 42, C-3
Wolf Run State Park, Caldwell, (740) 732-5035	140	●	●	●	●	●		●	10-horsepower limit.	Page 71, B-6

Wildlife

AFRICAN SAFARI WILDLIFE PARK – Port Clinton – (419) 732-3606 – Page 28, D-3 Drive-through safari. View zebras, giraffes, ostriches, lions, rhinoceroses, camels and rare white Bengal tigers. Reptiles. Tropical bird aviary. Turtle taxi. Elephant and pony rides.

AKRON STATE FISH HATCHERY – Akron – (330) 644-2293 – Page 41, D-6 Walleye egg incubation and hatching during four- to five-week period in March and April. Open year-round.

AKRON ZOOLOGICAL PARK – Akron – (330) 375-2525 – Page 41, D-6 Animals from North and South America including llamas, aoudads, tamarins, monkeys, big horn sheep, eagles and exotic birds.

AULLWOOD AUDUBON CENTER & FARM – Dayton – (937) 890-7360 – Page 65, B-5 200-acre environmental education center with woods, meadows and pasture. Farm includes animals, barn and exhibit buildings. Foot trails. Guided and self-guided field trips.

BLUEBIRD MANAGEMENT TRAIL – Delaware State Park – (740) 369-2761 – Page 58, A-1 More than 90 boxes have been placed to attract relatively rare bluebird and other cavity-nesting birds. Interpretive programs and trails. *(See Parks.)*

BUNN'S LAKE WILDLIFE AREA – Westlake – (330) 351-6300 – Page 40, A-3 5.5-acre lake encircled by a 0.6-mile nature trail, located in Bradley Woods Reservation *(see Parks).* Fishing for largemouth bass, sunfish, catfish and rainbow trout. Mallard, black and wood ducks. Canada geese.

CEDAR BOG – Urbana – (614) 297-2606 – Page 56, D-2 Alkaline bog harbors brook trout, endangered spotted turtle and massasauga (swamp) rattlesnake. Some distinctive butterflies. Over 100 species of birds. National Natural Landmark. *(See Unique Natural Features.)*

CINCINNATI ZOO & BOTANICAL GARDEN – Cincinnati – (513) 281-4700 – Page 74, C-3 World-famous zoo, including white Bengal tigers, red pandas, lowland gorillas, reptiles and insects. Aquarium. Nocturnal House. Walk-through aviary. Children's zoo. Elephant and camel rides.

CLEVELAND METROPARKS ZOO – Cleveland – (216) 661-6500 – Page 41, A-5 Fifth oldest zoo in US. Over 1,300 animals including elephants, giraffes, zebras, kangaroos, ostriches, leopards, monkeys, reindeer and tortoises. Zootrain. Children's farm.

CLIFTON GORGE – Clifton – (614) 265-6453 – Page 66, B-2 Glacial remnant along Little Miami River. Small mammals, reptiles and amphibians. Migratory songbirds, woodpeckers, and flycatchers. *(See Unique Natural Features.)*

COLUMBUS ZOO AND AQUARIUM – Powell – (614) 645-3550 – Page 58, C-1 Over 6,000 animals including elephants, giraffes, lions, tigers, gorillas, lesser pandas, kangaroos, polar bears, penguins, sharks, manatees, sea turtles, reptiles and birds. Train and boat rides. Petting barn.

CRANE CREEK EXPERIMENTAL STATION – Oak Harbor – (419) 898-2495 – Page 27, D-7 Freshwater marsh harbors waterfowl, birds of prey and warblers including egrets, coots, bald eaglesand short-eared owls.

EAGLE CREEK – Garrettsville – (614) 265-6453 – Page 42, B-3 Watershed supports many reptiles and amphibians including rare and endangered spotted turtle and four-toed salamander. Wetland habitat includes deer, fox, raccoon and opossum. Large beaver ponds provide migratory stops for Canada geese. Herons, hawks and owls.

FOWLER WOODS – 6 mi. NW of Olivesburg – (614) 265-6453 – Page 49, A-6 133.5-acre preserve. Varied habitats. Abundance of lesser mammals supports several predatory birds. Barred owl, sharp-shinned hawk, Cooper's hawk and turkey vultures. Eight species of non-poisonous snakes including rare northern copperbelly. Spotted salamanders. Nature trails. *(See Unique Natural Features.)*

GOLL WOODS – Archbold – (614) 265-6453 – Page 25, D-5 Virgin woodlands reminiscent of northwestern Ohio's primeval Black Swamp. Large variety of wildflowers. White-tailed deer. Red fox. Great horned and barred owls. Spotted salamanders and turtles. *(See Unique Natural Features.)*

HACH–OTIS SANCTUARY – Willoughby Hills – (614) 265-6453 – Page 31, D-7 Wooded forest of beech, maple and oak. Clay banks along Chagrin River are ideal nesting spots for bank swallows and kingfishers. Pileated woodpeckers, great horned and barred owls. Deer and foxes. Spectacular spring wildflower bloom. *(See Unique Natural Features.)*

HEBRON STATE FISH HATCHERY – Hebron – (740) 928-8092 – Page 69, A-5 Produces walleye, saugeye, muskellunge, bluegills and flathead minnows, sauger and channel catfish. Birdwatching. 252 bird species recorded. Nature trails.

IRWIN PRAIRIE – 5 mi. W of Toledo – (614) 265-6453 – Page 26, C-2 Wet prairie habitat supports large and small mammals. Nesting area for mallards and wood ducks. Pied-billed grebes, least bitterns, rails and common snipes. Endangered spotted turtle. *(See Unique Natural Features.)*

KINCAID HATCHERY – Latham – (740) 493-2717 – Page 77, D-6 Fish-rearing ponds and indoor concrete raceway. Muskellunge, walleye, striped bass, coho salmon, rainbow and golden trout.

LAKE ERIE NATURE AND SCIENCE CENTER – Bay Village – (440) 871-2900 – Page 40, A–3 Located on 103-acre Huntington Reservation *(see Parks).* Reptile room. Deer run. Animal yard. Greenhouse and Schuele Planetarium.

LONDON STATE FISH HATCHERY – London – (740) 852-1412 – Page 67, A-4 33 ponds and 800-foot earthen raceway produce 500,000 fingerlings annually. Stock fish include coho and chinook salmon; rainbow, golden and brown trout; muskellunge, walleye, saugeye and largemouth bass.

MAGEE MARSH WILDLIFE AREA – Oak Harbor – (419) 898-0960 – Page 27, D-7 2,600-acre marshland located at crossing point of Mississippi and Atlantic Flyways, two major migratory paths. Abundant waterfowl. Whistling swans, sandhill cranes, egrets and great blue herons. Bird trail and observation tower. Interpretive center houses decoy and hunting equipment display.

MAUMEE BAY STATE PARK – Oregon – (419) 836-7758 – Page 27, C-5 Meadows, wet woodlands and marshes form natural habitat for birds. Unusual species include dickcissels, bobolinks, western meadow larks and short-eared owls. *(See Parks.)*

MENTOR MARSH – Mentor – (614) 265-6453 – Page 32, C-1 644 acres of decomposing forest returning to marshland. Bird species include long-billed marsh wren, Virginia and king rails. Nesting area for wood ducks, eastern bluebirds and rare prothonotary warbler. Non-poisonous snakes and small mammals. *(See Unique Natural Features.)*

NORTH CHAGRIN RESERVATION – Mayfield Village – (440) 473-3370 – Page 31, D-7 1,912 acres of marshland, forest and meadow. Ten walking trails. Waterfowl include black and wood ducks, pintails, common mergansers, mallards and Canada geese. Deer, rabbits and other mammals. Information, maps and trail guides available at nature center. *(See Parks.)*

OLD WOMAN CREEK SANCTUARY – East Huron – (419) 433-4601 – Page 39, A-5 Environmental interpretive facility. Aquarium. Visitor center, observation deck and trail system enable visitors to view marshlands, open water, barrier sand beach, upland forests and fields. Shorebirds and migratory waterfowl. *(See Unique Natural Features.)*

OTTAWA NATIONAL WILDLIFE REFUGE – Oak Harbor – (419) 898-0014 – Page 27, D-7 Refuge complex containing 8,000 acres of swamp, forest and marsh. Migratory stop for waterfowl on Atlantic and Mississippi Flyways. Bald eagles, whistling swans, Canada geese, pheasant and varieties of ducks, herons, hawks and songbirds. Mammals include deer, muskrat, raccoon, fox, rabbit and mink. Interpretive foot trails.

PUT-IN-BAY FISH HATCHERY – Put-in-Bay – (419) 285-3701 – Page 28, C-3 Indoor concrete raceways exhibiting coho salmon, walleye and rainbow trout. Educational display depicting hatchery operations from egg collection to stocking.

ROCKBRIDGE – Rockbridge – (614) 265-6453 – Page 69, D-6 Old field transformation to mature woodlot. Habitat for deer, fox and beaver. Grouse and turkeys. Nature trails. *(See Unique Natural Features.)*

SHAKER LAKES REGIONAL NATURE CENTER – Cleveland – (330) 321-5935 – Page 41, A-6 300-acre park. Four miles of trails which lead to old Shaker dams, and along edge of ravine. Herons. Birdwatching.

ST. MARYS STATE FISH HATCHERY – St. Marys – (419) 394-5170 – Page 45, D-4 Warm and cool water hatchery. Fish-rearing ponds. Largemouth bass, northern pike, walleye, saugeye and channel catfish. Large flock of Canada geese. Migratory waterfowl and shorebirds.

STAGE'S POND – Ashville – (614) 265-6453 – Page 68, C-2 Glacial (kettle) lake harboring migrating waterfowl. Marsh areas provide rookeries for great blue heron and other shorebirds. Oak–hickory uplands and open fields support quail, pheasant and several species of hawks. Nature trails. *(See Unique Natural Features.)*

TOLEDO ZOO – Toledo – (419) 385-5721 – Page 26, D-4 Elephants, birds, bears, reptiles and cats. Exhibits feature ten endangered species including cheetahs, orangutans, gorillas and snow leopards. Freshwater and saltwater aquariums. Spanish Colonial architecture. Conservatory. Botanical gardens. Children's zoo.

WAHKEENA NATURE PRESERVE – Lancaster – (740) 746-8695 – Page 69, C-5 150-acre preserve featuring forested sandstone cliffs. Native orchids. 100 different species of birds. 15 species of mammals. Nature trails.

WILD ANIMAL REHABILITATION PROGRAM – Hueston Woods State Park – (513) 523-6347 – Page 64, D-1 Rehabilitation program for injured or orphaned birds of prey. Nature center exhibits small native animals. Larger wildlife in outdoor exhibit which features flight cage for birds of prey and large pen for deer. *(See Parks.)*

Spectator Sports

BEULAH PARK – Grove City – Page 68, A-1 Thoroughbred and quarterhorse racing.

CINCINNATI BENGALS – Cincinnati – Page 74, D-3 NFL football team. Plays at Paul Brown Stadium.

CINCINNATI REDS – Cincinnati – Page 74, D-3 National League baseball team. Plays at Great American Ball Park.

CLEVELAND BROWNS – Cleveland – Page 31, D-5 NFL football team. Plays at Cleveland Browns Stadium.

CLEVELAND CAVALIERS – Cleveland – Page 41, A-5 NBA basketball team. Plays at Gund Arena.

CLEVELAND FORCE – Cleveland – Page 41, A-5 National Professional Soccer League team. Plays at Cleveland State University Convocation Center.

CLEVELAND INDIANS – Cleveland – Page 31, A-5 American League baseball team. Plays at Jacobs Field.

COLUMBUS CLIPPERS – Columbus – Page 68, A-1 International League AAA baseball farm team for New York Yankees. Plays at Cooper Stadium.

COLUMBUS MOTOR SPEEDWAY – Columbus – Page 68, A-2 Stock car racing on 1/3-mile asphalt oval track.

DRAG WAY 42 – West Salem – Page 50, A-2 Automobile drag racing on 1/4-mile strip. National championships.

FREMONT SPEEDWAY – Sandusky – Page 38, B-1 Sprint car and dirt truck racing on 3/8-mile clay oval track.

LEBANON RACEWAY – Lebanon – Page 75, A-6 Harness racing.

LORAIN COUNTY SPEEDWAY – Lorain – Page 40, B-1 Stock car racing on 3/8-mile asphalt track.

MID-OHIO SPORTS CAR COURSE – Lexington – Page 49, C-4 Automobile racing. IROC, vintage car, Trans-Am, Indy car and 24-hour endurance races.

NATIONAL TRAIL RACEWAY – Hebron – Page 69, A-5 Championship automobile drag racing. National Hot Rod Association. Spring Nationals.

NORTHFIELD PARK – Cleveland – Page 41, B-6 Harness racing.

NORWALK RACEWAY PARK – Norwalk – Page 39, C-5 Automobile drag racing. Superpro, stock and pro bike on 1/4-mile track.

PRO FOOTBALL HALL OF FAME – Canton – Page 51, B-7 Displays honoring famous professional football players. Related artifacts. Audio-visual presentations and movie theater.

RACEWAY PARK – Toledo – Page 27, C-4 Harness racing.

RIVER DOWNS – Cincinnati – Page 75, D-4 Thoroughbred and quarterhorse racing.

SANDUSKY SPEEDWAY – Sandusky – Page 38, A-4 Automobile drag racing on 1/2-mile asphalt track. Stock car racing.

SCIOTO DOWNS – Columbus – Page 68, B-2 Harness racing.

THISTLEDOWN – Randall – Page 41, A-6 Thoroughbred racing.

TOLEDO MUD HENS BASEBALL CLUB – Toledo – Page 27, C-4 International League AAA baseball farm team for Detroit Tigers. Plays at Fifth Third Field.

TOLEDO SPEEDWAY – Toledo – Page 27, C-4 Oval track automobile racing on asphalt. Late-model, figure-eight and Detroit iron racing.

TRAPSHOOTING HALL OF FAME – Vandalia – Page 65, A-6 Displays feature trophies, photographs and memorabilia of accomplished individuals in the sport.

Covered Bridges

In the United States, Ohio is second only to Pennsylvania in the number of authentic covered bridges still standing. Most of these are located in the southern half of the state, with concentrations in Washington and Fairfield Counties, although Ashtabula County, on Lake Erie, also boasts a large collection of bridges. The majority of Ohio's covered bridges were built in the second half of the 19th century.

Wood has been used in bridge-building since ancient times. Only with the invention of the truss system in the 19th century, however, did wood come into its own. By using variations on interlocking triangles of timber, great spans supporting heavy loads could be achieved. Common truss types include kingpost, queenpost, multiple kingpost, Burr arch, Howe and arch. There are many variations in the truss system, as modifications and reinforcements were developed by local craftsmen and builders.

Wooden bridges were cheaper to build than stone or iron, and thus were ideally suited to meeting the needs of small communities. As they evolved, they were roofed over to protect the trusses from weathering.

Over 125 covered bridges are located and named in this Atlas. This is only a fraction of the number of bridges that once existed. Road improvements for increasing traffic and heavier loads, fire and floods have all contributed to the gradual decline in the number of these notable landmarks. Fortunately, the cultural and historical value of these bridges has been realized, and many people are now working to preserve them.

Several of Ohio's most scenic covered bridges are listed below.

GERMANTOWN BRIDGE, Page 65, C-5 In Montgomery County, crosses Little Twin Creek. Bowstring suspension. Built in 1870. Listed in National Register of Historic Places.

ISLAND RUN BRIDGE, Page 70, C-3 In Morgan County, crosses Island Run. Multiple kingpost. Built in 1867.

JOHNSON BRIDGE, Page 69, D-4 In Fairfield County, crosses Clear Creek. Howe truss. Built in 1887.

SCOFIELD BRIDGE, Page 83, C-5 In Brown County, crosses Beetle Creek. Multiple kingpost with arch. Built in 1875.

For more information about covered bridges in Ohio, contact the Southern Ohio Covered Bridge Association, 3155 Whitehead Road, Columbus, OH 43204.

Amish Country

The Amish people of Ohio have preserved the beliefs and lifestyles of their past. Originally followers of Mennon Simons, the Amish split with the Mennonites before coming to America in the 17th century. Through simple living and dedication to religious ideals, the Amish have been able to maintain their heritage in an increasingly complex world.

ALPINE HILLS HISTORICAL MUSEUM – Sugarcreek – (330) 852-4113 – Page 51, D-5 Displays depict Swiss and Amish heritage of Sugarcreek community (*see below*). Farm tools and machinery. Cheese house replica. Slides and audio-visual presentations. Information Center.

AMISH COUNTRY CRAFT VILLAGE – Walnut Creek – (216) 852-4382 – Page 51, D-5 Candle making and quilting. Photography and Tool Museum. Crafts emphasizing dyeing and pioneer folklore. Demonstrations, lessons and supplies.

AMISH COUNTRY DRIVE – Millersburg – Page 50, D-3 *See Excursions/Scenic Drives, for complete description.*

AMISH COUNTRY FARM – Berlin – (216) 893-2951 – Page 51, D-4 1900's Amish home. Animal barn. Museum and blacksmith shop. Quilts and antiques. Restaurant, bakery and gifts.

AMISH HOME – Millersburg – (330) 893-2541 – Page 51, D-5 100-acre Amish farm. Tour two complete homes. Animal petting and milking. Buggy rides and hayrides. Local crafts.

HEINI'S PLACES – Berlin – (330) 893-2131 – Page 51, D-4 Tours of cheese house. Dutch farm furniture, smoked meats, quilts and gifts.

MENNONITE INFORMATION CENTER – Berlin – (330) 893-3192 – Page 51, D-4 20-minute slide show about local cultures. Seasonal.

PERSONALIZED TOURS OF AMISH COUNTRY – New Philadelphia – (216) 339-2936 – Page 61, A-7 Your car is driven by guide on backroads and country highways. Amish farms, furniture shops, one-room schools, cemeteries and cheese factories.

AMISH COMMUNITIES

BERLIN – Page 51, D-4 Amish farm tour. Mennonite Information Center. Quilt Museum. Local artists' gallery. Bakeries, restaurants and local crafts.

BOLIVAR – Page 51, C-7 Antiques, restaurant and farms.

CHARM – Page 51, D-4 Restaurants, cheese house, hickory rockers, harness shop and ice house.

MIDDLEFIELD – Page 42, A-3 Cheese house with viewing room and film. Restaurants, farms, ice house and harness shops. Amish clothing and fabrics.

MILLERSBURG – Page 50, D-3 Amish Home Tour, Rastetter Woolen Mill, buggy rides, crafts, quilts, bakeries and restaurants.

NEW PHILADELPHIA – Page 61, A-7 Personalized tours of Amish countryside. Historic Schoenbrunn Village. "Trumpet in the Land" (outdoor drama). Farms.

SHREVE – Page 50, C-2 Local crafts, restaurant, antiques, Kister Mill (last water-powered mill in Ohio).

SUGARCREEK – Page 51, D-5 Alpine Hills Historical Museum, cheese-making, restaurants, livestock auctions, antiques, bakeries, local crafts, Swiss Festival.

WALNUT CREEK – Page 51, D-5 Cheese and trail bologna, restaurants, grandfather clocks, Amish home tour, German Culture Museum, and candle-making factory.

WILMOT – Page 51, C-5 World's largest cuckoo clock. Dioramas, cheese-making, furniture, restaurants and farms.

Industrial Tours

BOYD'S CRYSTAL ART GLASS – Cambridge – **Page 61, D-6** Glass factory and showroom. Glass from molten form to finished product.

MOSSER GLASS – Cambridge – **Page 61, D-6** Glassmaking tours. Antique reproductions. Paperweights. Glass animals and collectibles. Showroom. Reservations recommended.

OHIO CERAMIC CENTER – Roseville – **Page 70, B-2** Museum displaying east-central Ohio ceramic wares, where visitors are invited to participate in pottery-making. Cluster of five buildings housing exhibits and demonstration area. Redware and stoneware.

THE PLAIN DEALER – Cleveland – **Page 31, D-5** One-hour tour of Ohio's largest daily newspaper, including newsroom, retail and classified advertising, circulation and press room. Audio-visual presentation. Children fourth grade and up allowed. Two-week advance notice for reservations.

QUAKER SQUARE – Akron – **Page 41, D-6** Self-guided tour through former mill buildings and silos of Quaker Oats Company, now Quaker Square Hilton and specialty shops. Mill Engineering, Quaker Oats Advertising and Mill Shipping offices are displayed. Listed in National Register of Historic Places.

ROBINSON–RANSBOTTOM POTTERY COMPANY – Roseville – **Page 70, B-2** Guided tour featuring natural and prepared clay, glaze preparation and several methods of forming potteryware. Periodic (old-fashioned) and tunnel (modern) kilns. Raw and finished pieces. Hand decorating.

ROSSI PASTA – Marietta – **Page 81, A-7** 30-minute demonstration at pasta-making company includes rolling, cutting and drying dough for capelli d'angelo, fettuccini, linguini and tagliarini. Samples. One-week advance notice required.

UNITED MUSICAL INSTRUMENTS – Cleveland – **Page 31, C-7** One-hour tour of instrument manufacturing operations. Follows procedures from raw brass to finished product. 150 different brass instruments manufactured. Two-week advance notice for reservations.

Amusements

THE BEACH WATERPARK – Mason – **Page 75, B-5** Water activities include waterslide, wave pool and inner tube rapids ride. Children's area.

CEDAR POINT – Sandusky – **Page 39, A-4** Amusement park with one of tallest and fastest roller coasters in U.S. Over 60 rides and attractions including 16 roller coasters. Live entertainment. Children's area.

CONEY ISLAND – Cincinnati – **Page 75, D-4** Water park featuring waterslides, pool and boating facilities. Children's area.

DOVER LAKE WATERPARK – Northfield – **Page 41, B-6** Water activities include seven waterslides, wave pool and swimming beach. Picnic area.

GEAUGA LAKE – Aurora – **Page 42, B-1** Amusement park with over 100 rides and attractions including wave pool, waterslide and roller coasters. Live entertainment. Children's area.

PARAMOUNT'S KINGS ISLAND – Kings Mills – **Page 75, B-5** Amusement park with eight major theme areas. Over 80 rides and attractions including 13 roller coasters and water park. Live entertainment. Children's area.

PREHISTORIC FOREST AND MYSTERY HILL – Marblehead – **Page 28, D-3** Park featuring optical illusions and accurate reproductions of dinosaurs.

PUTT N' POND SPEED PARK – Fostoria – **Page 37, C-5** Park featuring 350-foot-long waterslide. Water rides include bumper boats and hydro sleds. Swimming beach. Go-karts. 18-hole miniature golf course.

SURF'S UP AQUATIC CENTER – Sandusky – **Page 38, A-4** Wave pool with four-foot waves and whitewater. Marina and fishing piers.

WYANDOT LAKE AMUSEMENT PARK – Powell – **Page 58, C-1** Wave pool and roller coaster. Children's area.

Gardens

ADELL DURBIN ARBORETUM – Stow – (330) 688-8238 – **Page 41, C-7** 34.5-acre city park featuring 250 native and ornamental trees, flowers and shrubs. Self-guided nature trails.

BULL'S RUN ARBORETUM – Middletown – (513) 425-7841 – **Page 65, D-5** 11-acre natural area along creek. Remnant of forest once covering area. Over 30 species of trees. Guided tours.

CHADWICK ARBORETUM – Columbus –(614) 292-3854 – **Page 58, D-1** Located on Ohio State University campus. Arboretum established in 1980. Existing gardens feature labeled native plants and shrubs. Expansion plans include interpretive center and greenhouse.

CIVIC GARDEN CENTER OF GREATER CINCINNATI – Cincinnati – (513) 221-0981 – **Page 74, C-3** Four-acre garden and arboretum featuring labeled herb, rose and lily gardens. Greenhouse and library.

COLUMBUS PARK OF ROSES – Columbus – (614) 445-3300 – **Page 58, D-1** 13-acre park featuring wide variety of roses. Herb, daffodil and perennial gardens. Gazebo.

COX ARBORETUM AND GARDENS METROPARK – Dayton – (937) 434-9005 – **Page 65, C-6** 159 acres of native plants and shrubs. Collections include shade trees, crab apples, conifers, ivy and endangered plants. Herb, rock and shrub gardens. Greenhouse. Guided tours. Trail system through natural area.

CROSBY GARDENS – Toledo – (419) 536-8365 – **Page 26, C-3** 1837 Pioneer Homestead. Herb, rhododendron, azalea and rose gardens. Seasonal floral displays. Artists' village.

DAWES ARBORETUM – Newark – (740) 323-2355 – **Page 69, A-6** 950 acres of natural areas and formal gardens. Over 1,500 species of trees and shrubs. Japanese garden. Nature center and historic house museum.

FELLOWS RIVERSIDE GARDENS – Youngstown – (330) 740-7116 – **Page 43, D-6** Ten-acre formal garden featuring wide variety of roses. Victorian gazebo, fountain and statues. Rock, herb and shade gardens. Guided tours.

FRANKLIN PARK CONSERVATORY – Columbus – (614) 645-8733 – **Page 68, A-2** Horticultural landmark housing nine distinct climates ranging from Himalayan Mountains to tropical rain forest and desert. Guided tours.

GARDEN CENTER OF GREATER CLEVELAND – Cleveland – (216) 721-1600 – **Page 31, D-6** Variety of outdoor gardens feature perennials, herbs and roses. Japanese garden. Indoor displays. Library.

GARDENVIEW HORTICULTURAL PARK – Strongville – (440) 238-6653 – **Page 40, B-4** 16-acre garden park featuring formal gardens and arboretum. English Cottage gardening techniques highlighted. Flowering and ornamental trees underplanted with spring flowers.

GLASSHOUSE WORKS GARDENS – Stewart – (740) 662-2142 – **Page 80, B-3** Collections of rare tropical and temperate zone plants including ferns, succulents and carnivorous plants. Outdoor gardens feature plants imported from Japan and Europe.

HOLDEN ARBORETUM – Mentor – (440) 946-4400 – **Page 32, D-1** 2,900 acres of display gardens, natural woodlands, ponds, fields and ravines. Wildflower and rhododendron gardens. Hiking trails.

HOPEWELL FARMS – Manchester – (937) 549-2666 – **Page 83, C-7** Commercial herb grower. Formal gardens include culinary, fragrance and medicinal herbs. 60 varieties of herbs and scented geraniums in greenhouses. Guided group tours of farm and factory.

INNISWOOD – Westerville – (614) 895-6216 – **Page 58, D-2** 91-acre botanical garden and nature preserve. Flower beds, rock gardens and tended lawns. Foot trails.

KINGWOOD CENTER – Mansfield – (419) 522-0211 – **Page 49, B-5** 1926 estate of industrialist Charles Kelley King. 27 landscaped acres featuring formal gardens, greenhouses, gazebo, fountain and statues. Nature trail.

KROHN CONSERVATORY – Cincinnati – (513) 421-5707 – **Page 74, D-4** 1933 conservatory. Major displays include palms, orchids, tropical and desert plants. Seasonal floral displays.

MT. AIRY ARBORETUM – Cincinnati – (513) 541-8176 – **Page 74, C-3** 120-acre arboretum located within Mt. Airy Forest (*see Hiking: La Trainee De L'Explorateur*). Trees, flowers and woody plants. Labeled collections of rhododendrons, azaleas, vines, herbs and shrubs. Wildflower trail.

ROCKEFELLER PARK GREENHOUSE – Cleveland – (216) 664-3103 – **Page 31, D-5** Greenhouse displays of tropical plants, ferns, cacti and orchids. Talking garden for the blind, with tape recorded descriptions of plants and herbs. Japanese garden.

SECREST ARBORETUM – Wooster – (330) 263-3761 – **Page 50, B-3** 2,000 species of native and exotic trees, shrubs and plants. Rose garden. Flowering trees. Rhododendron display garden.

SPRING GROVE – Cincinnati – (513) 681-6680 – **Page 74, C-3** 733-acre cemetery and arboretum. Over 800 types of native and exotic trees and plants. Rose garden. Gothic architecture and sculpture. Guided tours.

STAN HYWET HALL AND GARDENS – Akron – (330) 836-5535 – **Page 41, D-6** 1915 estate of industrialist Frank A. Seiberling. 70 acres of lawns, gardens, meadows and lagoons. Tulip and daffodil display. Japanese and formal rose garden. Tudor Revival mansion. *(See Historic Sites/Museums.)*

TAPPAN SQUARE – Oberlin – (216) 775-8265 – **Page 40, B-1** Located on Oberlin College campus. 13 acres featuring 60 species of native trees, shrubs and labeled perennials. Collections of daffodils, tall grasses, cacti and nut trees. Pond. Sculpture. Guided tours.

TECUMSEH NATURAL AREA AND ARBORETUM – Lima – (419) 228-2641 – **Page 45, C-7** Located on Ohio State University campus. 200-acre preserve featuring wildflowers and deciduous trees. Foot trails.

Fishing

A sampling of Ohio's lake, stream and Great Lake fishing spots is listed below. Check ahead with local authorities for current regulations. For additional fishing information listed in this Atlas, see Parks, Forests and Campgrounds.

LAKES

Alum Creek Lake – Page 58, C-2 smallmouth and largemouth bass, walleye

Atwood Lake – Page 52, D-1 largemouth bass, northern pike

Barnesville Reservoir – Page 72, A-2 largemouth bass, rainbow trout

Berlin Lake – Page 42, D-4 smallmouth and largemouth bass, walleye

Bresler Reservoir – Page 45, C-6 smallmouth and largemouth bass, walleye

Buckeye Lake – Page 69, A-5 largemouth bass, muskellunge

Caesar Creek Lake – Page 65, D-7 smallmouth bass

Clendening Lake – Page 62, B-2 smallmouth and largemouth bass, muskellunge

Cowan Lake – Page 76, A-1 largemouth bass, muskellunge

Deer Creek Lake – Page 67, D-7 largemouth bass, muskellunge

Deer Creek Reservoir – Page 52, A-2 largemouth bass, muskellunge

Delaware Reservoir – Page 58, A-1 largemouth bass

Dillon Reservoir – Page 60, D-2 largemouth bass, muskellunge, walleye

Dow Lake – Page 80, B-2 largemouth bass, rainbow trout

East Branch Reservoir – Page 32, D-3 largemouth bass, northern pike

East Fork Lake – Page 75, D-6 smallmouth bass

Ferguson Reservoir – Page 45, C-7 smallmouth and largemouth bass, walleye

Findlay Reservoir 2 – Page 36, D-4 smallmouth and largemouth bass, walleye

Findley Lake – Page 40, C-1 largemouth bass, northern pike

Grand Lake–St. Marys – Page 44, D-4 largemouth bass

Greenfield Lake – Page 69, B-4 largemouth bass, northern pike

Guilford Lake – Page 53, B-4 largemouth bass, northern pike

Hammertown Lake – Page 78, D-4 largemouth bass, rainbow trout

Hargus Lake – Page 68, C-2 largemouth bass, muskellunge

Highlandtown Lake – Page 53, C-5 largemouth bass, northern pike, muskellunge

Hinckley Lake – Page 41, C-5 largemouth bass, northern pike

Hoover Reservoir – Page 58, C-2 smallmouth and largemouth bass, walleye

Indian Lake – Page 56, A-1 largemouth bass, northern pike, muskellunge, walleye

Jackson Lake – Page 86, A-1 largemouth bass, muskellunge

Julian Griggs Reservoir – Page 58, D-1 smallmouth and largemouth bass

Kiser Lake – Page 56, C-1 largemouth bass, walleye

Kokosing Lake – Page 49, D-5 largemouth bass, northern pike

Lake Aquilla – Page 32, D-2 largemouth bass, northern pike

Lake Logan – Page 69, D-6 largemouth bass, northern pike

Lake Medina – Page 40, C-4 largemouth bass, walleye

Lake Milton – Page 42, D-4 smallmouth and largemouth bass, muskellunge, walleye

Lake Rupert – Page 79, C-5 largemouth bass, northern pike, walleye

Lake Snowden – Page 80, C-1 largemouth bass, walleye

Lake White – Page 78, D-1 largemouth bass, muskellunge

Leesville Lake – Page 62, A-2 largemouth bass, muskellunge, walleye

M. J. Kirwan Reservoir – Page 42, C-3 smallmouth and largemouth bass, muskellunge, walleye

Mogadore Reservoir – Page 42, D-1 largemouth bass, muskellunge

Monroe Lake – Page 72, B-2 largemouth bass, rainbow trout

Mosquito Lake – Page 43, A-5 largemouth bass, northern pike, walleye

New Lexington Reservoir – Page 70, C-1 largemouth bass, rainbow trout

Nimisila Reservoir – Page 51, A-6 largemouth bass, northern pike, walleye

Oakthorpe Lake – Page 69, B-6 largemouth bass

O'Shaughnessy Reservoir – Page 57, C-7 largemouth bass

Paulding Reservoir – Page 34, D-3 smallmouth and largemouth bass, walleye

Piedmont Lake – Page 62, C-2 smallmouth and largemouth bass, muskellunge, walleye

Pleasant Hill Lake – Page 49, C-7 smallmouth and largemouth bass, muskellunge, walleye

Portage Lakes – Page 51, A-6 largemouth bass, muskellunge, walleye

Punderson Lake – Page 42, A-2 largemouth bass, rainbow trout

Pymatuning Reservoir – Page 33, D-7 smallmouth and largemouth bass, muskellunge, walleye

Rocky Fork Lake – Page 77, C-5 smallmouth and largemouth bass, muskellunge, walleye

Rush Creek Lake – Page 69, B-6 largemouth bass

Salt Fork Lake – Page 61, D-7 muskellunge, walleye

Seneca Lake – Page 71, A-7 largemouth bass, muskellunge, walleye

Shreve Lake – Page 50, C-2 largemouth bass, northern pike

Tycoon Lake – Page 86, A-3 largemouth bass, walleye

Wauseon Reservoir – Page 25, D-6 smallmouth and largemouth bass, walleye

Wellington Upground Reservoir – Page 40, C-1 smallmouth and largemouth bass, walleye

Willard Reservoir – Page 39, D-4 smallmouth and largemouth bass, walleye

Wolf Run – Page 71, B-6 largemouth bass, rainbow trout

LAKE ERIE

Bradstreet's Landing Park – Page 40, A-4 walleye

Catawba – Page 28, D-3 smallmouth bass, walleye

Conneaut City Park Dock – Page 33, A-7 smallmouth bass, salmon, rainbow trout

Eastlake Breakwall – Page 31, C-7 salmon, rainbow trout

Green Island Wildlife Area – Page 28, C-3 smallmouth and largemouth bass, walleye

Headlands Beach State Park – Page 32, B-1 salmon, rainbow trout

Madison Township – Page 32, B-3 salmon, rainbow trout

Perry Township – Page 32, B-2 largemouth bass, salmon, rainbow trout

Willow Point Wildlife Area – Page 38, A-2 largemouth bass, northern pike, walleye

STREAMS

Beaver Creek – Page 53, C-7 smallmouth bass

Grand River – Page 43, A-4 smallmouth and largemouth bass

Great Miami River, Taylorsville Dam – Page 65, A-6 smallmouth and largemouth bass

Huron River, Milan Wildlife Area – Page 39, B-4 smallmouth bass, salmon

Killbuck Creek – Page 50, C-3 largemouth bass, northern pike

Little Miami River, Fort Ancient – Page 75, A-7 smallmouth bass

Magee Marsh – Page 27, D-7 largemouth bass, northern pike, muskellunge

Maumee River, Buttonwood Access – Page 26, D-3 smallmouth bass, northern pike, walleye

Maumee River, Otsego Park – Page 36, A-2 smallmouth bass, northern pike, walleye

Maumee River, Providence Park – Page 36, A-2 smallmouth bass, northern pike, walleye

Maumee River, Walbridge Park – Page 26, D-4 largemouth bass, northern pike, walleye

Muskingum River, Lowell Dam Access – Page 71, D-6 largemouth bass

Muskingum River, Luke Chute Access – Page 71, D-5 largemouth bass, walleye

Muskingum River, Philo Dam Access – Page 70, B-3 largemouth bass, northern pike

Muskingum River, Rokeby Dam Access – Page 70, C-3 largemouth bass

Muskingum River, Stockport Access – Page 71, D-4 largemouth bass

Muskingum River, Zanesville Lock – Page 70, A-2 largemouth bass, northern pike

Ohio River, Coolville Access – Page 81, C-4 largemouth bass

Ohio River, Eagle Creek Access – Page 83, C-5 smallmouth and largemouth bass

Ohio River, Island Creek Access – Page 83, C-7 smallmouth and largemouth bass

Ohio River, Leading Creek Access – Page 87, A-5 largemouth bass

Ohio River, Ohio Brush Creek – Page 84, C-1 smallmouth and largemouth bass

Ohio River, Portsmouth Access – Page 85, C-4 largemouth bass

Ohio River, Steubenville Access – Page 63, B-7 largemouth bass, northern pike

Ohio River, White Oak Creek Access – Page 82, B-4 smallmouth and largemouth bass, salmon

Olentangy River – Page 58, D-1 smallmouth bass

Paint Creek – Page 77, B-5 largemouth bass

Sandusky River, Abbott Bridge – Page 37, C-7 smallmouth and largemouth bass, muskellunge

Sandusky River, Roger Young Park – Page 38, B-1 smallmouth bass, walleye

St. Joseph River, Montpelier Park – Page 24, D-3 smallmouth and largemouth bass, northern pike

Tuscarawas River, Dover Dry Dam – Page 51, D-7 largemouth bass, northern pike

Vermilion River – Page 39, A-7 smallmouth bass, northern pike, salmon, rainbow trout

Walhonding River, Mohawk Dry Dam – Page 60, B-2 smallmouth bass

FISHING HOT SPOTS®

Fishing Hot Spots® publishes large-scale, marked fishing maps of selected waters noted for excellent fishing. To locate Fishing Hot Spots waters in this atlas, look for the symbol on the left. For more information on Fishing Hot Spots maps for Ohio, call toll-free 1-800-255-6277 or write to: Fishing Hot Spots, P.O. Box 1167, Rhinelander, WI 54501.

 # Hunting

This chart represents a selected portion of public hunting areas in Ohio. It is the responsibility of the hunter to be familiar with all rules, regulations and restrictions before hunting in any of the areas listed below. For a comprehensive guide and licensing information, contact the Ohio Department of Natural Resources, Wildlife Division, 1840 Belcher Drive, Columbus, OH 43224-1300, (614) 265-6300. Individual wildlife area maps are also available. To purchase these maps, contact the Geologic Records Center, 4383 Fountain Square Drive, Columbus, OH 43224, (614) 265-6576. For additional public hunting areas in this Atlas, see Parks and Forests.

NAME, TOWN	SPECIES	ACREAGE	ATLAS LOCATION
Auburn Marsh Wildlife Area, Auburn Corners	pheasant, quail, rabbit	462	Page 42, A-2
Beach City Wildlife Area, Beach City	deer, rabbit, squirrel, raccoon, muskrat, beaver	1,214	Page 51, D-6
Beaver Creek Wildlife Area, 5 mi. NE of Bryan	pheasant, rabbit, squirrel	153	Page 24, D-3
Berlin Lake Wildlife Area, Deerfield	pheasant, quail, rabbit, raccoon, squirrel, woodchuck, opossum, muskrat, mink, waterfowl	8,518	Page 42, D-3
Big Darby Public Hunting Area, Darbydale	rabbit, squirrel	800	Page 67, B-7
Big Island Wildlife Area, New Bloomington	pheasant, quail, woodcock, rabbit, squirrel, waterfowl	1,904	Page 47, D-6
Brush Creek Wildlife Area, Monroeville	grouse, rabbit, squirrel	2,546	Page 53, D-5
Caesar Creek Wildlife Area, Harveysburg	deer, quail, rabbit, squirrel, woodchuck	2,257	Page 66, D-1
Clark Lake Wildlife Area, 2 mi. NE of Harmony	raccoon, muskrat, woodchuck, waterfowl, rabbit	284	Page 66, A-3
Cooper Hollow Wildlife Area, Centerville	deer, grouse, woodcock, squirrel	4,201	Page 86, A-1
Darke Wildlife Area, New Harrison	quail, rabbit, raccoon, squirrel, woodchuck	316	Page 54, D-3
Deer Creek Wildlife Area, Mt. Sterling	deer, pheasant, quail, rabbit, squirrel, woodchuck	3,710	Page 67, C-6
Delaware Wildlife Area, 8 mi. N of Delaware	pheasant, quail, rabbit, raccoon, squirrel, woodchuck, opossum, muskrat, mink, waterfowl	4,670	Page 58, A-1
Dillon Reservoir Wildlife Area, Nashport	deer, rabbit, quail, grouse, woodchuck, raccoon	3,952	Page 60, D-1
East Fork Wildlife Area, 4 mi. SE of Batavia	deer, squirrel, rabbit, quail, woodchuck	2,248	Page 75, D-7
Fallsville Wildlife Area, New Vienna	pheasant, quail, rabbit, raccoon, squirrel, woodchuck, opossum, muskrat	1,212	Page 76, B-3
Fox Lake Wildlife Area, 4 mi. W of Athens	deer, grouse, quail, rabbit, squirrel, woodchuck	421	Page 80, B-1
Grand River Wildlife Area, West Farmington	deer, grouse	6,277	Page 42, A-4
Grant Lake Wildlife Area, 2 mi. S of Mt. Orab	rabbit, quail, squirrel, waterfowl	412	Page 76, D-1
Hambden Orchard Wildlife Area, Hambden	pheasant, rabbit, raccoon, squirrel, woodchuck, opossum, muskrat, mink	842	Page 32, D-3
Highlandtown Wildlife Area, 4 mi. E of Salineville	rabbit, squirrel, waterfowl, woodcock	2,105	Page 53, C-5
Indian Creek Wildlife Area, Fayetteville	quail, rabbit, squirrel, waterfowl	1,691	Page 76, C-1
Killbuck Marsh Wildlife Area, Shreve	rabbit, raccoon, muskrat, waterfowl	4,642	Page 50, C-3
Killdeer Plains Wildlife Area, Marseilles	deer, rabbit, quail, pheasant, squirrel, waterfowl, raccoon, muskrat, woodcock	8,627	Page 47, C-6
Knox Lake Wildlife Area, Fredericktown	rabbit, squirrel	286	Page 59, A-5
Kokosing Lake Wildlife Area, Fredericktown	squirrel, rabbit, woodchuck, quail, pheasant, waterfowl	1,323	Page 49, D-5
Lake La Su An Wildlife Area, Bridgewater Center	deer, rabbit, squirrel, pheasant, waterfowl	1,161	Page 24, C-2
Leesville Lake Wildlife Area, 2 mi. SE of Sharrodsville	rabbit, raccoon, squirrel	2,861	Page 62, A-2
Liberty Wildlife Area, Big Rock	deer, grouse, squirrel, rabbit, raccoon	140	Page 78, D-3
Little Portage Wildlife Area, 6 mi. W of Port Clinton	woodcock, rabbit, waterfowl	357	Page 38, A-1
Magee Marsh Wildlife Area, 10 mi. N of Oak Harbor	muskrat, mink, raccoon, waterfowl	2,131	Page 27, D-7
Mercer Wildlife Area, Montezuma	waterfowl	1,408	Page 54, A-3
Metzger Marsh Wildlife Area, Bono	muskrat, mink, raccoon, waterfowl	558	Page 27, C-6
Milan Wildlife Area, 3.5 mi. W of Milan	squirrel, raccoon, opossum	296	Page 39, B-4
Missionary Island Wildlife Area, 2 mi. SW of Waterville	deer, rabbit, squirrel	326	Page 36, A-3
Mohican Wildlife Area, Brinkhaven	deer, grouse, squirrel, rabbit, quail, woodchuck	405	Page 60, A-1
Monroe Lake Wildlife Area, Miltonsburg	squirrel, rabbit, raccoon	1,333	Page 72, B-2
Mosquito Creek Wildlife Area, North Bloomfield	waterfowl	8,525	Page 43, A-5
New Lyme Wildlife Area, South New Lyme	deer, woodcock, grouse, squirrel, raccoon	530	Page 33, D-6
Oldaker Wildlife Area, Russel	rabbit, quail, squirrel, woodchuck, raccoon, muskrat, opossum	141	Page 76, C-3
Orwell Wildlife Area, 2 mi. N of Orwell	grouse, rabbit, squirrel, raccoon	193	Page 33, D-5
Oxbow Lake Wildlife Area, 5 mi. NW of Defiance,	deer, rabbit, quail, woodcock, waterfowl	415	Page 34, B-4
Paint Creek Wildlife Area, Greenfield	deer, rabbit, squirrel	6,188	Page 77, C-6
Pater Lake Wildlife Area, Bunker Hill	rabbit, quail	192	Page 74, A-2
Pleasant Valley Wildlife Area, 3 mi. NW of Chillicothe	deer, squirrel, rabbit, raccoon	1,465	Page 78, A-1
Powelson Wildlife Area, 4 mi. N of Zanesville	deer, grouse, squirrel, rabbit, waterfowl	2,697	Page 60, D-2
Resthaven Wildlife Area, Castalia	rabbit, quail, pheasant, woodcock, raccoon, woodchuck, muskrat, waterfowl	2,210	Page 38, A-3
Ross Lake Wildlife Area, 3 mi. E of Chillicothe	deer, quail, squirrel, grouse, rabbit	1,124	Page 78, B-2
Rush Run Wildlife Area, Somerville	rabbit, quail, pheasant, squirrel, woodchuck, raccoon, fox, muskrat, opossum, waterfowl	1,174	Page 64, D-3
Salt Fork Wildlife Area, 7 mi. NE of Cambridge	deer, squirrel, quail, grouse, rabbit	8,279	Page 61, D-7
Shenango Wildlife Area, Kinsman	deer, rabbit, squirrel, grouse, raccoon, muskrat, beaver	4,845	Page 43, A-7
Shreve Lake Wildlife Area, Shreve	deer, rabbit, pheasant	228	Page 50, C-2
Spencer Lake Wildlife Area, Spencer	rabbit, pheasant, quail, squirrel	618	Page 40, D-2
Spring Valley Wildlife Area, Spring Valley	rabbit, pheasant, quail, squirrel, woodchuck, raccoon, muskrat, opossum	842	Page 65, D-7
Toussaint Wildlife Area, 6 mi. N of Oak Harbor	waterfowl, woodcock, muskrat, mink, raccoon	236	Page 27, D-7
Tranquility Wildlife Area, Tranquility	squirrel, rabbit, quail, woodchuck, raccoon	3,818	Page 77, D-4
Trimble Wildlife Area, Glouster	deer, squirrel, rabbit, grouse	2,094	Page 70, D-1
Tycoon Lake Wildlife Area, 5 mi. N of Rio Grande	squirrel	684	Page 86, A-3
Waterloo Wildlife Experiment Station, 10 mi. W of Athens	squirrel, deer, grouse, turkey	1,361	Page 79, B-7
Wellington Wildlife Area, Wellington	deer, rabbit, squirrel, woodchuck, pheasant	200	Page 40, C-1
Wellston Wildlife Area, Hambden	deer, rabbit, quail, grouse, squirrel, woodchuck, waterfowl	1,150	Page 79, C-5
Willard Marsh Wildlife Area, Celeryville	deer, rabbit, quail, pheasant, squirrel	1,676	Page 38, D-3
Willow Point Wildlife Area, 7 mi. W of Sandusky	deer, muskrat, raccoon, mink, woodchuck, opossum, waterfowl	645	Page 38, A-3
Wolf Creek Wildlife Area, 9 mi. SE of McConnelsville	deer, rabbit, quail, squirrel, grouse	3,638	Page 70, D-3
Woodbury Wildlife Area, 3 mi. S of Warsaw	deer, rabbit, squirrel, raccoon, grouse	1,960	Page 60, B-2
Wyandot Wildlife Area, 3 mi. S of Cary	pheasant, rabbit, raccoon, squirrel	338	Page 47, A-5
Zepernick Lake Wildlife Area, New Alexander	rabbit, quail, squirrel, woodchuck, pheasant	513	Page 52, B-4

Historic Sites/Museums

ADENA STATE MEMORIAL – Chillicothe – (740) 772-1500 – Page 78, B-1 Restored 1807 mansion of Thomas Worthington, sixth governor of Ohio. Period furnishings. Terraced gardens and estate buildings.

AIR FORCE MUSEUM – Wright-Patterson Air Force Base, Dayton – (937) 255-3284 – Page 65, B-7 Oldest and largest military aviation museum in world. Chronological layout traces aviation development from Wright Brothers to Space Age. Exhibits include 200 aircraft and missiles.

ALLEN COUNTY MUSEUM – Lima – (419) 222-9426 – Page 45, C-7 Exhibits on variety of historical topics including transportation, Indian culture and pioneer life. Extensive steam and electric railroad collection.

ARMS MUSEUM – Youngstown – (330) 743-2589 – Page 43, D-6 Collections include pioneer household and farm implements, guns, 19th- and 20th-century costumes, political memorabilia and Indian relics.

AUGLAIZE VILLAGE – Defiance – (419) 784-0107 – Page 34, B-4 Re-created 19th-century village including cider mill, blacksmith shop, post office and railroad station. Several museums house military artifacts, farm implements and items related to archaeology and natural history.

AUTO-AVIATION MUSEUM – Cleveland – (216) 721-5722 – Page 31, D-6 Over 200 antique automobiles and aircraft on display. Exhibits feature artifacts relating to development of automobile and aviation industries. Restoration shop.

BUCKEYE FURNACE STATE MEMORIAL – Wellston – (740) 384-3537 – Page 79, D-6 Restored 1852 charcoal-fired iron furnace. Exhibits housed in reconstructed company store. Foot trail along abandoned ore pits.

U.S. PRESIDENTS

GRANT BIRTHPLACE – Point Pleasant – (614) 297-2300 – Page 82, A-2 Restored home of General Ulysses S. Grant, 18th US president. Period furnishings.

HARDING HOME – Marion – (740) 387-9630 – Page 48, D-1 Restored turn-of-the-century home of Warren G. Harding, 29th US president.

HARDING TOMB – Marion – (740) 387-9630 – Page 48, D-1 Circular marble monument housing tomb of President Warren G. Harding and his wife, Florence.

HARRISON TOMB – North Bend – (614) 297-2300 – Page 74, C-1 Hilltop tomb of William Henry Harrison, 9th US President.

HAYES PRESIDENTIAL CENTER – Fremont – (419) 332-2081 – Page 37, B-7 Museum, library and Victorian house of Rutherford B. Hayes, 19th US president. Family memorabilia.

LAWNFIELD – Mentor – (440) 255-8722 – Page 32, C-1 Home of James A. Garfield, 20th US president. Two floors of original furnishings and artifacts tracing Garfield's career.

MCKINLEY MEMORIAL – Canton – (330) 455-7043 – Page 51, B-7 Tomb of William McKinley, 25th US president.

TAFT NATIONAL HISTORIC SITE – Cincinnati – (513) 684-3262 – Page 74, D-3 Birthplace and boyhood home of William Howard Taft, 27th US President. Visitor center houses related exhibits.

CAMPUS MARTIUS MUSEUM – Marietta – (740) 373-3750 – Page 81, A-7 Exhibits outline history and settlement of Northwest Territory. Restored Rufus Putnam home, oldest known residence in Ohio.

CANTON CLASSIC CAR MUSEUM – Canton – (330) 455-3603 – Page 51, B-7 Over 30 restored historic automobiles and related memorabilia. Restoration shop.

CARILLON PARK – Dayton – (937) 293-3412 – Page 65, C-6 65-acre park containing exhibits highlighting Dayton's contributions to transportation industry including *Wright Flyer III* (Wright Brothers' first practical airplane), covered bridge, restored canal lock, restored locomotive and historic buildings.

CENTURY VILLAGE – Burton – (440) 834-1492 – Page 42, A-2 Re-created 19th-century village including country store, blacksmith shop, railroad station, school, jail and historic houses.

CINCINNATI FIRE MUSEUM – Cincinnati – (513) 621-5553 – Page 74, D-3 Exhibits trace Cincinnati firefighting history. Artifacts from early 19th century to present. Participatory displays stress fire prevention.

DUNHAM TAVERN MUSEUM – Cleveland – (216) 431-1060 – Page 31, D-5 1819 stagecoach stop on Buffalo–Cleveland–Detroit route. Museum houses period items, recreating early 19th-century tavern.

FAIRPORT MARINE MUSEUM – Fairport Harbor – (440) 354-4825 – Page 32, B-1 Maritime museum housed in 1871 lighthouse. Exhibits include navigational instruments, ship models, lighthouse lens, charts and paintings.

FORT LAURENS – Bolivar – (330) 874-2059 – Page 51, C-7 Museum at site of only Revolutionary fort in Ohio. Artifacts from fort excavations and Revolutionary era. Audio-visual program.

FORT MEIGS – Perrysburg – (419) 874-4121 – Page 26, D-3 Reconstructed 1813 walled fort. War of 1812 exhibits. Military living-history demonstrations.

FORT RECOVERY – Fort Recovery – (419) 375-4649 – Page 54, A-1 Partly reconstructed 1793 fort of General Anthony Wayne. Museum houses military and Indian artifacts.

FRIENDS MEETING HOUSE STATE MEMORIAL – Mount Pleasant – (740) 769-2199 – Page 63, C-5 First Quaker meeting house west of Allegheny Mountains, built in 1814. Period and original furnishings.

GLENDOWER STATE MEMORIAL – Lebanon – (513) 932-5366 – Page 75, A-6 Example of Greek Revival architecture. Period furnishings.

GREAT LAKES MUSEUM – Vermilion – (440) 967-3467 – Page 39, A-7 Maritime museum containing artifacts relating to Great Lakes history. Ship models, navigational instruments, engines, lighthouse lens and marine paintings.

HALE FARM AND WESTERN RESERVE VILLAGE – Cuyahoga Valley National Recreation Area – (216) 721-5722 – Page 41, C-6 Restored 19th-century buildings including sawmill, church and schoolhouse. Working farm. Costumed guides. Craft demonstrations. *(See Parks.)*

HARRIET BEECHER STOWE MEMORIAL – Cincinnati – (513) 632-5120 – Page 74, C-4 Artifacts and memorabilia highlighting black history in Cincinnati housed in home of author of *Uncle Tom's Cabin.*

HARRIS DENTAL MUSEUM – Bainbridge – (614) 486-2700 – Page 77, C-6 Artifacts and exhibits documenting history of dentistry.

HISTORIC LYME VILLAGE – Bellevue – (419) 483-4949 – Page 38, B-3 Re-created 19th-century village. Seven buildings house period furnishings, antique farm equipment, weaving and spinning exhibits. 19th-century post office houses world's largest single collection of postmarks.

HOOVER HISTORICAL CENTER – Canton – (330) 499-0287 – Page 52, A-1 Birthplace of William H. Hoover, founder of Hoover Company. Exhibits include collection of antique cleaning devices, early electric sweepers and memorabilia related to growth and development of company.

INDIAN MILL – 3 mi. NE of Upper Sandusky – (419) 294-2675 – Page 47, B-6 Museum of milling in restored 1861 structure. Working model of water turbine mill.

JOHNSON-HUMRICKHOUSE MUSEUM – Coshocton – (740) 622-8710 – Page 60, B-3 General museum containing collections of Americana, Indian and Eskimo artifacts, Oriental art and decorative arts.

LOCKINGTON LOCKS – Lockington – (614) 297-2300 – Page 55, C-6 Preserved locks were part of 1845 Miami and Erie Canal System connecting Cincinnati to Toledo. Site includes lock master's house, dry-dock basin for boat repair and sawmill race.

MALABAR FARM STATE PARK – Lucas – (419) 892-2784 – Page 49, C-6 Former home of Louis Bromfield, Pulitzer Prize-winning author. 32-room country estate with original furnishings. Operational farm. *(See Parks.)*

MARBLEHEAD LIGHTHOUSE STATE PARK – Marblehead – (419) 734-4424 – Page 28, D-4 Oldest original lighthouse on Great Lakes, built in 1821. Made of native limestone. 75 feet high, 50 feet in diameter at base.

MILAN HISTORICAL MUSEUM – Milan – (419) 499-2968 – Page 39, B-5 Complex including museum, country store, blacksmith shop, 19th-century house and Memorial Arts Building. Main museum houses glass and doll collections. Guided tours.

MUSEUM OF HISTORICAL MEDICINE – Cleveland – (216) 368-3648 – Page 31, D-6 Historical artifacts related to medicine, dentistry, pharmacology and nursing. Exhibits trace medical developments in 19th and 20th centuries. Re-creation of early doctor's offices and pharmacy.

NATIONAL ROAD/ZANE GREY MUSEUM – Norwich – (740) 872-3143 – Page 70, A-4 Exhibits trace construction of National Road, authorized by Congress in 1806 and extending from Maryland to Illinois. Museum also commemorates life of Ohio-born author Zane Grey.

OHIO HISTORICAL CENTER – Columbus – (614) 297-2300 – Page 58, D-2 Archaeology exhibits feature prehistoric Ohio. History exhibits interpret development of transportation, architecture, communication and decorative arts. Natural history displays of extinct animals once indigenous to Ohio including bison, crane, passenger pigeon and mastodon.

OHIO RIVER MUSEUM – Marietta – (740) 373-3750 – Page 81, A-7 Exhibits examine early exploration of Ohio River, 19th-century steamboat era, shipbuilding and present day issues. *W. P. Snyder, Jr.*, last steam-powered, stern-wheeled towboat remaining in US, is on display.

OHIO STATE CAPITOL – Columbus – (614) 466-2125 – Page 68, A-1 Greek Revival building. Rotunda open to public. Tours by reservation. Bronze sculptures by Levi Scofield commemorating famous Ohioans including presidents and Civil War generals.

OHIO VILLAGE – Columbus – (614) 297-2300 – Page 58, D-2 Reconstructed 19th-century Ohio village including shops, offices and residences. Authentically costumed guides. Craft demonstrations.

OUR HOUSE – Gallipolis – (740) 446-0586 – Page 86, B-4 Restored 1819 Ohio River tavern with period furnishings. Guided tours.

PERRY'S VICTORY MEMORIAL – Put-in-Bay – (419) 285-2184 – Page 28, C-3 352-foot granite column commemorates American naval victory over British at 1813 Battle of Lake Erie and subsequent lasting peace between US and Britain. Observation platform and museum.

PIATT CASTLES – West Liberty – (937) 465-2821 – Page 56, B-3 1864 Castle Piatt Mac-A-Cheek, built in style of Norman-French chateau, contains original furnishings. 1879 Castle Mac-O-Chee is replica of Flemish chateau housing European art and furnishings.

PIQUA HISTORICAL AREA – 3.5 mi. NW of Piqua – (937) 773-2522 – Page 55, C-5 Early 19th-century farm buildings of Indian agent John Johnson. Historic Indian Museum featuring artifacts of Ohio tribes. Prehistoric Adena Indian ring-shaped earthwork. Pioneer cemetery.

RAILROAD MUSEUM – Conneaut – (440) 599-7878 – Page 33, A-7 Housed in former New York Central depot. Scale models of locomotives, railroad memorabilia, restored engine and caboose.

RANKIN HOUSE – Ripley – (937) 392-1627 – Page 83, B-5 Restored home of abolitionist Reverend John Rankin; stopping point for "underground railroad."

ROSCOE VILLAGE – Coshocton – (740) 622-9310 – Page 60, B-3 Restored 19th-century Ohio-Erie Canal town with homes and shops. Visitor center with audio-visual presentation and displays. Canal boat rides.

SAUDER MUSEUM FARM AND VILLAGE – Archbold – (419) 446-2541 – Page 25, D-5 Restored farm and pioneer village. Museum featuring farm implements, woodworking tools and household items. Traditional craft demonstrations.

SCHOENBRUNN – New Philadelphia – (330) 339-3636 – Page 61, A-7 Reconstructed 1772 Moravian mission to Ohio Indians. 19 log buildings. Costumed guides.

SHANDY HALL – Geneva – (440) 466-3680 – Page 32, B-4 Restored 1815 pioneer home. Original furnishings. Dining room features rare block-printed French wallpaper.

SLATE RUN FARM – Ashville – (740) 833-1880 – Page 68, B-3 Fully operating 1880's central Ohio farm. Work done using late 19th-century machinery, implements and methods.

STAN HYWET HALL AND GARDENS – Akron – (330) 836-5533 – Page 41, D-6 Tudor Revival home of Frank Seiberling, founder of Goodyear Tire and Rubber Company. Built in 1915. 65 rooms. Collections include Stuart and Tudor furniture, Flemish tapestries, antique silver, European sculpture and portraiture. *(See Gardens.)*

SUMMIT COUNTY HISTORICAL SOCIETY – Akron – (330) 535-1120 – Page 41, D-6 Perkins Mansion with displays depicting industrialization of agrarian society in late 19th century. Restored home of abolitionist John Brown houses period furniture. Local history exhibits in visitor center.

THOMAS EDISON BIRTHPLACE MUSEUM – Milan – (419) 499-2135 – Page 39, B-5 Boyhood home of inventor Thomas Alva Edison. Family furnishings and memorabilia. Guided tours.

USS COD SUBMARINE – Cleveland – (216) 566-8770 – Page 31, D-5 World War II submarine that made seven war patrols against Japanese. Tours.

WARREN COUNTY MUSEUM – Lebanon – (513) 932-1817 – Page 75, A-6 Shaker Gallery offers extensive collection of Shaker furniture and household items from Union Village settlement.

WESTERN RESERVE MUSEUM – Cleveland – (216) 721-5722 – Page 31, D-6 Antique furniture and decorative arts displayed in series of period rooms. Permanent exhibit traces history of Western Reserve from 1796 to 1870's.

WOLCOTT HOUSE MUSEUM COMPLEX – Maumee – (419) 893-9602 – Page 26, D-3 Historic building complex including log cabin, Federal-style house, Greek Revival house, salt box farm and railroad depot.

ZOAR VILLAGE – Zoar – (330) 874- 3011 – Page 51, D-7 Communal settlement founded in 1817 by German immigrants. Restored buildings include residence and shops. Historical museum. Formal gardens.

ANCIENT INDIAN CULTURES

The sites listed below feature earthworks and artifacts left behind by Ohio Indian cultures, including the prehistoric Adena (800 B.C. to 100 A.D.) and Hopewell (100 B.C. to 400 A.D.) Indians that once inhabited southern and central Ohio. The exact uses of these elaborate earthworks are not clear, although they are believed to have served social, religious and burial purposes.

ADENA MOUND – Enon – (937) 864-7756 – Page 66, A-1 Second largest Adena mound in Ohio. Adjacent 1820's log cabin.

CAMPBELL MOUND STATE MEMORIAL – Columbus – (614) 297-2300 – Page 68, A-1 Conical burial mound built by Adena Indians. 20 feet high, 100 feet in diameter. Stairs to top.

FLINT RIDGE STATE MEMORIAL – Newark – (740) 787-2476 – Page 69, A-7 Museum on site of ancient Indian flint quarry. Exhibits on geology, prehistoric man and flint quarrying. Nature preserve.

FORT ANCIENT MUSEUM – Oregonia – (513) 932-4421 – Page 75, A-7 Earthworks and museum of Hopewell and Fort Ancient Indian cultures. Nature trails.

FORT HILL STATE MEMORIAL – 3 mi. S of Cynthiana – (937) 588-3221 – Page 77, D-5 40-acre hilltop enclosure built by prehistoric Hopewell Indians. Stone and earthen wall approximately 1.5 miles long, 6 to 15 feet high and 40 feet wide at base. Nature trails.

INSCRIPTION ROCK – Kelleys Island – (614) 297-2300 – Page 28, D-4 Pictographs attributed to 17th-century Erie Indians. Etchings of birds and animals, and humans wearing headdresses.

LEO PETROGLYPH STATE MEMORIAL – Leo – (614) 297-2300 – Page 79, C-4 Prehistoric Indian inscriptions.

MIAMISBURG MOUND STATE MEMORIAL – Miamisburg – (614) 297-2300 – Page 65, C-5 Largest conical burial mound in Ohio, built by Adena Indians. 877 feet in circumference; originally more than 70 feet high. Stairs from base to summit.

MOUND CEMETERY – Marietta – no phone – Page 81, A-7 30-foot-high Hopewell Indian conical mound in cemetery containing graves of Revolutionary War soldiers.

MOUND CITY GROUP NATIONAL MONUMENT – Chillicothe – (740) 774-1125 – Page 78, A-1 23 burial mounds of prehistoric Hopewell Indians. Visitor Center. Observation platform.

MOUNDBUILDERS EARTHWORKS – Newark – (740) 344-1920 – Page 59, D-6 Great Circle earthworks built by Hopewell Indians. Embankment is 1,200 feet in diameter with earthen walls 8 to 14 feet high, and enclosing 26-acre area. Ohio Indian Art Museum displays artifacts representing all prehistoric cultures of Ohio.

OCTAGON EARTHWORKS – Newark – (614) 297-2300 – Page 59, D-6 Eight-sided earthworks, enclosing 50 acres, is joined by parallel walls to circular embankment enclosing 20 acres.

SEIP MOUND – 3 mi. E. of Bainbridge – (614) 297-2300 – Page 77, C-7 Geometric Hopewell Indian burial mound. 240 feet long, 160 feet wide and 30 feet high. Central mound of group of geometric earthworks.

SERPENT MOUND STATE MEMORIAL – Peebles – (937) 587-2796 – Page 77, D-5 Largest serpent effigy mound in US. Built by Adena Indians. 20 feet wide, nearly 0.25 mile long. Represents uncoiling serpent. Museum houses pottery artifacts, implements and models depicting mound's construction.

STORY MOUND – Chillicothe – (614) 297-2300 – Page 78, B-2 Large rounded earthen mound standing 19.5 feet high, 95 feet in diameter at base. Built by Adena Indians. 19th-century excavations unearthed circular timber structure, first recognized example of Adena architectural style.

TARLETON CROSS MOUND STATE MEMORIAL – Tarleton – (614) 297-2300 – Page 68, D-3 90-foot mound in shape of cross, believed to have been built by Hopewell Indians.

WRIGHT EARTHWORKS – Newark – (614) 297-2300 – Page 59, D-6 Small section of large square enclosure built by Hopewell Indians.

Art Museums/Science Centers

AKRON ART MUSEUM – Akron – (330) 376-9185 – Page 41, D-6 Italian Renaissance-style building houses permanent collections. American and European painting, sculpture, photographs and prints from 1850 to present. Tours.

ALLEN MEMORIAL ART MUSEUM – Oberlin – (216) 775-8665 – Page 40, B-1 Located on Oberlin College campus. Over 10,000 works of art including 20th-century American and European paintings, contemporary prints, sculpture, Japanese woodcuts, costumes and textiles.

ART CENTER – Zanesville – (740) 452-0741 – Page 70, A-2 European, Oriental and American art including painting, drawing and photography. Local ceramics and glass.

ART INSTITUTE – Dayton – (937) 223-5277 – Page 65, B-6 Collections include European and American painting and sculpture; classical, Oriental and pre-Columbian primitive objects; prints, ceramics and decorative arts. Exhibits housed in Italian Renaissance Revival building. Guided tours.

ART MUSEUM – Cincinnati – (513) 721-5204 – Page 74, D-4 Located in Eden Park. Over 100 galleries exhibit paintings, prints, sculpture, drawings, musical instruments, costumes, period rooms, decorative arts and photography. Tours.

BUTLER INSTITUTE OF AMERICAN ART – Youngstown – (330) 743-1711 – Page 43, D-6 Collections include American art from colonial times to present. Major works by Copley, Homer, Hopper, Remington, Shahn and Warhol. Nautical paintings. Western art.

CAMBRIDGE GLASS MUSEUM – Cambridge – (740) 432-3045 – Page 61, D-6 Over 4,000 pieces of glass and pottery made between 1901 and 1954. Tours.

CANTON ART INSTITUTE – Canton – (330) 453-7666 – Page 52, B-1 Over 1,900 works of art in permanent collection. European and American painting, sculpture, graphics and decorative arts. Japanese garden.

CENTER FOR CONTEMPORARY ART – Cleveland – (216) 421-8671 – Page 31, D-6 Changing exhibits of contemporary art by national and regional artists.

CENTER OF SCIENCE AND INDUSTRY – Columbus – (740) 221-2674 – Page 68, A-2 Participatory museum with focus on science, industry, health and history. Exhibits include time tunnel. transparent talking woman, coal mine, weather station and computers. Live science demonstrations. Traveling exhibits. Planetarium.

CHILDREN'S MUSEUM – Cleveland – (216) 791-5437 – Page 31, D-6 Hands-on museum for ages 3–12. Exhibits focus on building construction and bridges. Changing exhibits.

CINCINNATI OBSERVATORY – Cincinnati – (937) 321-5186 – Page 75, C-4 First US observatory, founded in 1842. Moved from Mt. Adams in 1873 due to increased pollution.

CONTEMPORARY ARTS CENTER – Cincinnati – (513) 721-0390 – Page 74, D-3 Changing contemporary art exhibits ranging from painting, sculpture, photography and architecture to multimedia installations and conceptual, experimental and video art.

DAYTON POWER AND LIGHT MUSEUM – Dayton – (937) 227-2241 – Page 65, C-6 Historic artifacts related to gas and electric utility industries, including 1905 Edison phonograph, 1820 gas street light and hand-operated washing machine.

DEGENHART PAPERWEIGHT AND GLASS MUSEUM – Cambridge – (740) 432-2626 – Page 61, D-6 Collections include midwestern pattern glass, 20th-century paperweights; blown, cut and art glass.

HEALTH EDUCATION MUSEUM – Cleveland – (216) 231-5010 – Page 31, D-6 Hands-on exhibits explore health topics including the brain, dental health, childbirth, aging and human senses. Guided tours.

JAPANESE EDUCATION CENTER – Westerville – (614) 882-2964 – Page 58, D-2 Japanese home, garden, Shinto shrine, dolls, toys, pottery and art pieces.

MASSILLION MUSEUM – Massillion – (216) 833-4061 – Page 51, B-6 Collections include American and European fine and decorative arts, folk arts, photographs and household items relating to local history and contemporary art.

MCKINLEY MUSEUM – Canton – (330) 455-7043 – Page 51, B-7 General museum featuring exhibits tracing US and local industrial history. Science hall includes 75 hands-on displays exploring electricity, transportation and physical sciences. Hoover-Price Planetarium.

MIAMI UNIVERSITY ART MUSEUM – Oxford – (937) 529-2232 – Page 64, D-2 Collections include American painting, 20th-century sculpture, decorative arts, folk art and African, Oceanic and pre-Columbian art. Tours.

MUSEUM OF ART – Cleveland – (216) 421-7340 – Page 31, D-6 Permanent collections include Western painting, Oriental art, medieval artifacts, decorative arts, painting and drawings. Sculpture court. Special exhibitions.

MUSEUM OF ART – Columbus – (740) 221-6801 – Page 68, A-2 Major works from many historical periods. Oriental art, Native American artifacts, African and Oceanic objects, Eskimo carvings. Changing exhibits. Tours.

MUSEUM OF ART – Toledo – (419) 255-8000 – Page 27, C-4 European and American painting and decorative arts, sculpture, prints and graphics. Glass collection.

MUSEUM OF NATURAL HISTORY – Cincinnati – (513) 621-3889 – Page 74, D-4 Exhibits focus on Ohio archaeology, anthropology, plants and wildlife. Full-scale replica of cavern with waterfall. Planetarium. Nature center.

MUSEUM OF NATURAL HISTORY – Cleveland – (216) 231-4600 – Page 31, D-6 Exhibits trace development of life on planet, including dinosaurs, geological displays, artifacts from North American Indian cultures, live animals and garden featuring native plants. Ralph Mueller Planetarium. Tours.

MUSEUM OF NATURAL HISTORY – Dayton – (937) 275-7431 – Page 65, B-6 Exhibits and live animals emphasizing Miami Valley area. Apollo observatory with 50-centimeter telescope. Planetarium.

MUSEUM OF NATURAL SCIENCES – Toledo – (419) 385-5721 – Page 26, D-4 Collections explore anthropology, geology and animal life. "Diversity of Life" exhibit. Guided tours.

NASA VISITOR INFORMATION CENTER – Cleveland – (216) 433-2001– Page 40, A-4 Aeronautics and space museum located on grounds of NASA Lewis Research Center. Communications satellites and space shuttles on display. Guided tours by advance reservation.

NATIONAL HEISEY GLASS MUSEUM – Newark – (740) 345-2932 – Page 59, D-6 Glassware made by A. H. Heisey and Company from 1895 to 1957. Glassmaking tools. Factory memorabilia and records.

NEIL ARMSTRONG AIR AND SPACE MUSEUM – Wapakoneta – (419) 738-8811 – Page 45, D-6 Displays and artifacts of air and space achievements, with focus on contributions by Ohioans. Exhibits include historic aircraft, hot air balloon and spacecraft. Audio-visual presentations.

OHIO CERAMIC CENTER – Crooksville – (740) 697-7021 – Page 70, B-2 Exhibits trace development of pottery industry from 1750 to present. Displays and demonstrations on pottery making.

ORTON GEOLOGICAL MUSEUM – Columbus – (614) 292-4473 – Page 68, A-1 Located on Ohio State University campus. Exhibits examine minerals, fossils and Ohio geological history. 10,000-year-old skeleton of giant ground sloth.

PERKINS OBSERVATORY – Delaware – (740) 363-1257 – Page 58, C-1 32-inch reflecting telescope. Public programs.

SOUTHERN OHIO MUSEUM AND CULTURAL CENTER – Portsmouth – (740) 354-5629 – Page 85, C-5 Collections include American, folk and decorative arts. Guided tours.

TAFT MUSEUM – Cincinnati – (937) 241-0343 – Page 74, D-3 Collections include portraits by Rembrandt, Hals, van Dyck and Goya; landscapes by Gainsborough and Ruisdael; Chinese porcelains and French Renaissance enamels. Formal gardens. Guided tours.

WARTHER CARVINGS – Dover – (330) 343-7513 – Page 51, D-7 Hand-carved works by Ernest Warther in ebony, ivory and pearl. Carvings trace history of steam-powered devices and engines from 250 B.C. to present.

A Campgrounds

To locate campgrounds in this Atlas, look on the appropriate map for the campground symbol and corresponding four-digit number. Members of the Ohio Campground Owners Association (OCOA) are listed here.

#	NAME, TOWN	Campsites	Electricity	Propane	Shower	Laundry	Store	Pets	Recreation Hall	Dump Station	Fishing	Swimming	Boating	ATLAS LOCATION
2000	Airport RV Park, Hebron	119	●		●			●	●	●				Page 69, A-5
2001	Alken Lakes, Bellefontaine	145	●	●	●	●	●	●	●	●	●			Page 56, A-3
2002	Amish Country Campsite, Winesburg	60	●		●				●					Page 51, D-5
2003	Auburn Lake Park, New Washington	112	●		●		●	●	●	●	●			Page 48, A-3
2006	Audubon Lakes Campground, Geneva	125	●		●	●	●	●	●	●	●	●	●	Page 32, B-4
2009	Austin Lake Park & Campground, Toronto	150	●	●	●	●		●	●	●	●	●		Page 63, A-6
2015	Barn Yard Campsite, Cambridge	50			●				●					Page 61, D-7
2018	Bass Lake Family Recreation, Springfield	95	●		●		●	●	●	●		●		Page 66, A-2
2021	Bay Shore, Andover	500	●		●		●	●	●	●	●	●	●	Page 33, D-7
2023	Baylor Beach Park, Canton	50	●		●		●	●	●	●		●		Page 51, C-6
2025	Bayshore Estates Campground, Sandusky	430	●		●	●	●	●	●	●	●			Page 39, A-4
2027	Beck's Family Campground, Wooster	100	●	●	●		●	●	●	●	●			Page 50, A-3
2030	Berkshire Campgrounds, Columbus	400	●		●	●	●	●	●	●	●	●		Page 58, C-2
2035	Blue Lagoon Campground & Canoe Livery, Mansfield	42	●	●	●	●	●	●	●	●	●	●	●	Page 49, D-6
2039	Bob Boord Park, East Rochester	250	●	●	●	●	●	●	●	●	●			Page 52, B-3
2041	Brunswick Lake Recreation, Brunswick	250	●		●				●		●			Page 41, C-4
2043	Buccaneer Campsites, Jefferson	170	●		●		●	●	●	●	●			Page 33, B-5
2044	Buckeye Lake KOA/Columbus East, Buckeye Lake	205	●	●	●	●	●	●	●	●	●	●		Page 69, A-6
2045	Buffalo Trail Camping Area, Chillicothe	85	●		●		●	●	●	●	●	●		Page 78, B-3
2046	Camp America, Oxford	24	●		●		●	●	●	●				Page 64, D-1
2048	Camp Coonpath, Lancaster	149	●	●	●		●	●	●	●		●		Page 68, B-4
2051	Camp Toodik Family Campground & Canoe Livery, Loudonville	185	●		●	●	●	●	●	●	●	●	●	Page 50, C-1
2057	Campbell Cove Camping, Logan	98	●					●	●		●			Page 69, D-6
2060	Camper Village—Cedar Point, Sandusky	430	●		●	●	●	●		●				Page 38, A-4
2063	Cave Lake Park, Sinking Spring	400	●	●	●		●	●	●	●	●	●		Page 77, D-6
2069	Cedarbrook Campground, Lebanon	150	●		●		●	●	●	●				Page 75, A-6
2070	Cedarlane Campground, Port Clinton	350	●		●	●	●	●	●	●	●			Page 28, D-3
2071	Chaparral Family Campground, Salem	225	●	●	●	●	●	●	●	●	●	●	●	Page 53, A-5
2073	Charlie's Place, Lisbon	80	●		●		●	●	●	●				Page 53, C-6
2075	Cherokee Park, Akron	100	●	●				●	●	●	●			Page 42, D-1
2078	Clare-Mar Lakes Campground, Wellington	500	●		●		●	●	●	●	●		●	Page 39, D-7
2081	Clinton Lake Camping, Republic	160	●		●		●	●	●	●	●			Page 38, C-1
2084	Country Acres Campground, Ravenna	200	●	●	●	●	●	●	●	●	●	●		Page 42, C-3
2088	Country Stage Campground, Nova	100	●		●		●	●	●	●	●			Page 39, D-7
2093	Crawford's Market & Campground, Springfield	300	●		●	●	●	●	●					Page 66, A-3
2096	Crystal Springs, Cleveland	96	●		●			●	●	●	●	●	●	Page 40, B-3
2099	Cutty's Sunset Camping Resort, Louisville	575	●				●	●	●	●	●			Page 52, A-2
2103	Dayton Tall Timbers KOA, Dayton	235	●	●	●	●	●	●	●	●	●	●		Page 65, B-4
2104	Deer Creek Camping Resort, Mount Sterling	450	●	●	●	●	●	●	●	●	●			Page 67, D-7
2105	Dogwood Valley Camp, Mt. Gilead	225	●		●	●	●	●	●	●	●	●	●	Page 48, D-3
2111	E-Z Camp Area, Wapakoneta	50	●		●		●	●	●	●				Page 53, A-5
2114	Enon Beach, Springfield	150	●		●		●	●	●	●	●	●		Page 66, A-1
2115	Evergreen Lake Park, Conneaut	300	●	●	●		●	●	●	●	●	●		Page 33, A-7
2117	Fort Ancient Campground, Lebanon	98	●		●		●	●	●	●				Page 75, A-7
2120	Fox's Den Campground, Put-In-Bay	64	●		●	●	●	●	●	●				Page 28, C-3
2123	Foxfire Family Campground, Nevada	160	●				●	●	●	●	●	●		Page 48, B-1
2126	Friendship Acres Park, Randolph	100	●	●	●		●	●	●	●	●			Page 42, D-2
2132	Good's Woods Campground, Carrollton	150	●	●	●		●	●	●	●	●			Page 52, D-4
2135	Happy Hills Family Campground, Nelsonville	60	●	●	●		●	●	●	●	●	●		Page 79, A-7
2136	Heritage Acres, Bowling Green	92	●		●		●	●	●	●	●			Page 36, B-3
2137	Heritage Hills Campground, Thompson	250	●		●		●	●	●	●	●			Page 32, C-3
2138	Hickory Grove Lake Campground, Marion	200	●		●		●	●	●	●	●	●		Page 47, D-7
2141	Hickory Hill Lakes, Sidney	128	●		●		●	●	●	●	●	●		Page 55, B-5
2144	Hidden Acres Campground, West Salem	185	●	●	●		●	●	●	●	●			Page 50, A-1
2147	Hidden Cove Resort, Deerfield	170	●					●	●	●	●	●		Page 42, D-3
2150	Hidden Valley Campground, Ravenna	140	●	●	●		●	●	●	●	●	●		Page 42, C-1
2159	Hide-A-Way Lakes Campground, Ashtabula	200	●		●		●	●	●	●	●	●		Page 33, B-5
2162	Hillside Park of Clinton, Clinton	150	●		●	●	●	●	●	●				Page 51, A-6
2166	Hillview Acres Campground, Cambridge	125	●		●		●	●	●	●	●	●		Page 61, D-6
2171	Honey-Do Campground, Spencer	220	●	●			●	●	●	●	●			Page 40, D-2
2172	Honeycreek Valley Campground, Bellville	70	●		●				●	●	●			Page 49, D-5
2174	Huron River Valley Campground & Marina, Huron	200	●		●		●	●	●	●	●		●	Page 39, B-5
2177	Indian Creek Camping Resort, Geneva-on-the-Lake	561	●	●	●	●	●	●	●	●	●	●		Page 33, B-4
2180	Indian Mound Campground, Athens	50	●		●				●	●				Page 80, B-1
2181	Indian Trail Campground, New London	169	●		●	●	●	●	●	●	●			Page 39, D-6
2186	Jackson Lake Park, Columbus	200	●		●		●	●	●	●	●			Page 68, B-3
2190	Kenisee's Grand River Camp & Canoe, Geneva	300	●		●		●	●	●	●	●	●	●	Page 33, B-4
2197	Kool Lakes Family Camping, Parkman	200	●		●		●	●	●	●	●	●	●	Page 42, B-3
2200	L. B. Camping, Bainbridge	50	●	●				●	●					Page 77, C-7
2204	Lake Hill, Chillicothe	200	●	●			●	●	●	●	●	●	●	Page 77, A-7
2210	Lake Snowden Recreation Area, Albany	112	●					●	●	●	●	●		Page 80, C-1
2213	Lake Wapusun Campground, Loudonville	400	●	●			●	●	●	●	●	●		Page 50, C-2
2215	Lakeview RV Park & Campground, Lancaster	46	●		●			●	●	●	●			Page 69, C-5
2216	Lazy R Campground, Granville	195	●		●		●	●	●	●	●			Page 59, D-6
2222	Long Lake Park, Loudonville	225	●		●		●	●	●	●	●	●		Page 50, C-1

18

CAMPGROUNDS, *continued*

To locate campgrounds in this Atlas, look on the appropriate map for the campground symbol and corresponding four-digit number. Members of the Ohio Campground Owners Association (OCOA) are listed here.

	NAME, TOWN	CAMPSITES	ELECTRICITY	PROPANE	SHOWER	LAUNDRY	STORE	PETS	RECREATION HALL	DUMP STATION	FISHING	SWIMMING	BOATING	ATLAS LOCATION
2225	Long's Retreat Family Campground, Latham	450	•	•	•	•	•	•	•	•	•	•	•	Page 77, D-6
2234	Maple Lakes Campground, Seville	225	•	•	•				•	•	•			Page 40, D-4
2235	The Maples, Grafton	25	•	•			•			•	•			Page 40, C-2
2237	Mar-Lynn Lake Park, Streetsboro	250	•	•	•	•			•	•	•	•		Page 41, C-7
2238	Meadow Lake Park, Wooster	165	•					•	•	•	•			Page 50, A-3
2240	Meadow Lake Resort, Urbana	170	•	•				•	•	•	•			Page 56, C-2
2246	Mohican Reservation Campgrounds & Canoeing, Loudonville	175	•		•			•	•	•	•		•	Page 50, D-1
2249	Mohican Wilderness, Loudonville	240	•		•	•	•	•	•	•	•		•	Page 50, D-1
2258	Olentangy Indian Caverns, Columbus	200	•		•		•	•		•	•			Page 58, C-1
2261	Olive Branch Campground, Lebanon	140	•	•		•	•	•	•	•	•	•		Page 75, A-7
2270	Paradise Lake Park, East Rochester	600	•	•	•	•	•		•	•	•	•	•	Page 52, B-4
2273	Paradise Valley Campground, Cambridge	70	•		•			•		•	•	•		Page 61, C-6
2276	Pier-Lon Park, Medina	350	•		•		•	•	•	•	•	•		Page 40, D-2
2279	Pin Oak Lake Park, Milan	230	•		•		•	•	•	•	•	•		Page 39, B-6
2282	Pine Lakes Campground, Orwell	275	•		•		•	•	•	•	•	•		Page 33, D-5
2294	Pleasant View Recreation, Van Buren	300	•	•	•	•	•	•	•	•	•			Page 36, C-3
2296	Plymouth Shore RV Park & Marina, Marblehead	107	•					•		•	•	•	•	Page 28, D-3
2300	Ridge Ranch, Warren	250	•	•		•	•	•	•	•	•	•	•	Page 42, C-4
2303	Rippling Stream Campground, Baltimore	150	•	•			•	•	•	•	•			Page 69, B-4
2306	River Run Family Campground, Loudonville	160	•		•		•	•	•	•	•	•		Page 49, D-7
2312	Rustic Knolls Campsites, Mt. Vernon	150	•		•		•	•	•	•	•			Page 59, B-5
2315	Rustic Lakes Campgrounds, Wellington	275	•		•	•		•	•	•	•	•		Page 40, D-1
2316	Scenic Hills RV Park, Berlin	34	•					•		•	•			Page 51, D-4
2318	Schaun Acres Campground, Oberlin	98	•	•	•	•	•	•	•	•	•	•		Page 39, C-7
2321	Sea Lake Resort, Aurora	300	•		•	•	•		•	•	•	•		Page 42, B-1
2324	Seneca Campground, Clyde	188	•		•		•	•	•	•	•	•		Page 38, C-1
2327	Shady Lake Campground, Findlay	109	•		•		•	•	•	•	•	•	•	Page 36, D-3
2328	Shady Trails Campground, Hillsboro	150	•		•		•	•	•	•				Page 77, C-5
2330	Shawnee Lake Park, Spencer	218	•					•	•	•	•	•		Page 40, D-2
2333	Sherwood Forrest, Lodi	96	•				•		•	•	•	•	•	Page 40, D-2
2335	Smith's Hickory Lakes, Ashland	180	•	•	•	•	•	•	•	•	•	•		Page 50, B-1
2337	Smith's Pleasant Valley Family Campground, Loudonville	170	•		•		•	•	•	•	•	•	•	Page 50, D-1
2338	Spring Valley Campground, Cambridge	130	•		•		•	•	•	•	•	•		Page 71, A-6
2340	Spring Valley Frontier Campground, Waynesville	200	•		•	•		•	•	•	•	•		Page 65, D-7
2342	Stillwater Beach Campground, Piqua	100	•				•	•	•	•	•			Page 54, C-4
2345	Stony Ridge KOA Kampground, Toledo	58	•	•	•	•		•	•	•				Page 27, D-5
2348	Sun Valley Campground, Chillicothe	45	•		•			•	•	•	•	•		Page 78, A-1
2349	Sun Valley Family Campground, Harrod	185	•	•	•	•	•	•	•	•	•			Page 46, C-1
2351	Sunset Lake Campground, Spencer	200	•	•	•	•	•	•	•	•	•	•	•	Page 40, D-2
2357	Tamsin Park Camping Resort, Peninsula	250	•	•	•		•	•	•	•	•			Page 41, C-7
2363	Terrace Lakes Campground, Sullivan	145	•		•		•	•	•	•	•			Page 50, A-1
2365	Timashamie Family Campground, Salem	175	•	•	•	•	•	•	•	•	•			Page 52, B-4
2366	Top O' The Caves, Logan	200	•		•	•		•	•	•	•			Page 79, A-5
2369	Town & Country Camp Resort, West Salem	200	•		•	•	•	•	•	•	•	•		Page 50, A-2
2371	Traveland Family Campground, Sandusky	250	•	•	•	•	•	•	•	•	•			Page 38, A-3
2372	Tree Haven Campground, Westerville	130	•		•		•		•		•			Page 58, C-3
2374	Tri-Country Kamp Inn, Chardon	240	•		•		•	•	•	•	•			Page 32, D-3
2375	Tucaway Lake, Ravenna	184	•		•		•	•	•	•	•	•		Page 42, C-1
2378	Twin Lakes Park, Bluffton	85	•		•		•	•	•	•	•	•	•	Page 46, A-2
2381	Twin Valley Campground, Carrollton	120	•		•			•	•	•	•			Page 52, D-4
2384	Valley Lake Park, Warren	100	•		•			•	•	•	•	•	•	Page 42, B-4
2387	Valleyview Lake Resort, Streetsboro	225	•		•		•	•	•	•	•			Page 42, C-1
2390	Wagon Wheel Campground, Shelby	95	•		•		•	•	•	•	•			Page 48, A-4
2393	Walnut Grove Campground, Tiffin	230	•		•	•	•	•	•	•	•	•	•	Page 37, D-7
2396	Wapakoneta/Lima South KOA, Wapakoneta	75	•	•		•	•	•	•	•	•			Page 45, D-6
2399	Whip-Poor-Will Hills, Brinkhaven	100	•		•		•		•	•	•	•		Page 60, A-1
2401	Whispering Hills Recreation, Shreve	300	•	•	•	•	•	•	•	•	•			Page 50, C-2
2403	Wild Wings Marina & RV Park, Oak Harbor	450	•	•	•	•	•	•	•	•	•		•	Page 28, D-1
2405	Wild Wood Lakes Campground, Homerville	275	•		•	•	•	•	•	•	•	•		Page 40, D-2
2406	Wildcat Woods Campground, Greenville	100	•		•		•	•	•	•	•			Page 54, D-1
2411	Willow Lake Park, Brunswick	250	•		•		•	•		•	•	•		Page 40, C-4
2414	Windrush Hollow, Huntsburg	175	•		•		•		•	•	•			Page 32, D-3
2419	Woodbridge Campground, Paulding	140	•		•		•	•	•	•	•			Page 34, D-4
2420	Wooded Acres Campground, Fremont	130	•	•				•	•	•	•	•		Page 37, A-7
2423	Woodside Lake Park, Streetsboro	300	•			•	•	•		•	•	•	•	Page 42, B-1
2424	Yogi Bear's Jellystone Park, Bellevue	100	•	•	•	•	•	•	•	•				Page 38, B-3
2425	Yogi Bear's Jellystone Park Camp Resort, Mansfield	250	•	•	•	•	•	•	•	•	•	•		Page 49, D-5
2427	Yogi Bear's Jellystone Park Camp Resort, Mantua	500	•	•	•	•	•	•	•	•	•	•	•	Page 42, B-1
2435	Yogi Bear's Jellystone Park—Kings Island, Cincinnati	350	•	•	•	•	•	•	•			•		Page 75, B-5

Hiking

BACKPACK TRAIL – Lake Vesuvius Recreation Area – Page 85, D-7 – 16 miles Located in Wayne National Forest *(see Forests)*. Trailhead at Vesuvius boat dock. Moderately strenuous loop trail follows lakeshore and ridgetops and passes through hilly, wooded terrain. Marked with yellow diamonds. Camping on national forest land outside recreation area boundaries. *(See Parks.)*

BLACKHAND GORGE STATE NATURE PRESERVE – Toboso – Page 60, D-1 – distances vary System of trails through 970-acre preserve featuring narrow Blackhand Gorge *(see Unique Natural Features)*. Rugged terrain includes exposed sandstone formations, wooded slopes and ravines. Remains of Ohio-Erie Canal, Ohio Railroad and electric interurban trolley line dot the area.

BUCKEYE TRAIL – Hocking Hills State Park – Page 79, A-5 – 1,200 miles Loop trail encircling state, open to non-motorized use. Route passes through urban, rural and wilderness areas. Off-road portions follow abandoned railroad right-of-ways, old canal towpaths, rivers, lake shores and flat farmland. Designated portion of North Country National Scenic Trail, connecting states from Vermont to North Dakota. Marked with blue blazes and distance markers. Camping in designated areas only. Information available from Buckeye Trail Association, Inc., P.O. Box 254, Worthington, OH 43085.

BURR OAK BACKPACK TRAIL – Burr Oak State Park – Page 70, D-2 – 29 miles Loop trail encircling Burr Oak Reservoir. Trailhead at boat dock Number 4. Terrain varies from slight inclines to very steep slopes. Route through forest passes unusual rock outcrops, caves and scenic vistas. Backpackers must register at check-in station. Camping in designated areas only. Intersects Buckeye and Wildcat Hollow Trails *(see above and below)*.

DEER TRAIL – 3 mi. S of Cynthiana – Page 77, D-5 – 5 miles Strenuous loop trail beginning at parking lot and crossing Baker Fork, Reed Hill and Jarnigans Knob to natural bridge. Route circles Fort Hill for return to starting point. Marked with blue blazes.

EAST FORK BACKCOUNTRY TRAIL – East Fork State Park – Page 75, D-7 – 37 miles Moderately strenuous loop trail crossing variety of habitats from woodlands to marshy meadows. Trailhead at camp check-in station. Registration required for backpackers and overnight horsemen. Marked with green blazes. Two primitive campsites and one developed campground along route. CAUTION: During rainy weather, Army Corps of Engineers may open flood gates on East Fork River, and rising river level may be unsafe for hikers at two river crossings. *(See Parks.)*

GRANDMA GATEWOOD TRAIL – Hocking Hills State Park – Page 79, A-5 – 6 miles Popular hike connecting Old Man's Cave, Cedar Falls and Ash Cave *(see Unique Natural Features)*. Trailhead at Upper Falls at Old Man's Cave. Route passes gorge, caves, waterfalls and high cliffs. Pathway includes steps and bridges. Section of Buckeye Trail *(see above)*. *(See Parks.)*

JOHN BRYAN STATE PARK – 2 mi. W of Clifton – Page 66, B-2 – distances vary Ten miles of hiking trails along Little Miami River and through scenic Clifton Gorge *(see Unique Natural Features and Parks)*.

LA TRAINEE DE L'EXPLORATEUR – Cincinnati – Page 74, C-3 – 10 miles Wilderness hiking trail through 1,500-acre Mt. Airy Forest. Route follows ridges, crosses ravines and streams, and passes through hardwood and evergreen forests. Points of interest include 120-acre Mt. Airy Arboretum *(see Gardens)*, scenic views, fossil beds and sinkholes.

LITTLE MIAMI SCENIC TRAIL – Milford – Page 75, C-5 – 47 miles Paved multi-use trail extending through five counties along Little Miami River. *(See Parks and Bicycle Routes.)*

LOGAN TRAIL – Tar Hollow State Park – Page 78, A-4 – 23 miles Strenuous trail through Tar Hollow State Forest made up of northern and southern loops. Trailhead at Pine Lake Picnic Area. Route passes through woodlands and follows ridgetops. Marked with red blazes. One campsite along southern loop. *(See Parks and Forests.)*

MIAMI AND ERIE CANAL TRAIL – Independence Dam State Park – Page 35, B-5 – 3 miles Hiking trail along towpath of historic Miami and Erie Canal. Working lock located at west end of park. *(See Parks.)*

OHIO VIEW TRAIL – Beaverton – Page 73, C-7 – 7 miles Located in Wayne National Forest *(see Forests)*. Trailhead 0.25 mile north of Beaverton on State Route 7. Parking. Trail wanders north along ridges in scenic hill country. Route passes sandstone cliffs, caves and Ohio River overlook. Trail ends at State Route 260 near Yellow House.

SHAWNEE BACKPACK TRAIL – Shawnee State Park – Page 84, C-3 – 43 miles Strenuous trail over rugged terrain in Shawnee State Forest *(see Forests)*. Trailhead and parking for two loops at self-registration area in state park. Steep ascents to wooded ridgetops. Marked with orange blazes. Side trail to wilderness area marked with white blazes. Camping in designated areas only. Drinking water at seven hydrants along route. Trail map available from Shawnee State Forest, Route 5, Box 151C, Portsmouth, OH 45662. *(See Parks.)*

TOWPATH TRAIL – Cuyahoga Valley National Recreation Area – Page 41, C-6 – 2.5 miles National Recreation Trail along original towpath for Ohio-Erie Canal. Trailhead on Pine Hill Road. Scenic, flat hike north along path between waters of Cuyahoga River and canal. Route passes through pine forest.

VIRGINIA KENDALL PARK – Cuyahoga Valley National Recreation Area – Page 41, C-6 – distances vary Trail system leading to geological features including rock ledges, hanging gardens and Icebox Cave. Woodlands and meadows. Visitor center. Trails vary from easy to strenuous. *(See Parks.)*

WILDCAT HOLLOW BACKPACKING TRAIL – 3 mi. SE of Ringgold – Page 70, D-2 – 13 miles Scenic, marked loop trail located in Wayne National Forest *(see Forests)*. Trailhead and parking lot on County Route 58. Trail follows ridgetops and streambeds. Route passes white pine forests, open meadows, old roads and rock outcroppings.

ZALESKI BACKPACK TRAIL – 5 mi. N of Zaleski – Page 79, B-7 – 23.5 miles Parking and self-registration at trailhead on State Route 278 across from ruins of Hope Furnace. Numbered posts along trail correspond to interpretive brochure available from Zaleski State Forest, Zaleski, OH 45698 *(see Forests)*. Route follows old roads past abandoned mines, former farm and Indian ceremonial mound. Trail marked with orange blazes. Side trails marked with white blazes. Camping in designated areas only.

Unique Natural Features

ADAMS LAKE PRAIRIE – West Union – (937) 544-3927 – Page 83, B-7 Remnant of dry prairie once covering large expanses of Ohio. Shallow, dry soil. Characterized by sparse vegetation including shortgrasses, prairie wildflowers and red cedars. Foot trails.

ALLEN KNOB – Lancaster – (614) 265-6453 – Page 69, C-4 Located in Shallenberger State Nature Preserve. 240-foot peak of highly resistant sandstone. Views of central Ohio and lowland plains to west. Hiking trails.

ASH CAVE – Hocking Hills State Park – (740) 385-6841 – Page 79, A-5 Largest rock shelter in Ohio. 700-foot-long horseshoe-shaped ledge. 90-foot waterfall. Cave named for mounds of ashes discovered there by early settlers. *(See Parks.)*

BIGELOW CEMETERY PRAIRIE – Chuckery – (614) 265-6453 – Page 57, D-5 0.5-acre remnant of native Ohio prairie containing colonies of prairie grasses and wildflowers.

BLACKHAND GORGE –Toboso – (740) 763-4411 – Page 60, D-1 Narrow east–west gorge cut by Licking River through Black Hand sandstone formation. Black Hand sandstone named after dark, hand-shaped Indian petroglyph engraved on sandstone cliff face. *(See Hiking.)*

CAESAR CREEK GORGE – Waynesville – (614) 265-6453 – Page 75, A-7 Glacially reversed valley. 100-foot-high exposed limestone walls. Oak woodlands overlooking gorge. Prairie vegetation along dry bluffs on south side of gorge.

CANTWELL CLIFFS – Hocking Hills State Park – (740) 385-6841 – Page 69, D-5 Rugged area of cliffs, waterfalls and gorges. Hiking trail. *(See Parks.)*

CEDAR BOG – Urbana – (937) 297-2606 – Page 56, D-2 National Natural Landmark. Excellent example of marl swamp. Stand of white cedar, unique in bog setting. *(See Wildlife.)*

CEDAR FALLS – Hocking Hills State Park – (740) 385-6841 – Page 79, A-5 Hemlock-shaded gorge and 50-foot waterfall over cliff face. Region named for giant hemlocks settlers mistook for cedars. *(See Parks.)*

CLEARFORK GORGE – Mohican State Park – (419) 994-5125 – Page 49, D-7 National Natural Landmark. 400-foot-deep gorge along Clear Fork of Mohican River. Ecosystem typical of Canada found along northern rim, including virgin stand of white hemlock. Hiking trails. *(See Parks and Canoe Trips.)*

CLIFTON GORGE – Clifton – (614) 265-6453 – Page 66, B-2 National Natural Landmark. Limestone gorge cut by Little Miami River. Deepest point 100 feet. Waterfalls. White cedar grows from gorge walls. Hiking trails and overlooks.

CONKLES HOLLOW – 3 mi. S of Gibsonville – (614) 265-6453 – Page 79, A-5 Gorge cut through Black Hand sandstone by Pine Creek. 200 feet deep, 100 feet wide in places. Numerous waterfalls.

CRADLE IN THE ROCK – 4 mi. W of Athens – (740) 594-2211 – Page 80, B-1 Large rock outcrops form small cave-type shelters on north side of lake. Buffalo sandstone, formed 300 million years ago, overlies upper and lower Brush Creek limestones.

CRANBERRY BOG – Buckeye Lake State Park – (740) 763-4411 – Page 69, A-6 National Natural Landmark. Floating island is actually piece of ancient glacial bog that rose as area was flooded in early 1800's. Only known area in world where bog is surrounded by lake. Flora includes rare orchids, sundew and carnivorous pitcher plant. Written permission required for access; write: Ohio Department of Natural Resources, Division of Natural Areas and Preserves, Fountain Square, Building F-1, Columbus, OH 43224. *(See Parks.)*

CRYSTAL CAVE – Put-in-Bay – (419) 285-2811 – Page 28, C-3 Located at Heineman Winery *(see Wineries)*. Deposit of Celestite crystals forms immense geode characterized by hollow center, spherical shape and inward projecting crystals. *(See Excursions/Scenic Drives.)*

DYSART WOODS – 4.5 mi. SE of Bethesda – no phone – Page 72, A-4 National Natural Landmark. Largest known remnant of unglaciated terrain in southeastern Ohio. 51-acre virgin oak forest with trees 300–400 years old. Foot trails.

FOWLER WOODS – 6 mi. NW of Olivesburg – (614) 265-6453 – Page 49, A-6 Terminal moraine or ridge, formed when edge of glacier remained stationary for about a century in its final retreat, depositing vast quantities of till. Ground moraine formed when glacial till was deposited evenly during glacial advance, having generally smooth to gently rolling surfaces. *(See Wildlife.)*

GLACIAL GROOVES – Kelleys Island – (419) 746-2546 – Page 28, D-4 Furrows cut into bedrock by retreating glacier. 400 feet long, 25 feet wide and 10 feet deep. *(See Parks.)*

GOLL WOODS – Archbold – (614) 265-6453 – Page 25, D-5 80-acre example of primeval swamp forest dominated by black ash, red maples and silver maples. Nature trail. *(See Wildlife.)*

HACH-OTIS SANCTUARY – Willoughby Hills – (614) 265-6453 – Page 31, D-7 150-foot clay bluffs overlooking Chagrin River *(see Canoe Trips)*. Stream recutting old valley that was completely filled with glacial drift during last ice age. Foot trails along unstable cliffs. *(See Wildlife.)*

HEADLANDS DUNES – Mentor – (614) 265-6453 – Page 32, B-1 One of last dune ecosystems along Lake Erie.

HUESTON WOODS – Hueston Woods State Park – (513) 523-6347 – Page 64, D-1 National Natural Landmark. 200-acre stand of virgin beech–maple forest, remnant of original woodland that stretched diagonally across state. *(See Parks.)*

INDIAN TRAIL CAVERNS – Carey – (419) 387-7773 – Page 47, A-5 Cave descends 45 feet and travels 650 feet through passage 5 to 10 feet wide. Guided tours through lighted caverns along gravel walkways.

IRWIN PRAIRIE – 5 mi. W of Toledo – (614) 265-6453 – Page 26, C-2 172-acre remnant of wet meadow habitat. Ground water at or above ground level much of year. Variety of plants, birds and marsh-dwelling animals. Endangered spotted turtle. Boardwalk. *(See Wildlife.)*

JACKSON BOG – Massillon – (614) 265-6453 – Page 51, B-7 Six-acre fen, or alkaline bog, supporting plant community typical of glacial environment.

MENTOR MARSH – Mentor – (614) 265-6453 – Page 32, C-1 National Natural Landmark. Marsh contains wide variety of plant and animal life. Birdwatching. Trails. Nature center. *(See Wildlife.)*

NELSON KENNEDY LEDGES – Nelson – (440) 564-2279 – **Page 42, B-3** 50-foot Cascade Falls. Rugged cliffs of exposed sandstone. Hiking trails.

OHIO CAVERNS – West Liberty – (937) 465-4017 – **Page 56, C-3** Ohio's largest caverns. Colorful crystal formations including stalactites and stalagmites. Guided tours.

OLD MAN'S CAVE GORGE – Hocking Hills State Park – (740) 385-6841 – **Page 79, A-5** Long gorge cuts through entire depth of Black Hand sandstone. Geologic features include Devil's Bathtub pothole, Sphinx Head, Upper and Lower Falls and Old Man's Cave. *(See Parks.)*

OLD WOMAN CREEK SANCTUARY – 2 mi. E of Huron – (419) 433-4601 – **Page 39, A-5** Freshwater estuary where waters of Lake Erie and Old Woman Creek combine to form third type of water, chemically different from either lake or creek. Variety of aquatic and terrestrial habitats including marshlands,

open water, upland forests, barrier sand beach and old crop fields. Visitor center, trails and observation platform. National Estuarine Sanctuary. *(See Wildlife.)*

OLENTANGY INDIAN CAVERNS – Delaware – (740) 548-7917 – **Page 58, C-1** Three-level limestone cavern used by Olentangy Indians in 19th century. Guided tours. Indian museum and Frontier Land.

PERRY'S CAVE – Put-in-Bay – (419) 285-2405 – **Page 28, C-3** Single chamber 208 feet long, 165 feet wide and 3 to 10 feet high. 52 feet underground. Pool at eastern end rises and falls with level of Lake Erie. *(See Excursions/ Scenic Drives.)*

ROCK HOUSE – Hocking Hills State Park – (740) 385-6841 – **Page 79, A-5** Cave running horizontally to cliff face with "windows" formed from cracks intersecting main cave at right angles. *(See Parks.)*

ROCKBRIDGE – Rockbridge – (614) 265-6453 – **Page 69, D-6** Largest natural bridge in Ohio, made of Black Hand sandstone. 100 feet long, 10 to 20 feet wide, arching 50 feet across ravine. Hiking trail. *(See Wildlife.)*

SENECA CAVERNS – Bellevue – (419) 483-6711 – **Page 38, C-2** 250-foot earth crack through limestone. Slow-moving stream. Guided tours.

SEVEN CAVES – Bainbridge – (937) 365-1283 – **Page 77, C-6** Illuminated caves in wilderness area. Largest cave 315 feet long, 30 feet wide and 15 feet high. Waterfalls, cliffs and canyons. Paved walkways and handrails.

SHELDONS MARSH – Huron – (614) 265-6453 – **Page 39, A-5** Last remaining stretch of undeveloped shoreline in Sandusky Bay Region. Known to attract 200 species of birds. Wildflowers.

SMITH CEMETERY PRAIRIE – Plain City – (614) 265-6453 – **Page 57, D-6** Best example of tallgrass prairie that once covered much of Ohio, with over 30 species of native prairie plants.

ST. FRANCIS HOSPITAL AND SPRINGS – Green Springs – (419) 639-2626 – **Page 38, B-1** Largest sulphur springs in world. Springs never freeze. Rehabilitation hospital and park in wooded setting.

STAGE'S POND – Ashville – (614) 265-6453 – **Page 68, C-2** Kettle lake formed when chunk of receding glacier broke free and remained behind to be covered with glacial debris. When landlocked ice mass melted, it left 64-acre depression. Nature trails. *(See Wildlife.)*

TINKERS CREEK – Bedford – (216) 351-6300 – **Page 41, A-6** National Natural Landmark located in Bedford Reservation *(see Parks)*. Tinkers Creek drops total of 90 feet over course of two miles and cuts steep-walled gorge with depths ranging from 140 to 190 feet.

WHIPPS LEDGES – Hinckley – (216) 351-6300 – **Page 41, C-5** Ledges formed over 250 million years ago, rising 350 feet above lake. Due to ledge's water-bearing qualities, numerous springs and lush vegetation are present.

ZANE CAVERNS – Bellefontaine – (937) 592-0891 – **Page 56, A-3** Series of caves, tunnels and crystal formations. Unusual cave pearls of calcium carbonate formed around sand grains or pieces of rock. Walkways and stairs. Guided tours.

Wineries

NAME, TOWN	NATIVE AMERICAN	FRENCH-AMERICAN	EUROPEAN	OTHER FRUIT	ATLAS LOCATION
Anthony M. Greco, Middletown			●		Page 75, A-4
Breitenbach Wine Cellars, Dover	●	●	●	●	Page 51, D-6
Buccia Vineyards, Conneaut			●		Page 33, A-7
Cantwell's Old Mill Winery, Geneva	●	●			Page 32, B-4
Carl M. Limpert, Westlake	●				Page 40, A-3
Chalet Debonne Vineyards, Madison	●	●	●		Page 32, C-3
Colonial Vineyards, Lebanon	●	●			Page 65, D-6
Dankorona Winery, Aurora	●	●			Page 42, B-1
Dover Vineyards, Westlake	●	●	●	●	Page 40, A-3
E & K Winery, Sandusky	●				Page 38, A-4
Ferrante Wine Farm, Geneva	●	●			Page 32, B-4
Firelands Winery, Sandusky	●	●	●		Page 38, A-3
Grand River Wine Company, Madison	●	●	●		Page 32, C-3
Hafle Vineyards, Springfield	●	●			Page 66, A-2
Heineman Winery, Put-in-Bay	●	●			Page 28, C-3
Heritage Vineyards, West Milton	●	●			Page 65, A-5
Johlin Century Winery, Oregon	●	●	●	●	Page 27, C-5

Wineries listed here are open for tasting and retail sales, although hours and days may vary. While most have winery and/or vineyard tours, calling ahead for an appointment is recommended. In addition, most wineries offer a variety of styles, including, as indicated, wines made from native American, French-American and European grape varieties, as well as other types of fruit.

NAME, TOWN	NATIVE AMERICAN	FRENCH-AMERICAN	EUROPEAN	OTHER FRUIT	ATLAS LOCATION
John Christ Winery, Avon Lake	●	●			Page 40, A-2
Kelley's Island Wine Company, Kelleys Island		●	●		Page 28, D-4
Klingshirn Winery, Avon Lake	●	●			Page 40, A-2
Lonz Winery, Middle Bass Island	●	●	●	●	Page 28, C-3
Louis Jindra Winery, Jackson	●	●	●		Page 86, A-1
Markko Winery, Conneaut	●	●			age 33, A-7
McIntosh's Ohio Valley Wines, Bethel	●	●			Page 82, A-3
Meier's Wine Cellars, Silverton	●	●	●	●	Page 75, C-4
Mon Ami Champagne Company, Port Clinton	●	●	●		Page 28, D-3
Moyer Vineyards, Manchester			●		Page 83, C-6
Shamrock Vineyard, Waldo	●	●			Page 58, A-1
Steuk Wine Company, Sandusky	●	●	●		Page 38, A-3
Stillwater Wineries, West Troy	●	●		●	Page 55, D-6
Valley Vineyards, Morrow	●	●			Page 75, B-6
Vinterra Farm Winery, Houston	●	●		●	Page 55, B-5
The Winery at Wolf Creek, Norton			●		Page 41, D-5
Wyandotte Wine Cellar, Gahanna	●	●		●	Page 58, D-2

Forests

BLUE ROCK STATE FOREST – Blue Rock – (740) 674-4035 – **Page 70, B-4** 4,572 acres. Blue Rock State Park *(see Parks)* located within forest boundaries. Hunting, fishing, bridle trails and interpretive hiking trail.

BRUSH CREEK STATE FOREST – Peebles – (740) 858-6685 – **Page 84, A-2** 12,000 acres. Hunting, hiking and bridle trails.

DEAN STATE FOREST – Pedro – (740) 532-7228 – **Page 85, C-7** 2,745 acres. One of Ohio's first state forests, surrounded by Wayne National Forest. Hunting and bridle trails.

FERNWOOD STATE FOREST – Wintersville – (330) 339-2205 – **Page 63, B-6** 2,107 acres. Camping, hunting, fishing, hiking and interpretive nature trail. Trap shoot area, rifle and pistol range.

GIFFORD STATE FOREST – Chesterhill – (740) 554-3177 – **Page 80, A-3** 320 acres. Experimental seed orchard. Hunting.

HARRISON STATE FOREST – Cadiz – (330) 339-2205 – **Page 62, B-3** 1,345 acres. Camping, hunting, fishing, hiking, bridle trails and rifle range. Ronsheim Pond stocked with largemouth bass, bluegills and channel catfish.

HOCKING STATE FOREST – Rockbridge – (740) 385-4402 – **Page 79, A-5** 9,374 acres. Conkle's Hollow State Nature Preserve and Hocking Hills State Park *(see Unique Natural Features and Parks)* are located within forest boundaries. Camping, hunting, fishing, hiking and bridle trails. Buckeye Trail *(see Hiking)* passes through forest.

MAUMEE STATE FOREST – Swanton – (419) 822-3052 – **Page 26, D-1** 3,068 acres. Land elevation within forest varies less than 15 feet. Hunting and bridle trails. All-purpose-vehicle and snowmobile area.

MOHICAN–MEMORIAL STATE FOREST – Perrysville – (330) 339-2205 – **Page 49, D-7** 4,192 acres. Camping, hunting, fishing, hiking trails, bridle trails, snowmobile trails, cross-country skiing, skating, sledding. Clearfork Gorge *(see Unique Natural Features)*. 270-acre memorial Forest Park and shrine honoring Ohioans killed in defense of country. Covered bridge.

PERRY STATE FOREST – New Lexington – (740) 674-4035 – **Page 70, B-1** 4,567 acres. Hunting, bridle trails and all-purpose-vehicle area.

PIKE STATE FOREST – Latham – (740) 493-2441 – **Page 77, D-6** 11,621 acres.

Hunting, fishing, hiking, bridle trails and all-purpose-vehicle area. Buckeye Trail *(see Hiking)* passes through forest.

RICHLAND FURNACE STATE FOREST – Jackson – (740) 596-5781 – **Page 79, C-5** 2,343 acres. Hunting and all-purpose-vehicle area.

SCIOTO TRAIL STATE FOREST – Chillicothe – (740) 663-2538 – **Page 78, C-2** 9,371 acres. Rugged topography with ridges from 900 to 1,120 feet above sea level. 35 tree species found in forest, primarily oaks. No native evergreens. Scioto Trail State Park *(see Parks)* lies within forest boundaries. Hunting, hiking, bridle trails. Buckeye Trail *(see Hiking)* passes through forest. Fire tower lookout.

SHADE RIVER STATE FOREST – Reedsville – (740) 554-3177 – **Page 81, C-4** 2,601 acres. Adjacent to Forked Run State Park *(see Parks)*. Hunting. Interpretive trail.

SHAWNEE STATE FOREST – Portsmouth – (740) 858-6685 – **Page 84, A-4** 59,603 acres. Largest state forest in Ohio. Shawnee State Park *(see Parks)* within forest boundaries. Camping, hunting, fishing, hiking, bridle trails and scenic drive *(see Excursions/Scenic Drives: Panoram Scenic Drive)*. 8,000-acre

wilderness area. Shawnee Backpack Trail *(see Hiking)*.

SUNFISH CREEK STATE FOREST – Barlow – (740) 593-3341 – **Page 73, B-5** 637 acres. Hunting.

TAR HOLLOW STATE FOREST – Londonderry – (740) 663-2538 – **Page 78, B-4** 16,126 acres. Third largest state forest in Ohio. Tar Hollow State Park *(see Parks)* within forest boundaries. Camping, hunting, fishing, hiking and bridle trails. Buckeye Trail *(see Hiking)* passes through forest.

WAYNE NATIONAL FOREST – Ironton – (740) 753-0101 – **Page 85, D-7** Over 160,000 acres in southeast Ohio. Wooded, rolling hills. Lake Vesuvius Recreation Area *(see Parks)*. Camping, hunting, fishing and hiking *(see Hiking: Backpack Trail)*.

YELLOW CREEK STATE FOREST – Salineville – (330) 339-2205 – **Page 53, D-5** 756 acres. Hunting.

ZALESKI STATE FOREST – Zaleski – (740) 596-5781 – **Page 79, B-6** 26,313 acres. Camping, hunting, fishing, hiking and bridle trails. Zaleski Backpack Trail *(see Hiking)*.

Canoe Trips

Once vital as trade and transportation routes, Ohio river systems now provide many miles of scenic and recreational travel. Listed below are selected canoe routes scattered throughout the state. Since water levels change seasonally, check ahead for river conditions with local authorities. For a complete listing of canoe access sites contact the Department of Natural Resources, Division of Watercraft, 4435 Fountain Square Drive, Columbus, OH 43224-1362; (614) 265-6480. Information is also available from the Ohio Historical Canoe Route Association, P.O. Box 142039, Columbus, OH 43214-2039.

AUGLAIZE RIVER – Wapakoneta – Class I – Page 45, D-6 – 65 miles Put-in below State Route 198 bridge in Wapakoneta, below dam. Take-out at mouth of river at Kingsbury Park off Second Street in Defiance. Numerous dams and one canoe livery along route. River accessible to power boats above power dam in Defiance. Traffic continues upstream approximately ten miles.

BIG DARBY CREEK – Plain City – Class I – Page 57, D-6 – 42 miles Put-in at roadside rest area on State Route 736. Suitable for beginners. Dam to portage. Take-out at Big Darby Public Hunting Area *(see Hunting)* on State Route 665.

BLACK FORK – Mifflin – Class I – Page 49, C-7 – 14 miles Put-in at Charles Mill Reservoir Dam, west off State Route 603. Heavy use and many canoe liveries. Riverside stores and restaurants. Take-out at Riverside Park between State Route 39 and State Route 3 bridge in Loudonville. *(For longer trip combine with Mohican River in this section.)*

BLANCHARD RIVER – Findlay – Class I – Page 37, D-4 – 22 miles Put-in at Riverbend Parks/Big Oaks Access off Marion Township Road 208 southeast of Findlay. Suitable for beginners. River flows slowly and seasonally. Canoe livery at Riverside Park in Findlay. Take-out in Gilboa, 0.25 mile south of US 224, on Franklin Street. Parking available at both access sites.

CHAGRIN RIVER – Bentleyville – Class I–II – Page 41, A-7 – 26 miles Put-in at South Chagrin Reservation *(see Parks)* just north of Aurora confluence. Seasonal river, flow quickening near Lake County. Dams to portage. Take-out at Woodland Park off Woodland and Riverside Drives in Eastlake on Lake Erie.

CLEAR FORK – Perrysville – Class I – Page 49, D-7 – 3 miles Put-in at Mohican State Park Covered Bridge *(see Parks)*. Camping, parking and restrooms. Headwater of Mohican River. High water may present some Class II paddling. Logjams prevalent. Many canoe liveries in area.

CONNEAUT CREEK – Conneaut – Class I–II – Page 33, A-7 – 15 miles Put-in at Center Road Bridge south of Farnham. Seasonal paddling. Numerous broken weir dams along route. Scouting may be required near Conneaut. Sharp turns, unexpected rocks and narrow channels. Scenery includes covered bridges and waterfalls on neighboring streams. Take-out near Skippon Field on Center Street.

CUYAHOGA RIVER – Burton – Class I–II – Page 42, A-2 – 30 miles Winding route along river to Lake Rockwell. Put-in at State Route 87 bridge east of Burton. Moderate current until Hiram Rapids and submerged rock. Dam to portage. Mandatory take-out at State Route 303 bridge. Boating prohibited on Lake Rockwell. State-designated scenic river.

EAST BRANCH OF BLACK RIVER – 2 mi. E of Spencer – Class I – Page 40, D-2 – 23 miles Mandatory take-outs and waterfalls in Elyria on both East and West Branches. Put-in for East Branch at State Route 162 and Spencer Mills Road. Take-out on East River Road in Elyria. Scenic river with seasonal paddling.

EASTWOOD LAKE – Dayton – Page 65, B-6 – 3 miles Former gravel quarry offers lake-paddling for beginners. Some current present. Ten horsepower and under allowed on odd-numbered days. Fishing for bluegills and crappies. Located at Harshman Road and State Route 4.

GRAND RIVER – Farmington – Class I–II – Page 32, B-4 – 20 miles Put-in at Harpersfield Dam. Several alternate access sites. One canoe livery along route. Numerous dams to portage. Logjams and seasonal paddling prevalent in scenic upper reaches. Section from dam to take-out in Painsville Recreation Park is state-designated wild river.

GREAT MIAMI RIVER – Port Jefferson – Class I – Page 55, B-7 – 130 miles Put-in at roadside park off State Route 47 north of Port Jefferson. Many dams to portage, difficult at high water. Numerous access sites. Slow and wide paddling from Shelby County downstream. Take-out at Shawnee Lookout Park off County Road 170 before confluence with Ohio River.

HOCKING RIVER – Rockbridge – Class I–III – Page 69, D-5 – 54 miles Put-in at Rockbridge Road bridge. Natural arch called Rockbridge may be seen from river *(see Unique Natural Features)*. Short stretch of rocks and rapids at Falls Mill must be scouted. Dams to portage. Canoe liveries available. Take-out in Coolville at public access below Route 50 bridge, before joining Ohio River.

HURON RIVER – 3 mi. W of Milan – Class I – Page 39, B-4 – 10 miles Put-in at Milan Wildlife Area *(see Hunting)* on Lovers Lane. Flat lake-like paddling, suitable for beginners. Take-out at Huron Boat Basin off Main Street in Huron.

KILLBUCK CREEK – Wooster – Class I – Page 50, C-3 – 25 miles Put-in at Killbuck Marsh Wildlife Area *(see Hunting)*. Creek flows through Amish countryside, and joins with Walhonding River. Seasonal paddling. Roads must not be blocked with parked cars. Area floods easily.

KOKOSING RIVER – Mt. Vernon – Class I–III – Page 59, A-6 – 22 miles Put-in at Mt. Vernon Memorial Park. Gentle, flowing waters harbor Class II–III rapids depending on water level. Joins with Mohican River to form Walhonding River.

LICKING RIVER – Newark – Class I–III – Page 59, D-6 – 20 miles Put-in at Don Edwards Park. Passes Class II Rocky Run, and enters Blackhand Gorge State Nature Preserve *(see Unique Natural Features)*. Paddle through Dillon Lake to Dillon State Park *(see Parks)*. Rapids at Dillon Falls. Take-out at Dillon Falls Township Park.

LITTLE BEAVER CREEK – Beaver Creek State Park – Class I–III – Page 53, C-7 – 12 miles Put-in at state park. State-designated wild and scenic river. Remnants of locks from Sandy and Beaver Canals. Some fast spots along route. Hazards include downed trees, rocks and Class III rapids at Fredericksburg bridge. Scouting rapids necessary at high water from bridge to mouth of river. Canoe livery available in Calcutta. Current weakens as stream approaches Pennsylvania border and Ohio River. *(See Parks.)*

LITTLE MIAMI RIVER – John Bryan State Park – Class I – Page 66, B-2 – 73 miles Put-in at state park on State Route 370. State-designated wild and scenic river. Clifton Gorge *(see Unique Natural Features)* is directly upstream but off-limits to canoeing. Several canoe liveries and access sites along river. Historic sites along route. Caesar Creek, Todd and East Forks also scenic and paddleable rivers. Take-out at Lake Isabella Park off Interstate 275 in Loveland. *(See Parks.)*

LITTLE MUSKINGUM RIVER – Cline – Class I – Page 72, D-2 – 20 miles Put-in at Ring Mill access on Jerico–Low Gap Road. Scenic and remote route through Wayne National Forest *(see Forests)*. Take-out at Hune Bridge. Restrooms and camping available at both sites.

LOWER SCIOTO RIVER – Circleville – Class I – Page 68, D-2 – 95 miles Put-in at State Route 22 bridge. Historic sites in Chillicothe. Ohio-Erie Canal remains at Rushtown. Limited campsites along river. Take-out at Alexandria Park or Lower Scioto Ramp on left and right sides of river in Portsmouth.

MAHONING RIVER – 2.5 mi. N of Craig Beach – Class I–II – Page 42, C-4 – 12 miles Put-in below Lake Milton Dam near Mahoning–Trumbull county line on Cable Line–Newton Falls Road. Scenic and remote route. Newton Falls Covered Bridge. Dams to portage. Canoe livery available. Take-out in Packard Park off State Route 45 in Warren.

MAUMEE RIVER – 2 mi. SE of Sherwood – Class I–III – Page 34, B-3 – 75 miles Put-in at Bend Access off Bend Road Bridge, south of The Bend. Camping available at Independence Dam State Park *(see Parks)*. State-designated scenic river. Possible Class II–III rapids from Mary Jane Thurston State Park *(see Parks)* to Perrysburg. Spectacular foliage trip September–November. Wide and pleasant paddling. Take-out at Cullen Park off Summit Street in Toledo.

MOHICAN RIVER – Loudonville – Class I – Page 50, C-1 – 30 miles Put-in at Riverside Park on Black Fork, between State Route 39 and State Route 3 bridges. Black Fork joins with Clear Fork to form main branch of Mohican River *(see Black Fork above)*. Numerous canoe liveries allow camping and river access for private canoes. Passes through Mohican River Wildlife Area *(see Hunting)* and Mohican State Park *(see Parks)*. At confluence with Kokosing River name changes to Walhonding River.

MUSKINGUM RIVER – Coshocton – Class I – Page 60, B-4 – 100 miles Put-in at Lake Park on Walhonding River. Numerous dams to portage. With prior permission from Muskingum River Parkway, canoeists may pass through locks and make camping arrangements. Multiple access sites. Several historic sites along route. Powerboats and commercial activity. Take-out at mouth of river at Green Street Ramp in Marietta.

MUSKINGUM WATERSHED CONSERVANCY DISTRICT – Senecaville – Page 71, A-7 – distances vary Seneca Lake is one of ten MWCD man-made lakes. Located in 18 counties from Mansfield to Marietta. Lakes offer swimming, fishing and motorized boating in addition to canoeing. Atwood, Beach City, Charles Mill, Clendening, Leesville, Piedmont, Pleasant Hill, Seneca, Tappan and Wills Creek Lakes *(see Parks)*.

OHIO HISTORIC CANOE ROUTE ONE – Fremont – Page 38, A-2 – 300 miles For experienced canoeists. Route crosses central section of state. Sandusky Bay to Portsmouth on Ohio River. Follows Sandusky River, crosses 11-mile portage to Little Scioto River, then continues down Scioto River to Portsmouth.

OHIO HISTORIC CANOE ROUTE TWO – Cleveland – Page 41, A-5 – 245 miles For experienced canoeists. Route crosses eastern section of state from Cleveland to Marietta. Follows Cuyahoga River, crosses three-mile portage to Tuscarawas and Muskingum Rivers.

OHIO HISTORIC CANOE ROUTE THREE – Toledo – Page 26, D-4 – 300 miles For experienced canoeists. Route crosses western section of state from Toledo to Cincinnati. Follows Maumee River to Auglaize River, crosses eight-mile portage to Loramie Creek and continues down Great Miami River to Ohio River.

OLENTANGY RIVER – Delaware State Park – Class I–III – Page 58, B-1 – 22 miles Put-in at Delaware State Park Dam *(see Parks)*. Stretch of rapids begins south of Delaware. Numerous dams to portage. State-designated scenic river. Take-out at Olentangy River access on Wilson Bridge Road in Worthington.

PYMATUNING CREEK – Vernon – Class I – Page 43, A-7 – 4.5 miles Put-in at State Route 88 bridge. Access at Shenango Wildlife Area *(see Hunting)*. Canoe livery available in Orangeville. Take-out at Orangeville Park.

RACCOON CREEK – Vinton – Class I–II – Page 86, A-3 – 18 miles Put-in west off State Route 325. Longest creek in Ohio. Hazards include dams and waterfalls. Man-made and beaver dams to portage. Class II Cora Falls. Pristine and historic wilderness. Daniel Boone Cave just north of US 35. Take-out at Raccoon Creek County Park south of State Route 141 bridge. Canoe livery in Rio Grande offering camping, dining and canoe rentals.

SANDUSKY RIVER – 3 mi. NW of Upper Sandusky – Class I–III – Page 47, B-6 – 65 miles During high water, experienced canoeists only. Put-in at Indian Mill access on County Road 47. Scenic and remote river. Numerous dams to portage. Possible Class III rapids at high water downstream from Tiffin. Mandatory take-out on right side of river, at abandoned Chief Tarhe Park on Township Road 158, two miles southwest of Fremont. State-designated scenic river. Camping available along route.

ST. JOSEPH RIVER – Pioneer – Class I – Page 24, C-3 – 6 miles Put-in off US 20, one mile west of State Route 15. Moderate flow, suitable for beginners. Obstacles include downed trees and branches. Canoe livery and private campgrounds available. Take-out at Montpelier Park, south of State Route 107 in Montpelier.

STILLWATER RIVER – 2 miles NW of Covington – Class I – Page 55, C-4 – 32 miles Put-in at Stillwater Prairie Reserve off Range Line Road. Many dams to portage. State-designated scenic and recreational river. Some seasonal paddling. Take-out before joining Great Miami River at Triangle Park north of Dayton on Ridge Avenue.

SUGAR CREEK – Beach City – Class I–II – Page 51, C-6 – 9 miles Put-in at Beach City Dam. Seasonal paddling with some fast, rocky spots. Take-out at Francis Canoe Landing in Dover before confluence with Tuscarawas River. Camping available.

TIFFIN RIVER – 1 mi. NE of Stryker – Class I – Page 25, D-4 – 25 miles Put-in at Stryker Roadside Park. Flows southerly to Maumee River. Numerous logjams and steep banks. Scenic river with limited access. At confluence proceed downstream through Defiance to take-out at Kingsbury Park on Maumee River off Second Street.

TUSCARAWAS RIVER – Canal Fulton – Class I–II – Page 51, A-6 – 85 miles Put-in at Canal Fulton Park on Erie Avenue. Hazards include dams and rapids. Zoar Rapids, below State Route 212 bridge, must be scouted and portaged at high water. Many islands along route. Paddle one mile upstream on Walhonding River to take-out at Lake Park in Coshocton.

VERMILION RIVER – Birmingham – Class I–II – Page 39, B-7 – 12 miles Put-in at Birmingham Park, just north of State Route 113. Moderate flow. Scenic river. Seasonal paddling. Take-out at public dock on Huron and Main Streets near mouth of river.

WALHONDING RIVER – Newcastle – Class I – Page 60, B-2 – 15 miles Put-in at Mohawk Dam on State Route 715. Easy, year-round paddling. Dam to portage with permission. Camping available along route. Take-out at Coshocton Lake Park.

WILLS CREEK – 2 mi. S of Byesville – Class I – Page 71, A-6 – 55 miles Put-in at State Route 821 and Seneca Road Bridge. Seasonal paddling and numerous logjams. Take-out at Wills Creek Reservoir above dam at State Route 83.

Excursions/Scenic Drives

AMISH COUNTRY DRIVE – Millersburg – no phone – Page 50, D-3 State-designated scenic route from Millersburg to Sugarcreek. Drive begins on Route 39 in Millersburg, continues south to Charm on Route 557, loops back to Route 39, heading east to Berlin and Walnut Creek. At Walnut Creek drive branches north on Route 515 to Trail (famous for buggies and bologna), and returns to Route 39, finishing east at Sugarcreek. *(See Amish Country.)*

ARAWANNA STAR – Toledo – (419) 246-2628 – Page 27, C-4 Narrated sightseeing cruises on Maumee River.

AVIATION TRAIL – Dayton – (937) 443-0793 – Page 65, B-6 Self-guided tour connecting historic aviation sites. Includes areas where Wright brothers lived, worked and flew their early airplanes. Route begins at National Aviation Hall of Fame in Dayton Convention Center. Air Force Museum *(see Historic Sites/Museums).* Wright Memorial.

BB RIVERBOATS – Covington, Kentucky – (606) 261-8500 – Page 74, D-3 Sightseeing cruises on Ohio River in 19th-century-style sternwheeler.

BLUEBIRD PASSENGER TRAIN – Waterville – (419) 878-2177 – Page 26, D-3 20-mile round trip on vintage passenger train through northwestern Ohio farmland between Waterville and Grand Rapids, including spectacular views of Maumee River.

BUCKEYE SCENIC RAILROAD – 1.5 mi. W of Jacksontown – (740) 928-3827 – Page 69, A-6 Rail trips through central Ohio along original route of 1854 Shawnee Line. Renovated turn-of-the-century passenger cars include open coach, closed coach and gondola. 1948 locomotive and 1930 caboose.

CEDAR POINT FERRY – Sandusky – (419) 627-0198 – Page 38, A-4 Ferry service across Sandusky Bay.

DELTA QUEEN – Cincinnati – (800) 543-1949 – Page 74, D-3 3- to 14-day cruises on Ohio and Mississippi Rivers aboard paddlewheel steamboats.

FLY FERRY – Fly – no phone – Page 72, D-3 One of few remaining passenger and automobile ferries across Ohio River. Connects Fly, Ohio and Sistersville, West Virginia.

GENERAL HARRISON CANAL BOAT – Piqua – (937) 773-2522 – Page 55, C-5 Mule-drawn canal boat ride along Miami and Erie Canal. Replica of mid-19th-century mixed-cargo canal boat. Located in Piqua Historical Area *(see Historic Sites/Museums).*

GOODTIME II – Cleveland – (216) 861-5110 – Page 31, D-5 Sightseeing cruises along Cuyahoga River and Lake Erie aboard triple-decker sightseeing boat.

HOCKING VALLEY SCENIC RAILROAD – Nelsonville – (937) 335-0382 – Page 80, A-1 Weekend trips through hills of southeastern Ohio aboard 1916 steam locomotive. 10- and 25-mile trips.

MILLER BOAT LINE – Put-in-Bay – (419) 285-2421 – Page 28, C-3 Passenger and automobile service from Put-in-Bay on South Bass Island to Catawba and Middle Bass Islands.

MISS MAJESTIC – Lorain – (440) 244-2621 – Page 40, A-1 River and lake cruises.

MONTICELLO II – Coshocton – (740) 622-7528 – Page 60, B-4 Horse-drawn trips along historic Ohio-Erie Canal aboard replica of canal boat.

MV PELEE ISLANDER – Sandusky – (419) 625-4494 – Page 38, A-4 Passenger and automobile ferry across Lake Erie from Sandusky to Pelee Island, Canada.

NEUMAN BOAT LINE – Marblehead – (419) 626-5557 – Page 28, D-4 Passenger and automobile ferry from Marblehead to Kelleys Island.

PANORAM SCENIC DRIVE – 3 mi. W of Friendship – (740) 858-6685 – Page 84, C-3 Scenic drive through Shawnee State Forest *(see Forests).* Winding, narrow roads may be hazardous in winter. Panoramic view of Ohio River Valley. Especially colorful during fall foliage season.

PORTAGE PRINCESS – Akron – (330) 499-6891 – Page 51, A-6 Narrated cruise on Portage Lakes aboard paddle-wheeler.

PUT-IN-BAY BOAT LINE – Port Clinton – (419) 732-2800 – Page 28, D-2 Passenger ferry between Port Clinton and Put-in-Bay on South Bass Island.

PUT-IN-BAY TRANSPORTATION – Put-in-Bay – (419) 285-4855 – Page 28, C-3 Narrated tram tours of South Bass Island. Tour features Heineman Winery, Crystal and Perry's Caves and Perry's Victory Memorial *(see Wineries, Unique Natural Features and Historic Sites/Museums).*

SHAWNEE PRINCESS – Grand Rapids – (419) 531-0341 - Page 36, A-2 Boat ride on Maumee River aboard 1846 sternwheeler.

ST. HELENA III – Canal Fulton – (330) 854-3808 – Page 51, A-6 Narrated boat ride along historic Ohio-Erie Canal. Replica of canal freight barge pulled by mules. Sights include dry dock, where boats were built and repaired, and one of last working locks along canal.

TROLLEY TOURS OF MARIETTA – Marietta – (740) 373-2420 – Page 81, A-7 Narrated tours of historical sites and points of interest in Marietta aboard turn-of-the-century-style trolley car.

VALLEY GEM – Marietta – (740) 373-7862 – Page 81, A-7 Narrated sightseeing tour on Ohio and Muskingum rivers aboard sternwheeler.

Bicycle Routes

AKRON RAILROAD BIKEPATH – Sagamore Hills – Page 41, B-6 – 17 miles Limestone hike/bike path from Highland Road to Munroe Falls–Kent Road in Kent. Route follows railroad bed and some existing roads. Access points at road junctions. Parking on State Route 91 in Munroe Falls.

BICYCLE ROUTE A – Cincinnati – Page 74, C-1 – 239 miles Route connects Cincinnati and Maumee, crossing west side of Ohio. Flat to rolling terrain. Passes near Dayton and Middletown and follows Ohio and Miami Canal for many miles.

BICYCLE ROUTE B – Cincinnati – Page 74, C-1 – 240 miles Scenic route connects Cincinnati and Marietta. Hilly terrain at either end of route, nearly flat in middle section.

BICYCLE ROUTE C – Cincinnati – Page 74, D-3 – 294 miles Route connects Cincinnati and Cleveland. Southern end follows Little Miami Scenic Trail *(see below).* Middle section follows parts of Cardinal Trail *(see below)* over flat terrain. Route ends at intersection with Bicycle Route N *(see below).*

BICYCLE ROUTE E – Portsmouth –Page 85, C-5 – 494 miles In Ohio, route connects Portsmouth and Toledo. On southern end, trail extends to Pippa Passes, Kentucky. In north, trail extends to Milford, Michigan. Southern portions of route are hilly. Northern sections cross flat land.

BICYCLE ROUTE F – New Paris – Page 64, B-1 – 281 miles Route connects New Paris and Bellaire, following US Route 40. Route offers backcountry riding.

BICYCLE ROUTE J – Marietta – Page 81, A-7 – 244 miles Route connects Marietta and Conneaut over hilly terrain in eastern Ohio.

BICYCLE ROUTE K – McGill – Page 34, D-1 – 156 miles McGill to Mifflin connecting Indiana with Cardinal Trail *(see below).* Route crosses mainly flat terrain.

BICYCLE ROUTE N – McGill – Page 34, D-1 – 300 miles Northern route across Ohio connecting McGill and Pierpont. Posted every five miles and at turns.

CARDINAL TRAIL – New Paris – Page 64, B-1 – 314 miles Bicycle route across central Ohio from New Paris to New Middletown, through St. Paris, West Liberty, Prospect, Fredericktown, Haynesville, Canal Fulton and North Canton. Posted every five miles and at turns.

COVERED BRIDGE BIKEWAY – Canal Winchester – Page 68, B-3 – 36 miles Loop following county roads between Lancaster and Canal Winchester. Route begins two blocks west of Rising Park in Lancaster. Posted for travel in clockwise direction. Points of interest include four covered bridges and remains of former Ohio-Erie Canal.

DUBLIN BICYCLE LOOP – Dublin – Page 57, D-7 – 52 miles Loop along county roads between Dublin and Marysville. Posted for counterclockwise travel. Shorter (10- and 42-mile) loops also posted. Parking at municipal lot at Post and Coffman Roads. Covered bridge along route.

LITTLE MIAMI SCENIC TRAIL – Milford – Page 75, C-5 – 69 miles Paved Multi-use rail–trail mostly follows Little Miami State and National Scenic River. 47-mile-long southern section passes through Little Miami State Park *(see Parks).* Remainder of

trail extends from Hedges Road in Xenia to Springfield.

LOVELAND–MORROW BIKEPATH – Little Miami State Park – Page 75, B-5 – 13.5 miles Asphalt bikepath between Loveland and Morrow in Little Miami State Park *(see Parks and Hiking).* Path follows former railroad bed along river.

MANSFIELD LOOP – Mansfield – Page 49, C-5 – 22 miles Loop beginning at parking lot in John Todd Park. Route follows county roads and is posted for travel in either direction. Points of interest include quaint villages, scenic overlooks and Malabar Farm State Park *(see Parks and Historic Sites/Museums).*

MILAN CANAL BIKEWAY – Huron – Page 39, A-5 – 27 miles Posted loop along area roads beginning at Huron City Park on Ohio Street. Points of interest include scenic overlooks, wildlife sanctuary and historic sites including remnants of Milan Shipping Canal. Bikeway map available from Erie County, Osborn Park Office, 3916 East Perkins Avenue, Sandusky, OH 44870.

OLD MILL BIKEWAY – Clifton – Page 66, B-2 – 35 miles Loop following lightly traveled county roads. Posted for travel in counterclockwise direction. Points of interest include historic mills, nature preserve and John Bryan State Park *(see Parks).*

OLD MILLSTREAM BIKEWAY – Findlay – Page 36, D-3 – 39 miles Loop begins in Riverside Park. Pavement markings along county roads lead east around Findlay Reservoir, then south along Blanchard River to Mount Blanchard. Route continues west to Ar-

lington, then north for return to Findlay. Brochure available from Hancock Park District, 819 Park Street, 1833 Courthouse, Findlay, OH 45840.

OLENTANGY–LOWER SCIOTO BIKEWAY – Columbus – Page 68, A-1 – 12 miles Scenic commuter bikeway running length of city along Olentangy and Scioto Rivers. Route follows eight-foot-wide asphalt path and some existing roads.

RIVER BIKEWAY – Dayton – Page 65, B-6 – 24 miles North–south route along Great Miami and Stillwater Rivers. Route passes through Dayton, Moraine, West Carrollton, Miami Township and Miamisburg. Connections and extensions to other communities. Most of route follows eight-foot-wide paved pathway separated from traffic, but portions parallel or share roadways. Fairly flat terrain. Occasional flooding during heavy rains. Brochure available with self-addressed, stamped envelope, from River Bikeway, Dayton Area Chamber of Commerce, 1880 Kettering Tower, Dayton, OH 45423.

ROCKY RIVER RESERVATION – Rocky River – Page 40, A-4 – 10.5 miles Trail from scenic park (Detroit Road entrance) south to Cedar Point Road. Parking at numerous picnic areas along trail. All-purpose asphalt trail, for any non-motorized recreational activity. *(See Parks.)*

TOP OF OHIO – Bellefontaine – Page 56, B-2 – 45 miles Loop route following county roads. Posted for clockwise travel. Route includes some steep grades. Gradual climb past highest point in Ohio, 1,549 feet above sea level. Points of interest along route include historic sites and natural caves at Ohio and Zane Caverns *(see Unique Natural Features).*

Gazetteer continued on page 88

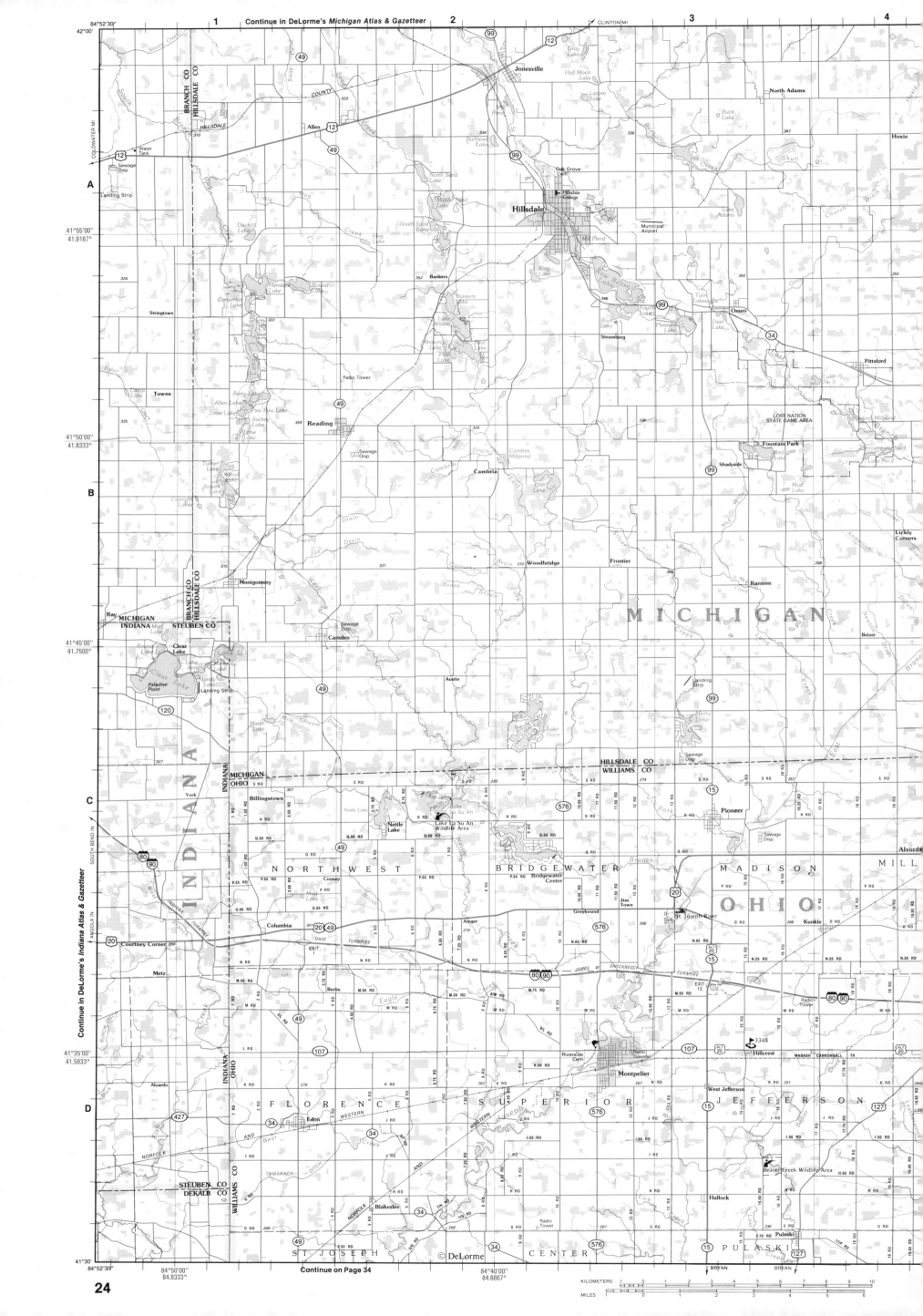

84°52'30"
42°00'

CLINTON MI

Jonesville

North Adams

Hoxie

Allen

A

Hillsdale

Hillsdale College

Osseo

Pittsford

41°55'00"
41.9167°

Municipal Airport

Bankers

LOST NATION STATE GAME AREA

Towns

Reading

Cambria

Fountain Park

41°50'00"
41.8333°

Shadyside

B

Woodbridge

Frontier

Ransom

Lickly Corners

Montgomery

MICHIGAN

Ray
MICHIGAN
INDIANA   STEUBEN CO

Camden

41°45'00"
41.7500°

Clear Lake

Austin

Landing Strip

120

HILLSDALE CO
WILLIAMS CO

MICHIGAN
INDIANA | OHIO

C

York

Billingstown

Nettle Lake

Lake La Su An
Wildlife Area

Pioneer

Alvordt

80
90

NORTHWEST

BRIDGEWATER

Bridgewater Center

MADISON

MILL

Cooney

Jim Town

20

Columbia

Greyhound

St. Joseph River

Kunkle

OHIO
TURNPIKE

Ainger

Courtney Corner

20

EXIT

80
90

JAMES W. SHOCKNESS TURNPIKE

EXIT 13

Metz

Berlin

Eagle

Radio Tower

80
90

107

41°35'00"
41.5833°

Riverside Cem

Radio Tower

107

Hillcrest

WABASH CANNONBALL

20

Alvarado

Montpelier

West Jefferson

127

427

D

FLORENCE

SUPERIOR

JEFFERSON

15

34

Edon

WESTERN

576

Beaver Creek Wildlife Area

STEUBEN CO
DEKALB CO

WILLIAMS CO

Hallock

Blakeslee

34

Radio Tower

Pulaski

49

34

ST. JOSEPH

CENTER

576

15 PULASKI

127

41°30'
84°52'30"

84°50'00"
84.8333°

© DeLorme

84°40'00"
84.6667°

BRYAN

BRYAN

KILOMETERS

MILES

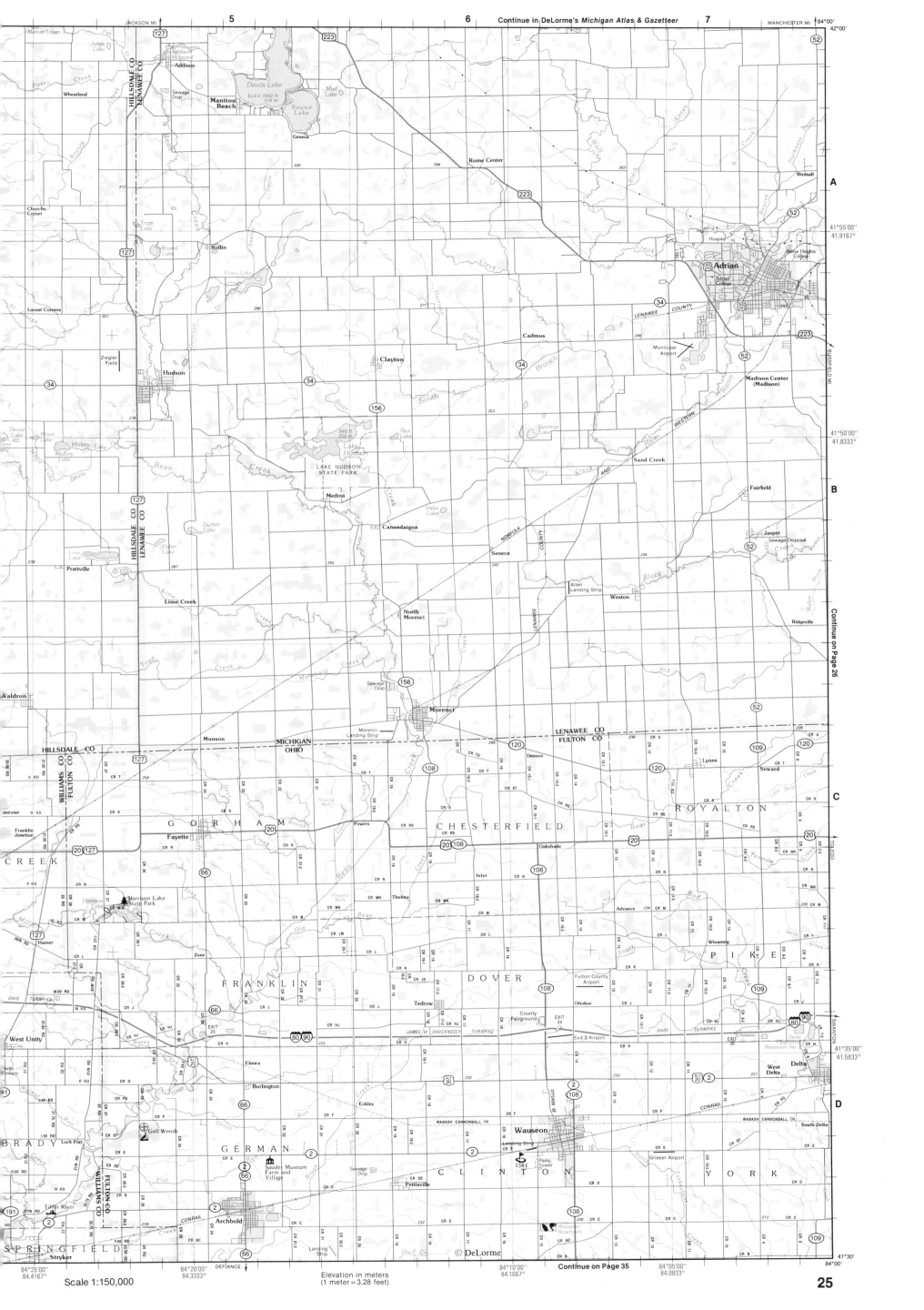

JACKSON MI   MANCHESTER MI 84°00'

42°00'

Mercer Lakes

Ames Lake

Posey Creek

Wheatland

Addison Millpond

Addison

Devils Lake

ELEV 1043 ft
318 m

Manitou Beach

Mud Lake

Round Lake

Geneva

Churchs Corner

Rome Center

Birdsall

41°55'00''
41.9167°

Hospital

Adrian

Siena Heights College

Adrian College

Tripp Lake

Rollin

Round Lake

Locust Corners

Ziegler Field

Hudson

Cadmus

Lenawee County

Municipal Airport

Madison Center (Madison)

Clayton

Devoe Lake

Moon Lake

Mallory Lake

Mallory Lake

Lake Hudson
STATE PARK

Rice Lake

Demings Lake

41°50'00''
41.8333°

Prattville

Fisher Lake

Durfee Lake

Medina

Canandaigua

Vales Lake

Seneca

Sand Creek

Fairfield

Jasper

Sewage Disposal

Lime Lake

Lime Creek

Allen Landing Strip

Weston

North Morenci

Lenawee

Ridgeville

Continue on Page 26

Waldron

Sewage Disp

Morenci

Morenci Landing Strip

HILLSDALE CO / LENAWEE CO

MICHIGAN
OHIO

Lenawee Co
Fulton Co

Denson

Lyons

Seward

Munson

Franklin Junction

Fayette

ROYALTON

HILLSDALE CO
WILLIAMS CO / FULTON CO

GORHAM

Powers

CHESTERFIELD

Oakshade

TOLEDO

41°35'00''
41.5833°

Harrison Lake State Park

Hamer

Zone

Inlet

Thelma

Advance

Winameg

PIKE

CREEK

FRANKLIN

DOVER

Fulton County Airport

Tedrow

Ottokee

West Unity

OHIO TURNPIKE

EXIT 25

JAMES W SHOCKNESSY TURNPIKE

County Fairground

EXIT 34

Exit 3 Airport

OHIO TURNPIKE

SWANTON

Delta

West Delta

South Delta

Elmira

Burlington

Eckley

WABASH CANNONBALL TR

WABASH CANNONBALL TR

CONRAIL

BRADY

Lock Port

Goll Woods

GERMAN

Sauder Museum Farm and Village

Wauseon

Landing Strip

Radio Tower

Grieser Airport

CLINTON

YORK

Pettisville

Wauseon Reservoirs

Tiffin River

Archbold

Landing Strip

SPRINGFIELD

Stryker

DEFIANCE

Continue on Page 35

41°30'

Scale 1:150,000   Elevation in meters
(1 meter = 3.28 feet)   25

84°25'00''
84.4167°   84°20'00''
84.3333°   84°10'00''
84.1667°   84°05'00''
84.0833°

© DeLorme

Continue on Page 25

Continue on Page 36

© DeLorme

KILOMETERS

MILES

FLAT ROCK MI   DETROIT MI

83°07'30"
42°00'

LAKE ERIE

APPROXIMATE MEAN LAKE ELEVATION 571 ft
174 m

MICHIGAN
OHIO

BOUNDARY

INDEFINITE

A
41°55'00"
41.9167°

B
41°50'00"
41.8333°

Continue on Page 28

C
41°40'00"
41.6667°

D
41°35'00"
41.5833°

POINT MOUILLE
STATE GAME AREA

Estral Beach

Oldport

Point Aux Peaux

Stony Point

Woodland Beach

Detroit Beach

STERLING STATE PARK

Monroe Harbor

Plum Creek Bay

Bolles Harbor

Avalon Beach

North Shores

Toledo Beach

Allens Cove

Luna Pier

Erie

Vienna

Western Basin

Turtle Island   Lighthouse

ERIE STATE GAME AREA

North Cape

MONROE CO
LUCAS CO

Maumee Bay

Cedar Point

Harbor View

Immergrun

South Shore Park

Maumee Bay State Park

Niles Beach

CEDAR POINT NATIONAL WILDLIFE REFUGE

MALLARD STATE WILDLIFE AREA

Reno Beach

Lakeland

Howard Farms Beach

METZGER MARSH STATE WILDLIFE AREA

Metzger Marsh Wildlife Area

Bono

OTTAWA NATIONAL

WILDLIFE REFUGE

Crane Creek State Park

Crane Creek Experimental Station

Ottawa National Wildlife Refuge

Magee Marsh Wildlife Area

Magee Marsh State Wildlife Area

Magee Marsh Wildlife Area

OREGON   JERUSALEM

Oregon

Pearson Metropark

Momeenetown

Fish Hatchery

Yondota

LUCAS CO
WOOD CO OTTAWA CO

Curtice

Northwood

Williston

Woodville

Yale

Blackberry Corner

Grodis Corner

Krause

Walbridge

Stanley

Woodville Gardens

Crescens Farms

East Lawn

ALLEN

Trowbridge

Toussaint Wildlife Area

Toussaint East

CARROLL

Metcalf Field

Millbury

Martin

Clay Center

BENTON

Elliston

Graytown

Limestone

Rocky Ridge

Moline

Latcha

Forest Park

CLAY

Genoa

HARRIS

Stony Ridge

TROY

DeLorme

SALEM

Oak Harbor

Toussaint

83°25'00"
83.4167°

Continue on Page 37

41°30'
83°07'30"

Scale 1:150,000

Elevation in meters
(1 meter = 3.28 feet)

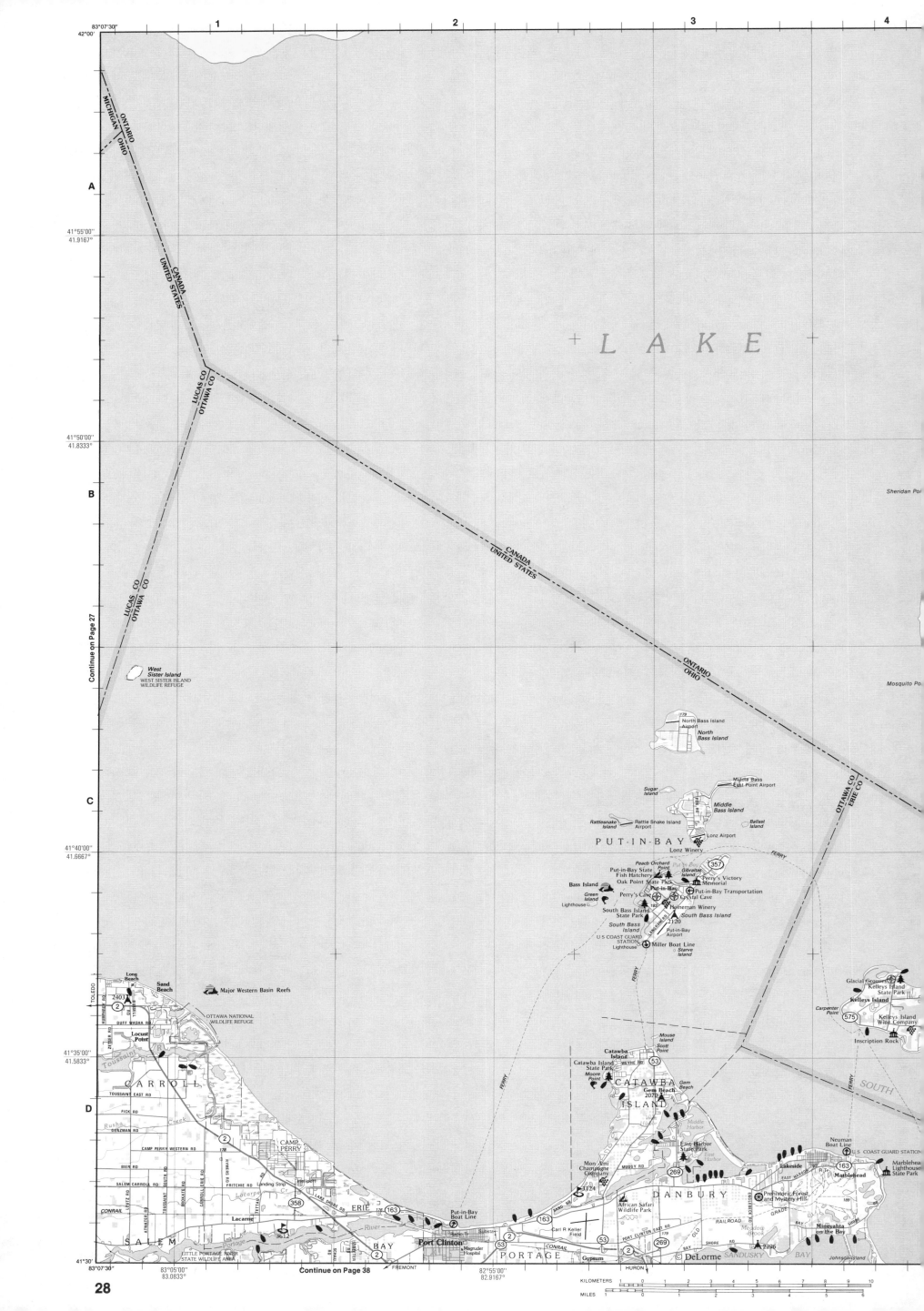

1   2   3   4

A

41°55'00"
41.9167°

MICHIGAN
OHIO

ONTARIO

CANADA
UNITED STATES

L A K E

B

41°50'00"
41.8333°

LUCAS CO
OTTAWA CO

Continue on Page 27

LUCAS CO
OTTAWA CO

CANADA
UNITED STATES

Sheridan Poi

West
Sister Island
WEST SISTER ISLAND
WILDLIFE REFUGE

ONTARIO
OHIO

Mosquito Po.

North Bass Island
Airport
North
Bass Island

Middle Bass
East Point Airport

OTTAWA CO
ERIE CO

C

Sugar
Island

Middle
Bass Island

Ballast
Island

Rattlesnake
Island

Rattle Snake Island
Airport

Lonz Airport

41°40'00"
41.6667°

P U T - I N - B A Y

Lonz Winery

357

FERRY

Peach Orchard
Point
Put-in-Bay State
Fish Hatchery
Oak Point State Park
Bass Island
Green
Island
Lighthouse
Put-in-Bay

Gibraltar
Island
Perry's Victory
Memorial
Put-in-Bay Transportation
Crystal Cave
Perry's Cave
Heineman Winery
South Bass Island
State Park
South Bass
Island
Put-in-Bay
Airport
U S Coast Guard
STATION
Lighthouse
Miller Boat Line
Starve
Island

Glacial Grooves
Kelleys Island
State Park

Kelleys Island

Carpenter
Point
575
Kelleys Island
Wine Company

Inscription Rock

Long
Beach
Sand
Beach
2403
2
TOLEDO
HUMPHREY RD
ZESIGER RD

Major Western Basin Reefs

OTTAWA NATIONAL
WILDLIFE REFUGE

Locust
Point
DUFF WASHA RD

SOUTH

Mouse
Island
Scott
Point

Catawba
Island
Catawba Island
State Park
Moore
Point
BEYHE RD
53

Gem
Beach
Gem Beach
207D

Neuman
Boat Line
U S COAST GUARD STATION
Marblehead
Lighthouse
State Park

41°35'00"
41.5833°

Toussaint

CARROLL

TOUSSAINT EAST RD

D

Rusha

Creek

FICK RD
GENZMAN RD

CAMP PERRY WESTERN RD

Lacarpe

2
CAMP
PERRY

Landing Strip

CATAWBA
ISLAND

Middle
Harbor

East Harbor
State Park

East Harbor

269

Lakeside

EAST HARBOR RD

163

Marblehead

163

Prehistoric Forest
and Mystery Hill

BIER RD
SALEM CARROLL SOUTH RD
CONRAIL
LIPELT RD
ATWATER RD
TOUSSANT SOUTH RD
PROATE RD
FRITCHIE RD

179
SHUMAN RD
358
LAKE SHORE DR

179

176
ERIE
163

Mon Ami
Champagne
Company
3124

African Safari
Wildlife Park

DANBURY

MUGGY RD

FORT CLINTON EAST RD

OLD

RAILROAD
Meadow
Brook

Minnyahta
on the Bay

SALEM

Lacarne

LITTLE PORTAGE RIVER
STATE WILDLIFE AREA

Little Portage

Portage River

3612

BAY

Port Clinton
2

FREMONT

Put-in-Bay
Boat Line
Substation
Magruder
Hospital

Carl R Keller
Field
163
53
53

PORTAGE

Gypsum

CONRAIL

269
BAY

SHORE

OLD

© DeLorme SANDUSKY BAY

2296

HURON

Johnson Island

41°30'
83°07'30"

83°05'00"
83.0833°

Continue on Page 38

82°55'00"
82.9167°

KILOMETERS   1   2   3   4   5   6   7   8   9   10

MILES   1   2   3   4   5

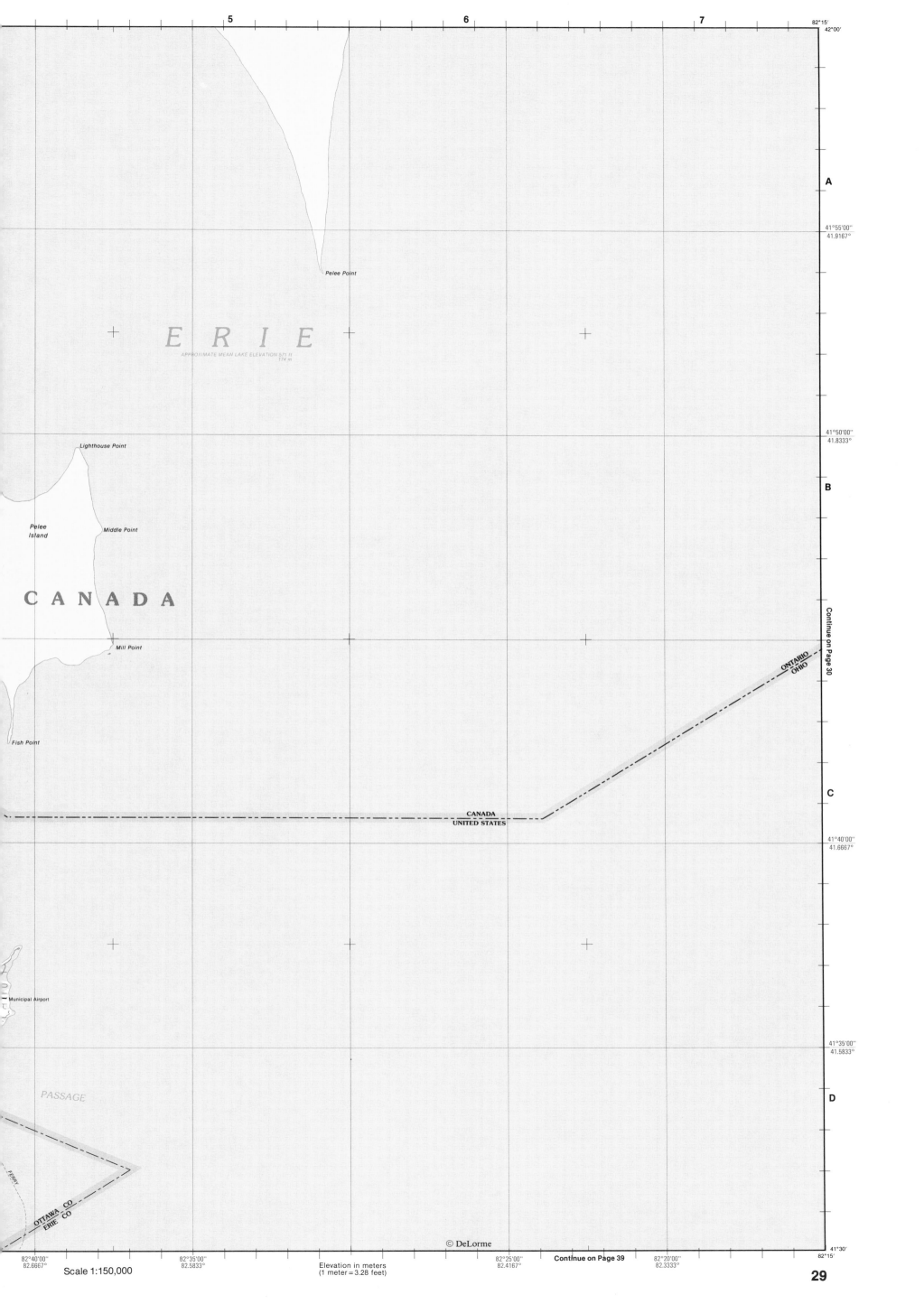

82°15'
42°00'

A

41°55'00''
41.9167°

Pelee Point

E R I E
APPROXIMATE MEAN LAKE ELEVATION 571 II
174 m

41°50'00''
41.8333°

B

Lighthouse Point

Pelee
Island

Middle Point

C A N A D A

Mill Point

Continue on Page 30

ONTARIO
OHIO

Fish Point

C

CANADA
UNITED STATES

41°40'00''
41.6667°

Municipal Airport

41°35'00''
41.5833°

D

PASSAGE

FERRY

OTTAWA CO
ERIE CO

© DeLorme

41°30'
82°15'

82°40'00''
82.6667°

Scale 1:150,000

82°35'00''
82.5833°

Elevation in meters
(1 meter = 3.28 feet)

82°25'00''
82.4167°

Continue on Page 39

82°20'00''
82.3333°

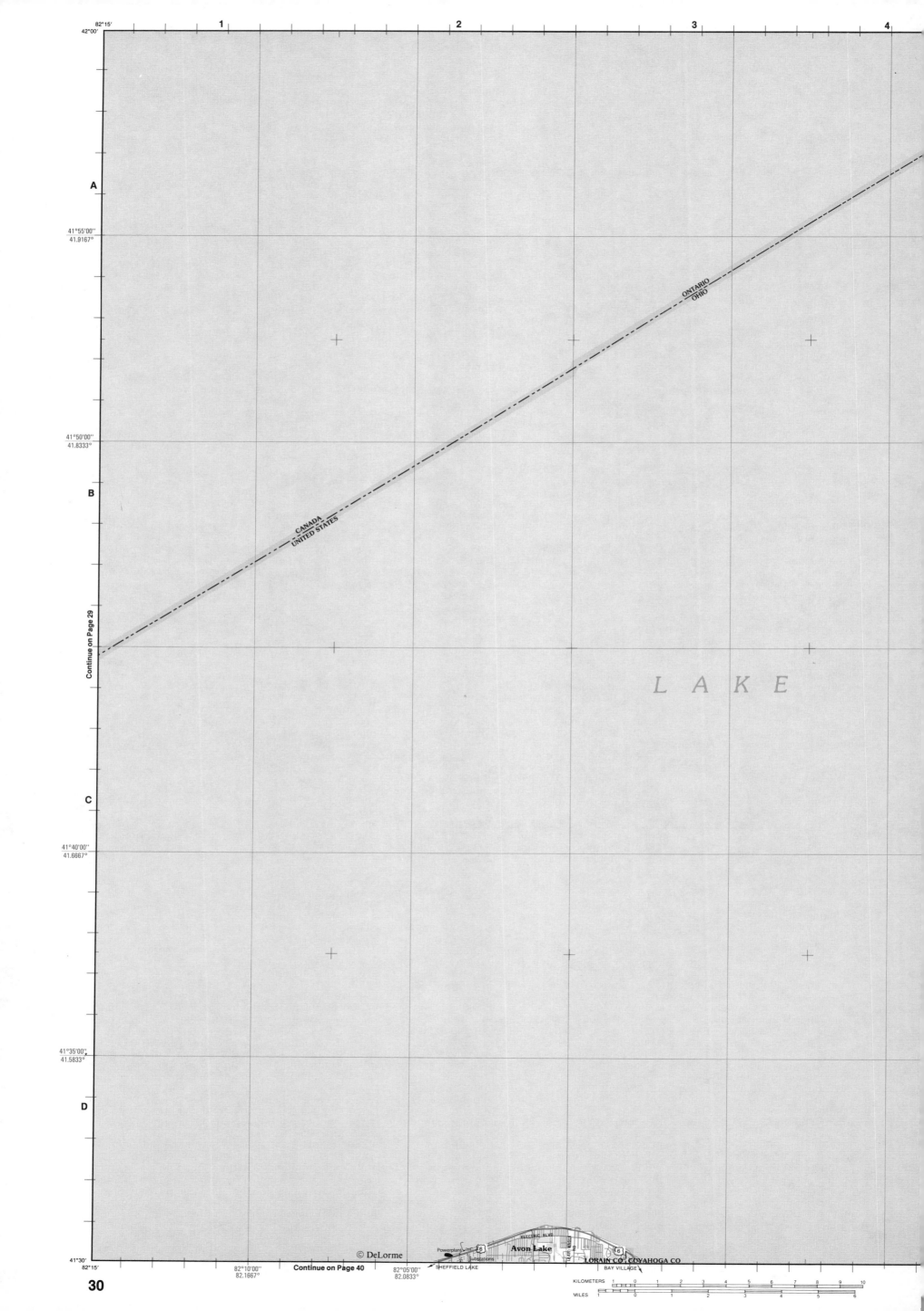

82°15'
42°00'

1   2   3   4

A

41°55'00''
41.9167°

ONTARIO
OHIO

41°50'00''
41.8333°

B

CANADA
UNITED STATES

Continue on Page 29

L A K E

C

41°40'00''
41.6667°

41°35'00''
41.5833°

D

ELECTRIC BLVD

Powerplant
Avon Lake
Substations
6   6   6
SHEFFIELD LAKE   LORAIN CO. CUYAHOGA CO
BAY VILLAGE

© DeLorme   Continue on Page 40

41°30'
82°15'   82°10'00''   82°05'00''
82.1667°   82.0833°

30

KILOMETERS   1   0   1   2   3   4   5   6   7   8   9   10
MILES   1   0   1   2   3   4   5   6

81°22'30"
42°00'

CANADA
UNITED STATES

A

41°55'00"
41.9167°

B

41°50'00"
41.8333°

Continue on Page 32

E R I E

APPROXIMATE MEAN LAKE ELEVATION 571 ft
174 m

Mentor on the Lake

C

LAKE SHORE BLVD

East Nation Airport

283

HODGSON RD

Powerplant

Timberlake

Ashtabula

Lakeline

ROBERTS RD

PAINESVILLE

2

Eastlake

91

STEVENS BLVD

Reynolds

20

84

MENTOR AV

VINE ST   640   VINE ST

United Musical
Instruments

90

Willowick

Willoughby

174

CUYAHOGA CO

LAKE CO

EUCLID AV

Hospital

Moss
Pt

LAKE SHORE BLVD

2

Wickliffe

Walte
Hill

Park

175

84

198

283

20

EXIT
188

River RD

3467

Hach-Otis
Sanctuary

AQUEDUCT

EXIT
189

90

EDDY

CHARDON

Euclid

EXIT
184A

90

84

175

CHARDON RD

6

174

CHARDON

Cleveland Lakefront
State Park

EXIT
184C

EXIT
182A

EXIT
182B

Willoughby Hills

271

91

North Chagrin
Reservation

LAKE CO
CUYAHOGA CO

GEAUGA CO
CUYAHOGA CO

D

CLSP

EXIT
180

EXIT
181

Euclid Creek
Reservation

Cuyahoga
County
Airport

84

6

CHARDON RD

BISHOP RD

WHITE RD

MAIN ST

Mayfield

Cave

205

WILSON ST

CHESTERLAND

Cleveland Lakefront
State Park

Light

EXIT
179

90

283

EXIT
178

Bratenahl

LAKESHORE BLVD

HOPKINS AV

SHAW AV

NOBLE RD

**Richmond
Heights**

**Highland
Heights**

RICHMOND RD

HIGHLAND RD

North Chagrin
Reservation

ROCKEFELLER RD

174

SHERMART
RD

Rockefeller Park
Greenhouse

Martin Luther King
Jr. Parkway

EXIT
177

MONTICELLO BLVD

WILSON MILLS RD

36

Gates Mill

322

Scotland

Burke Lakefront
Airport

EXIT
176

CLSP

90
374

Garden Center of
Greater Cleveland

Auto Aviation
Museum

**East
Cleveland**

Forest Hill Park

**South
Euclid**

RIDGEBURY BLVD

LANDER RD

Lyndhurst

**Mayfield
Heights**

91

BERKSHIRE RD

322

Goodtime II

USS Cod Submarine

The Plain
Dealer

6

Western Reserve
Museum

MAYFIELD RD

322

Cleveland Clinic

Lighthouse

BREAKWATER

Dunham
Tavern
Museum

Museum of Natural
History

Health
Education
Museum

Center for
Contemporary Art

**Cleveland
Heights**

GREEN RD

Notre Dame
College

271

2

Cleveland Browns

322

Euclid Av

Museum of
Historical Medicine

Children's Museum

WARRENSVILLE CENTER RD

CEDAR RD

© DeLorme

20

CLEVELAND

CLSP

BREAKWATER

CLSP

D

41°30'
41°22'30"

Scale 1:150,000   Elevation in meters
(1 meter = 3.28 feet)   Continue on Page 41   81°25'00"
81.4167°   **31**

BROOKLYN   81°35'00"
81.5833°

Continue on Page 31

Continue on Page 42

© DeLorme

KILOMETERS
MILES

LAKE   ERIE

APPROXIMATE MEAN LAKE ELEVATION 571 ft
174 m

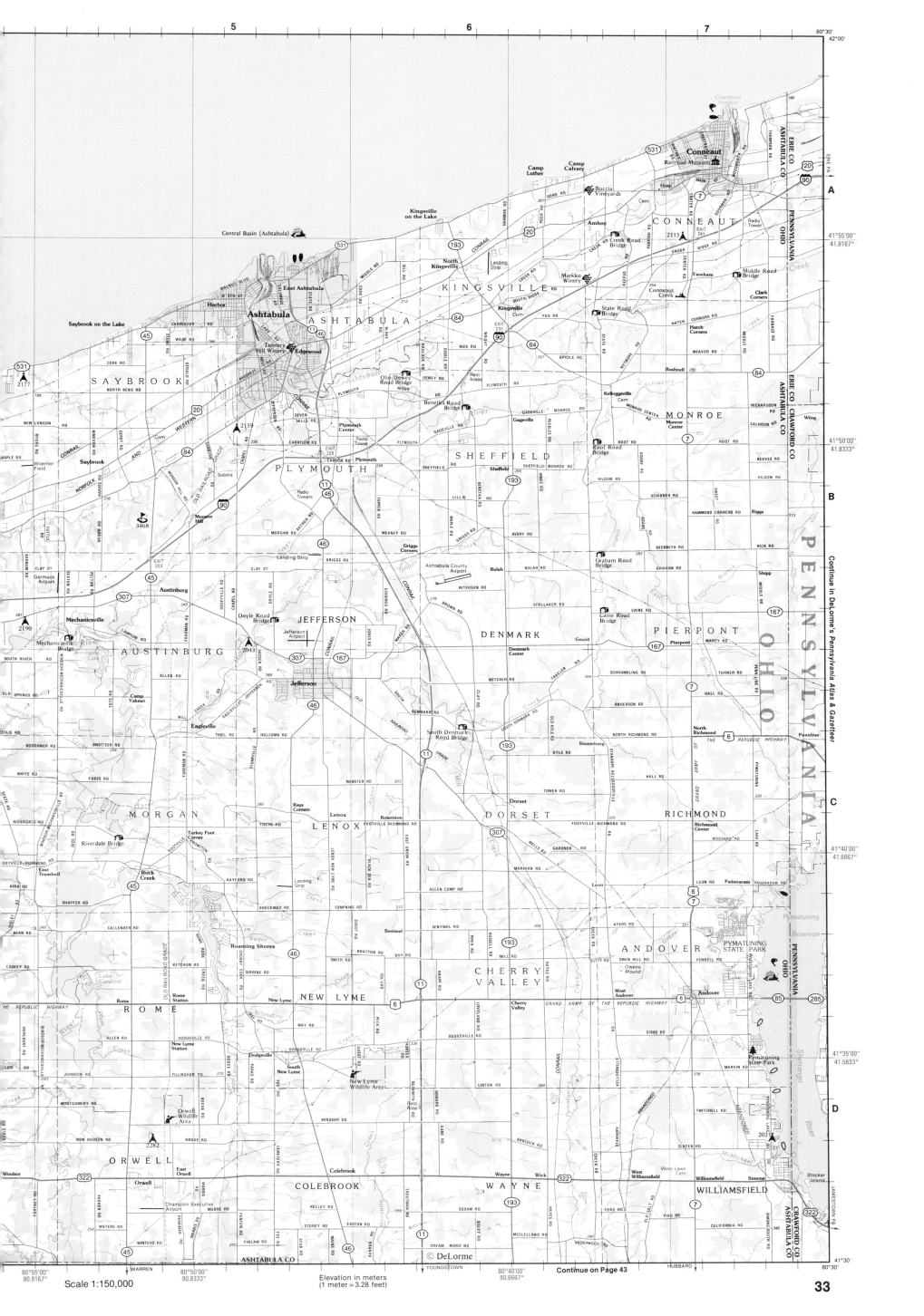

Continue in DeLorme's Pennsylvania Atlas & Gazetteer

Continue on Page 43

Scale 1:150,000

Elevation in meters
(1 meter = 3.28 feet)

© DeLorme

33

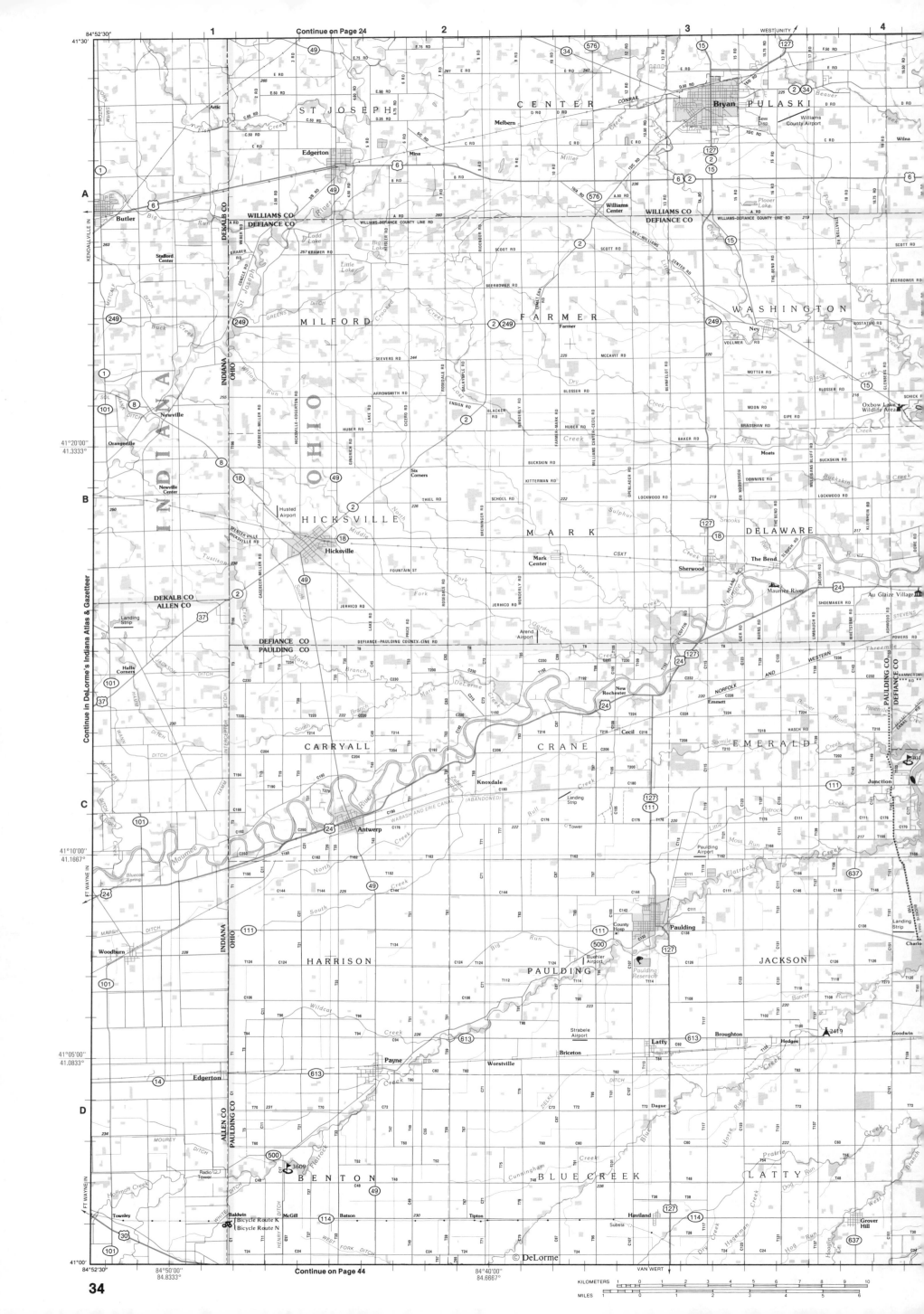

Continue in DeLorme's Indiana Atlas & Gazetteer

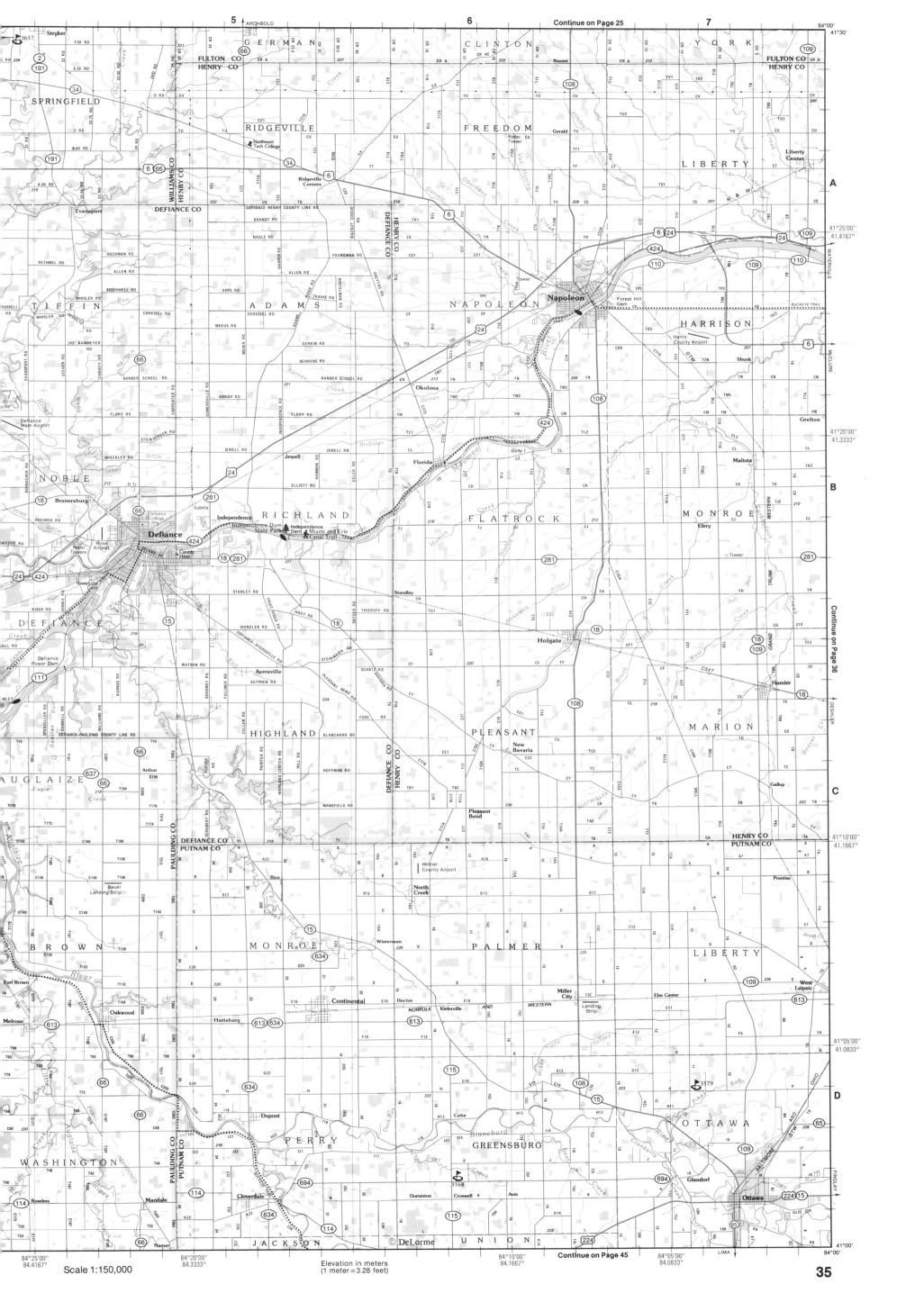

Continue on Page 25

Continue on Page 36

Continue on Page 45

Scale 1:150,000

Elevation in meters
(1 meter = 3.28 feet)

© DeLorme

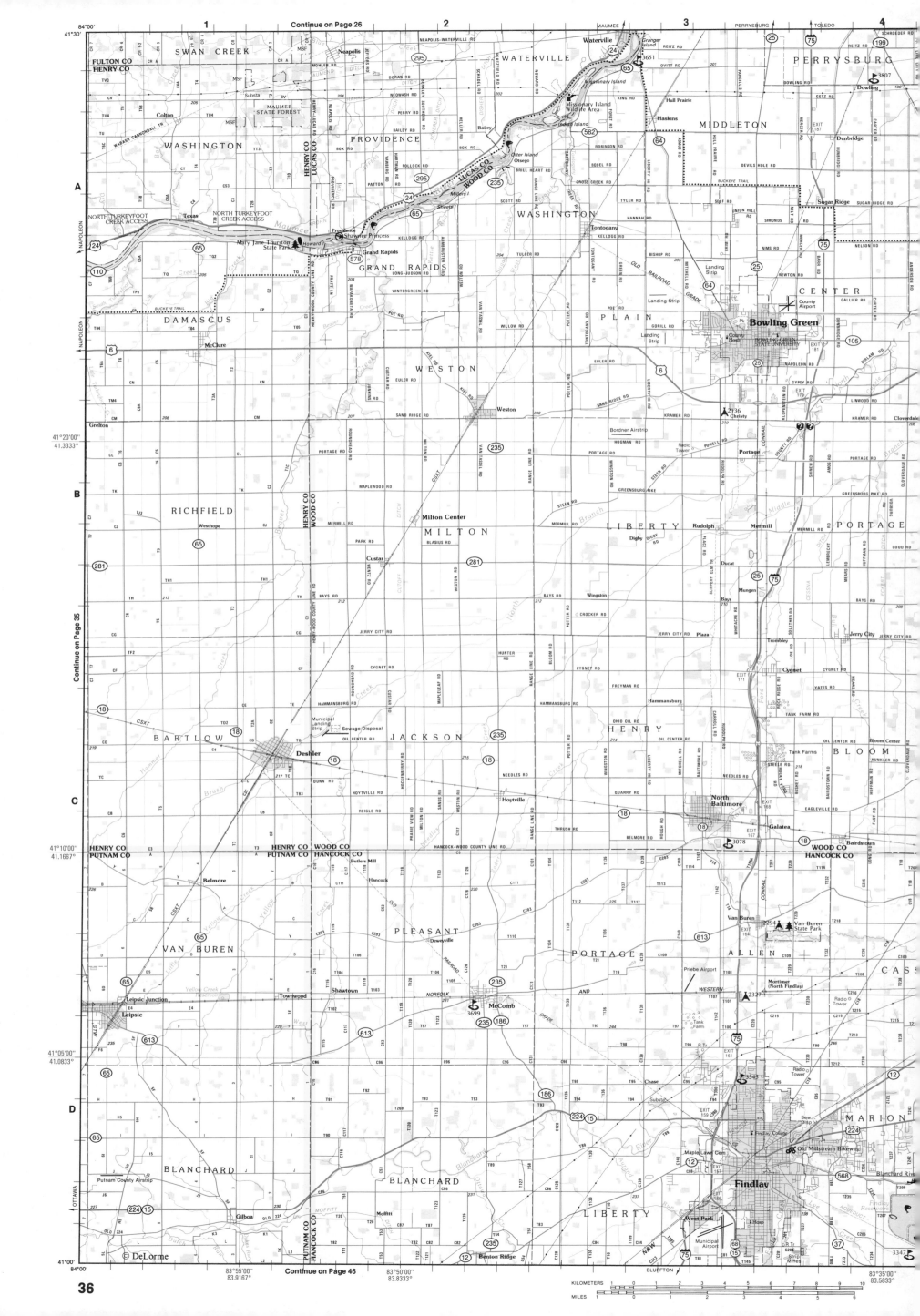

Continue on Page 35

© DeLorme

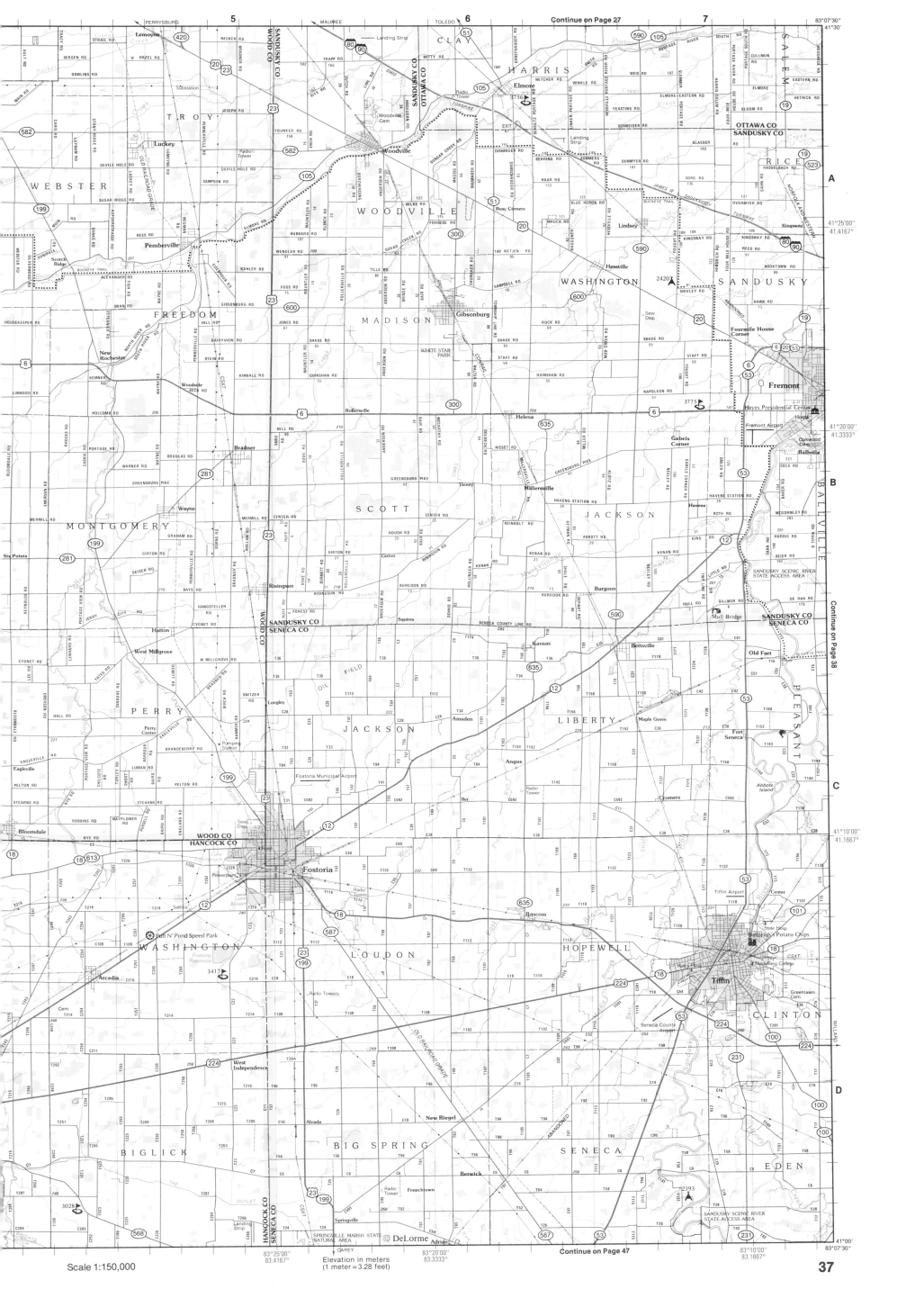

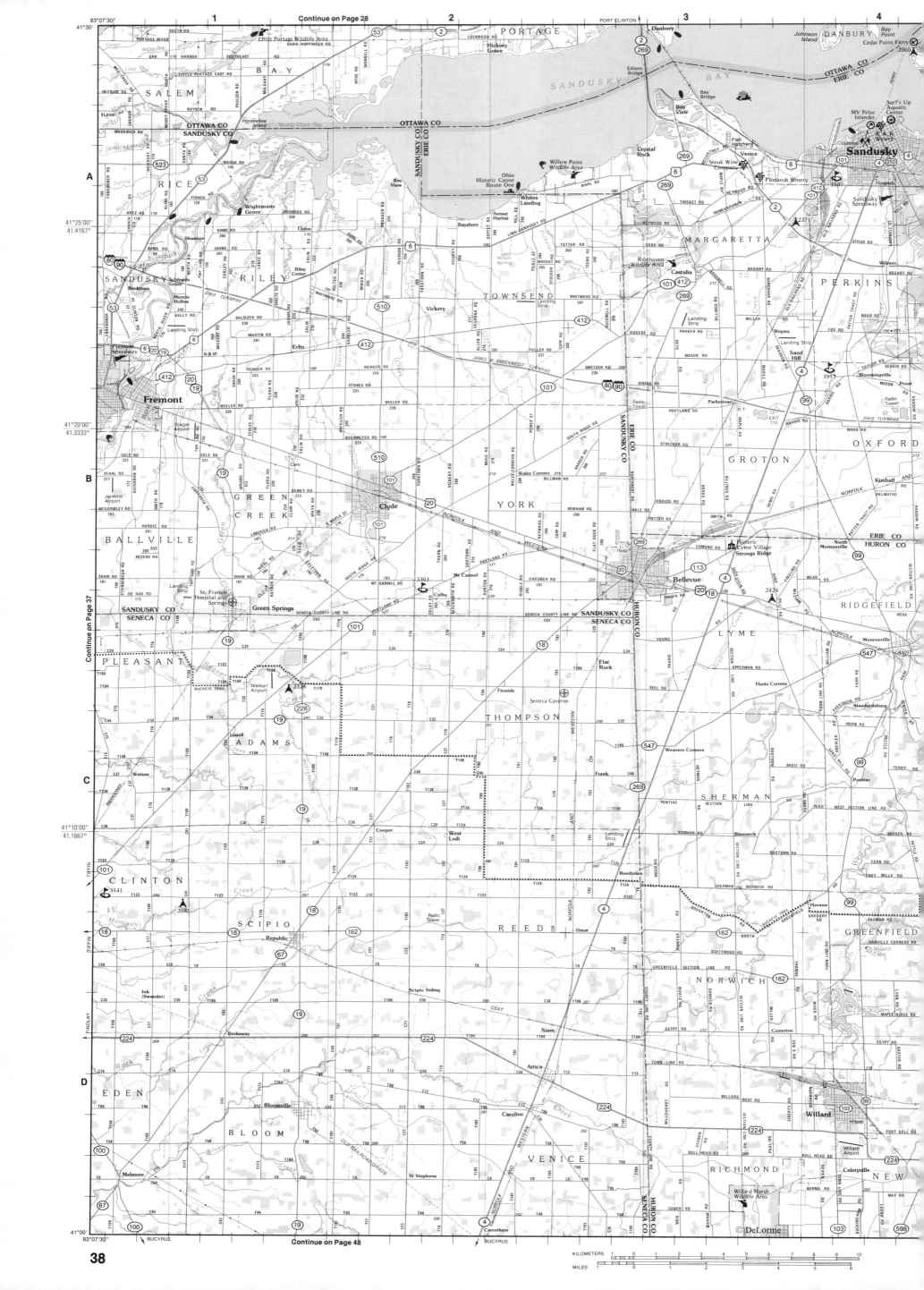

Continue on Page 37

Continue on Page 48

LAKE ERIE

Approximate Mean Lake Elevation 571 ft
174 m

©DeLorme

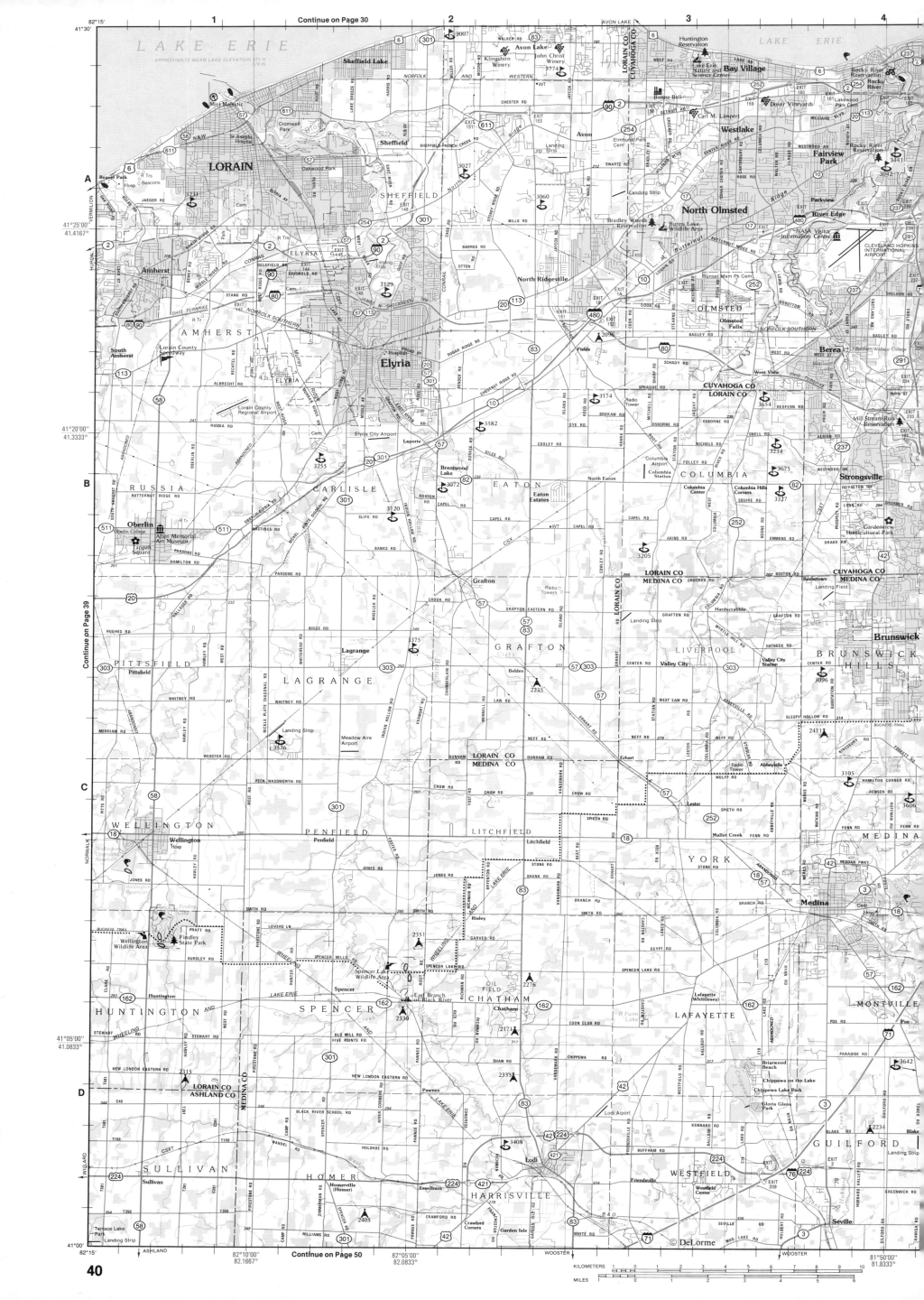

LAKE ERIE

APPROXIMATE MEAN LAKE ELEVATION 571 ft
174 m

Continue on Page 39

© DeLorme

Continue on Page 42

Scale 1:150,000

Elevation in meters
(1 meter = 3.28 feet)

© DeLorme

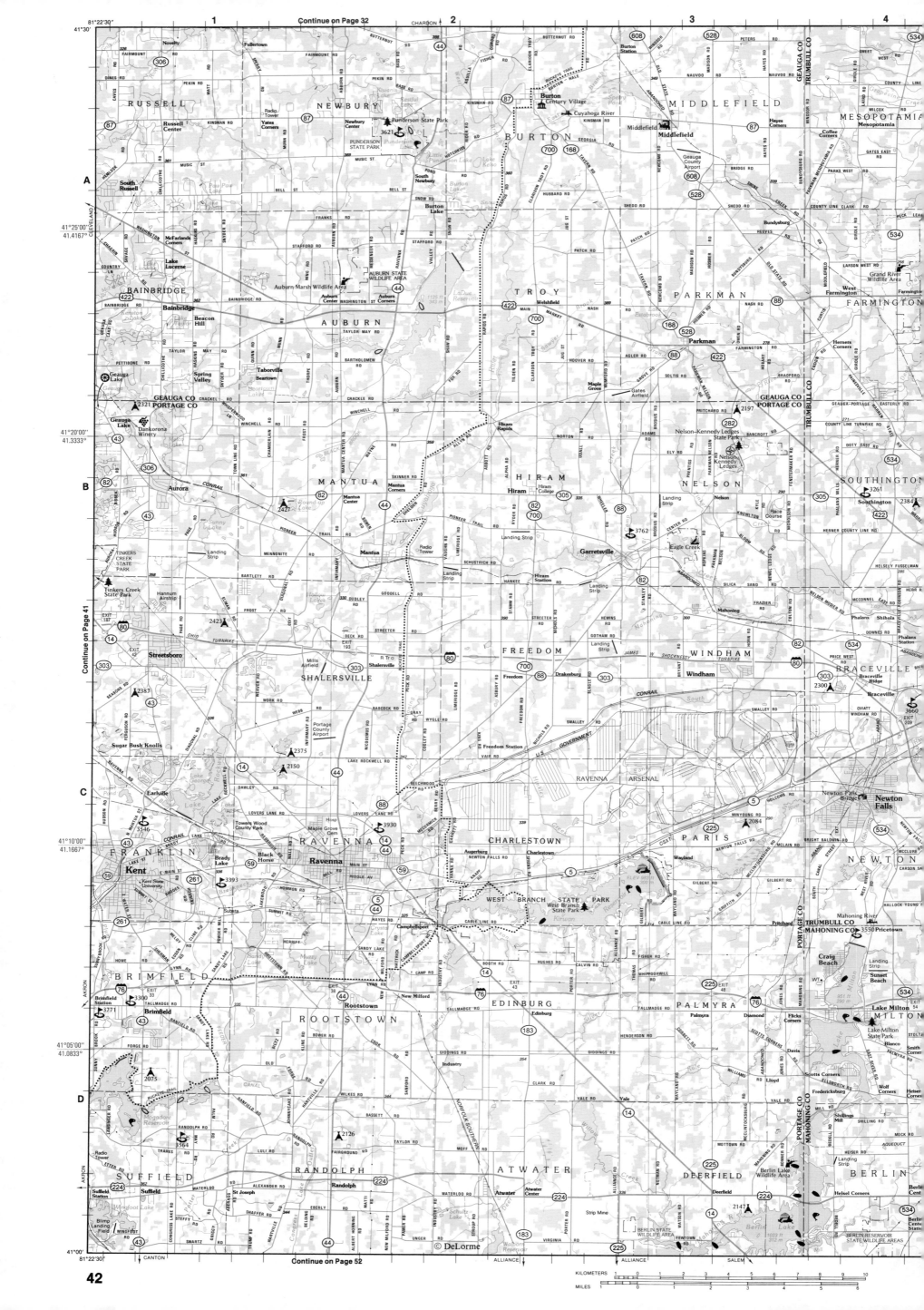

Continue on Page 41

© DeLorme

KILOMETERS
MILES

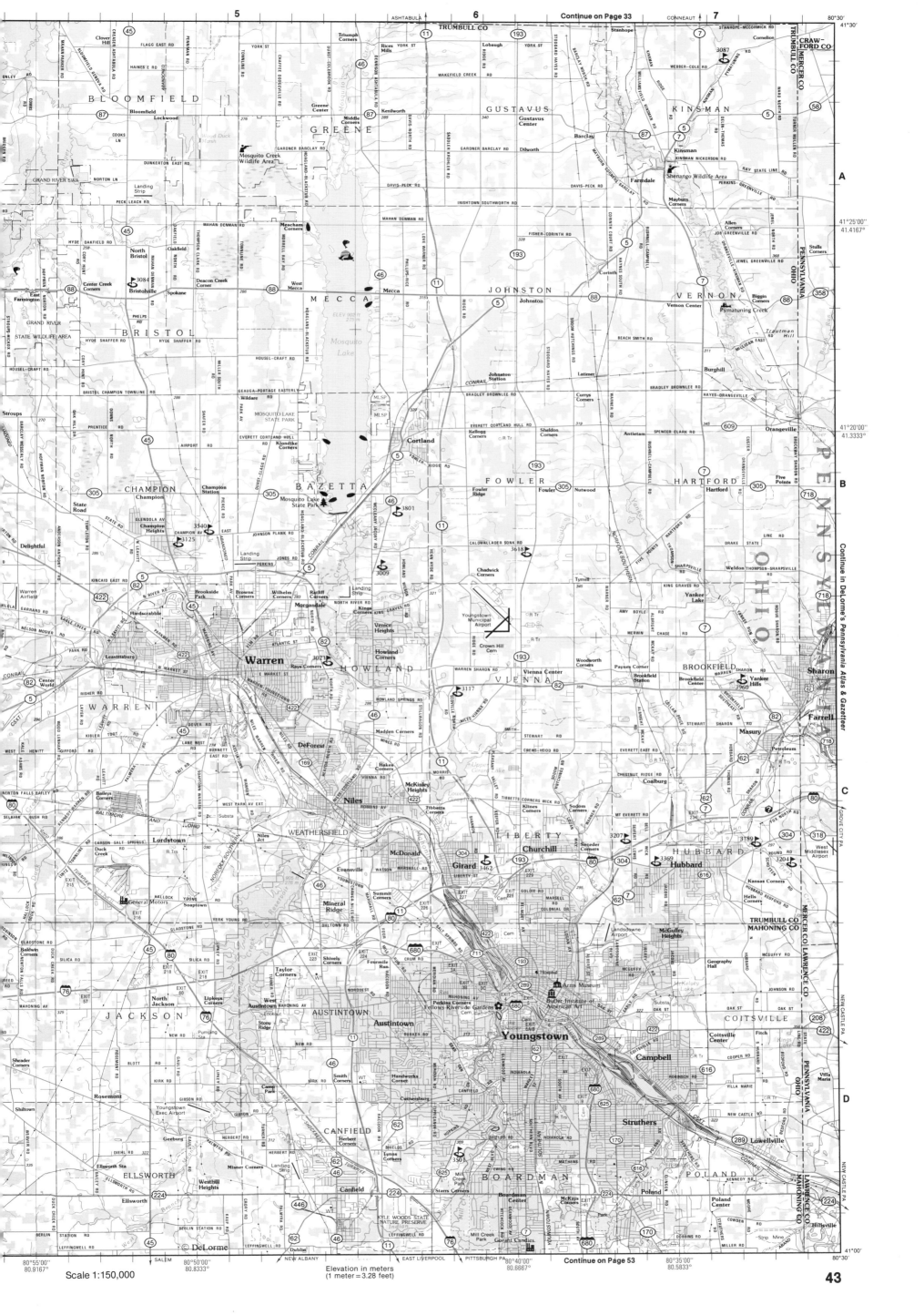

Continue in DeLorme's Pennsylvania Atlas & Gazetteer

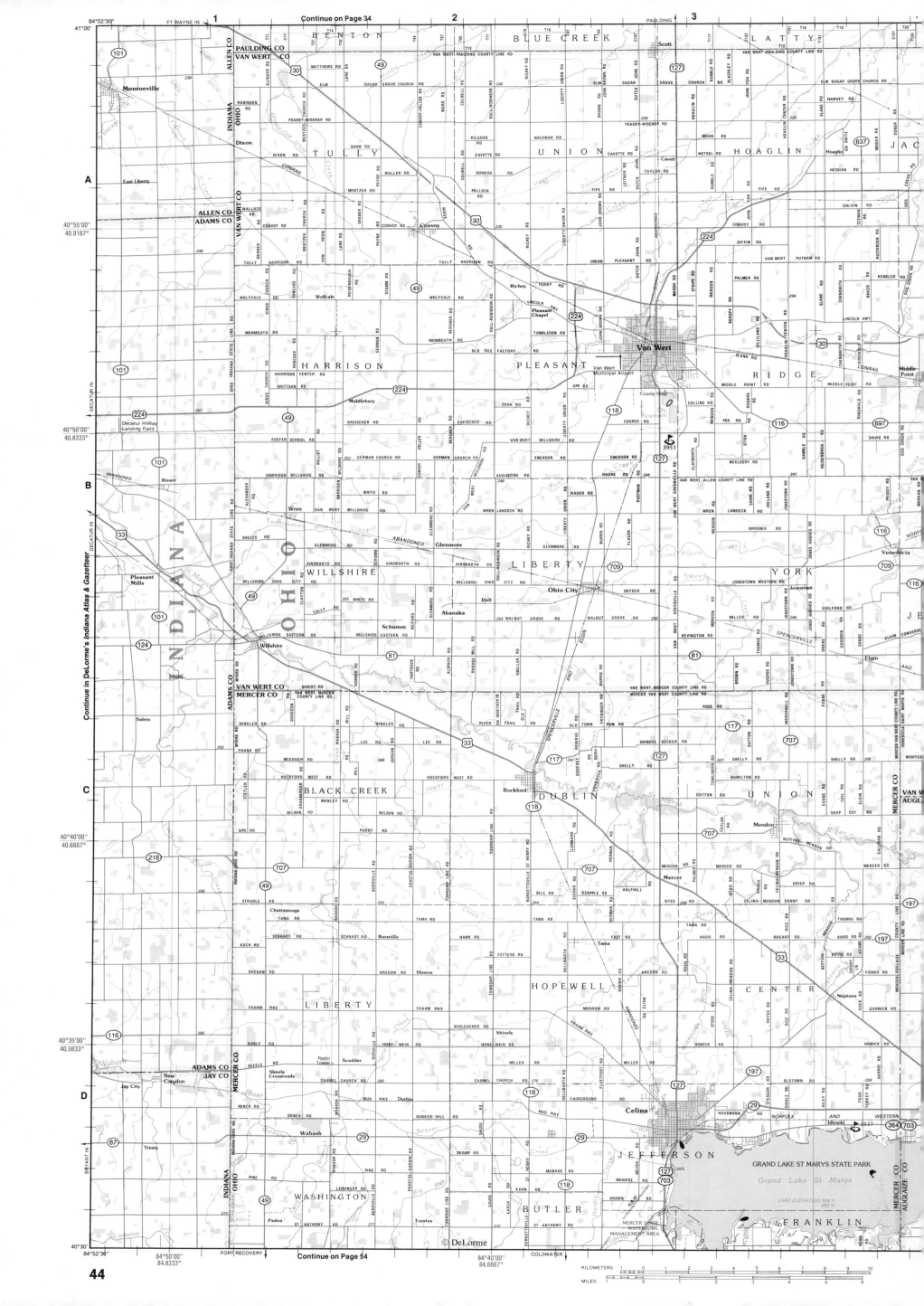

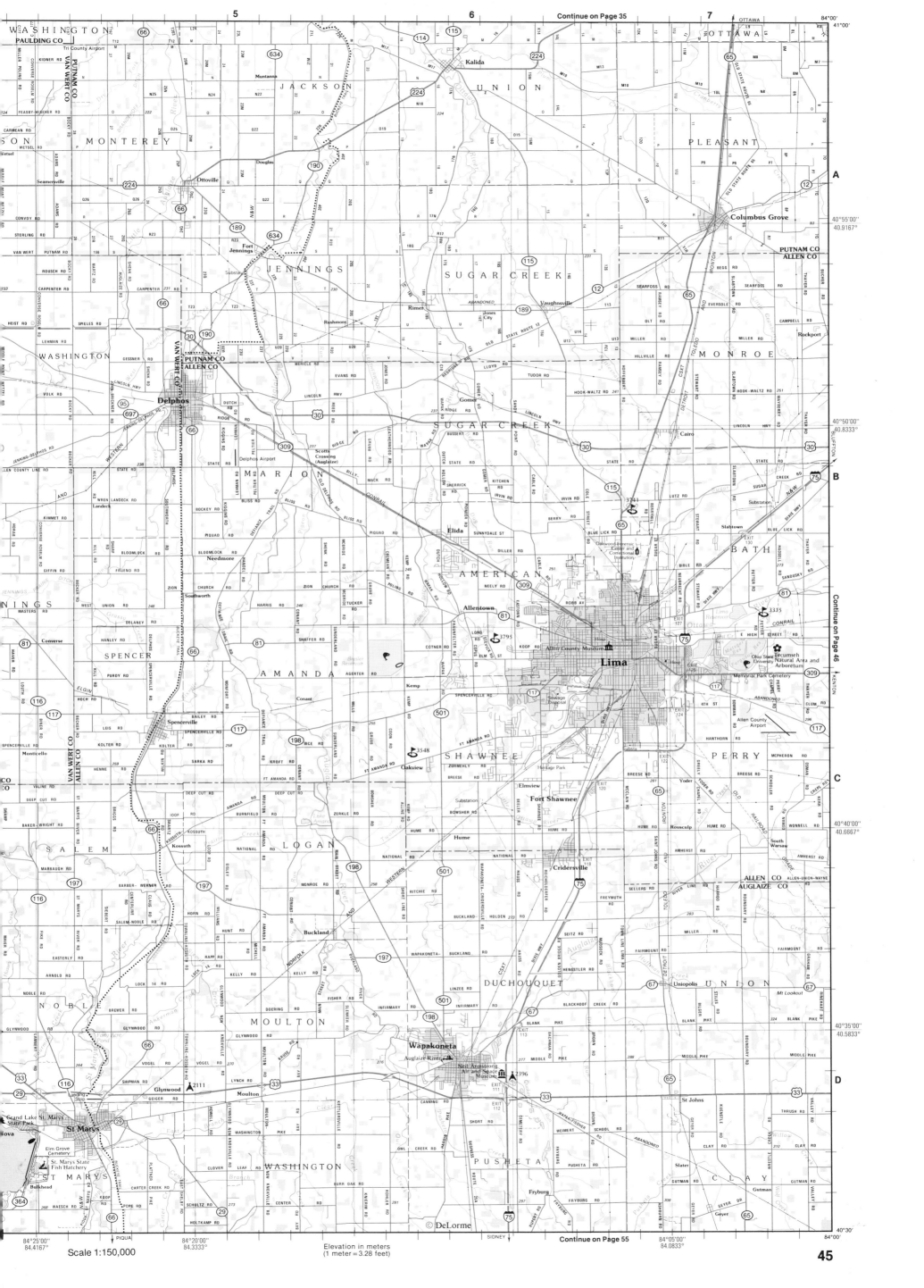

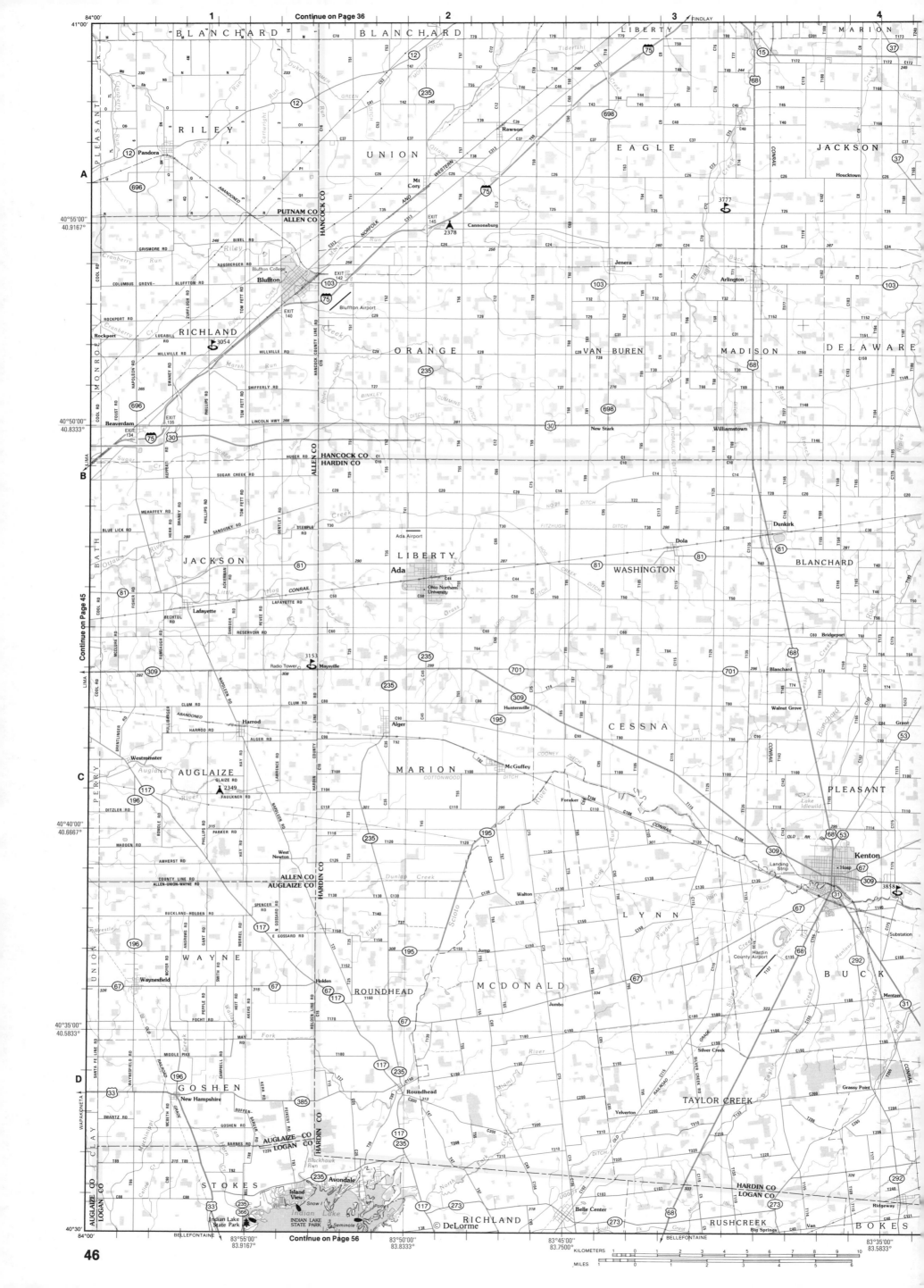

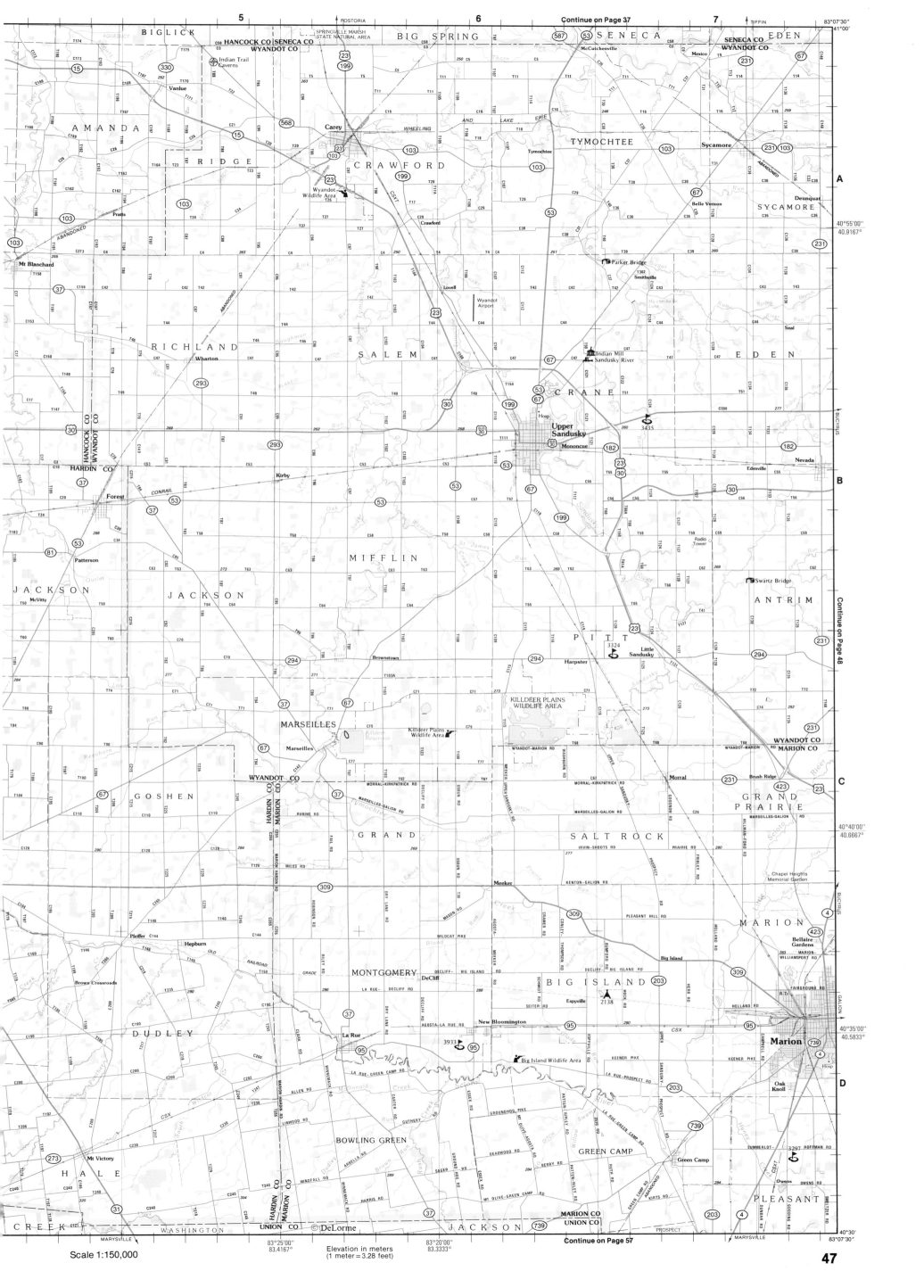

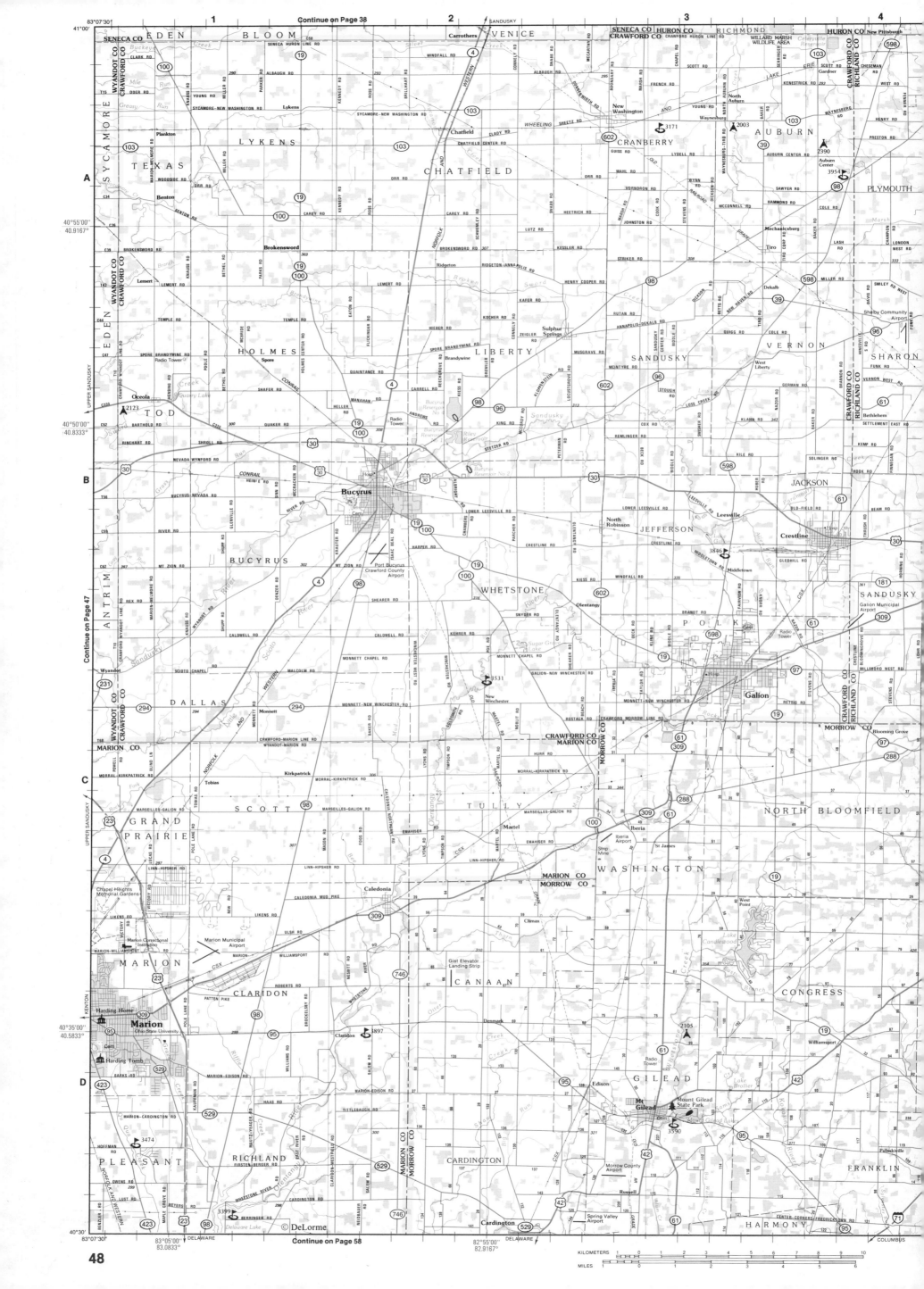

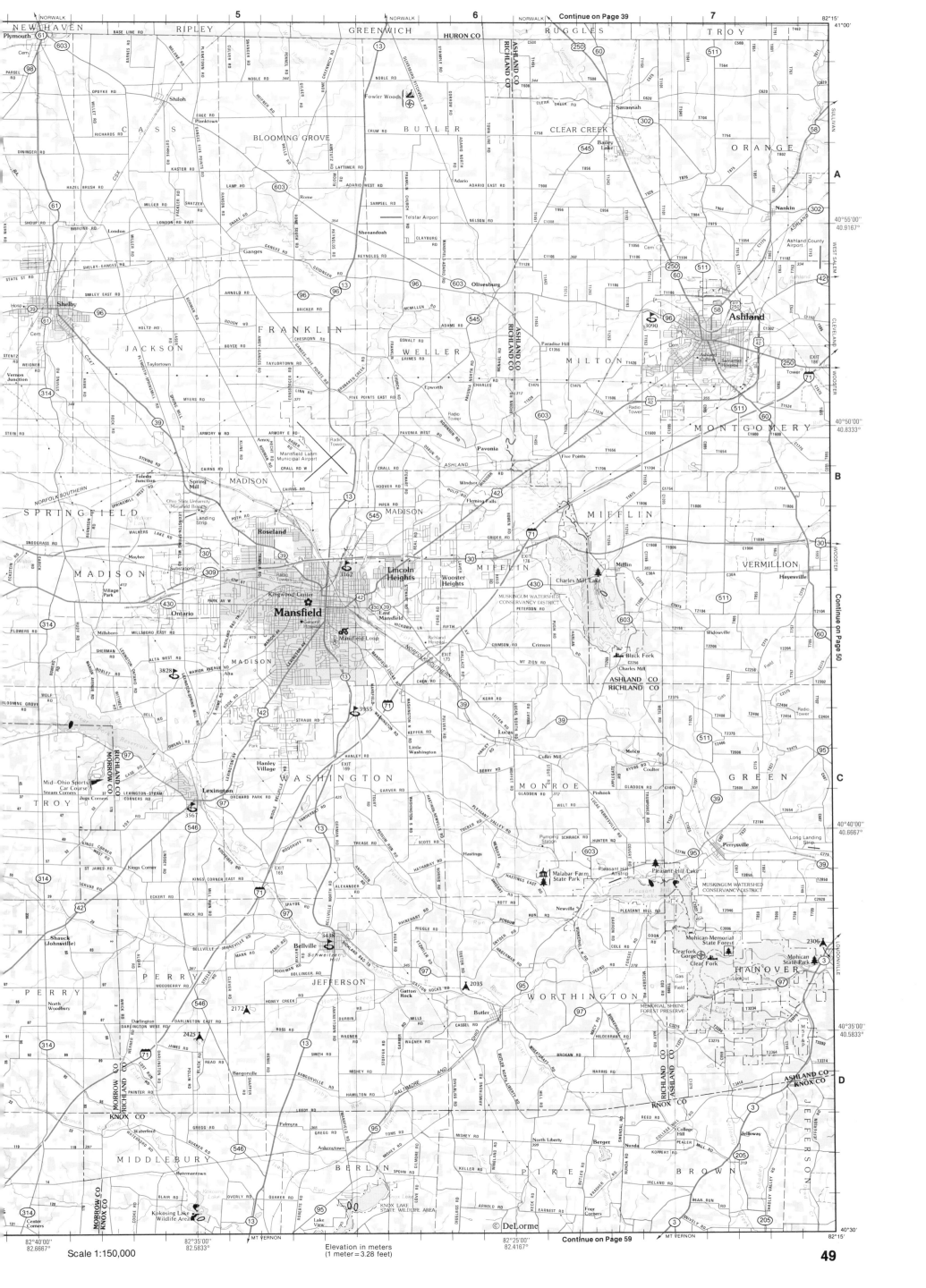

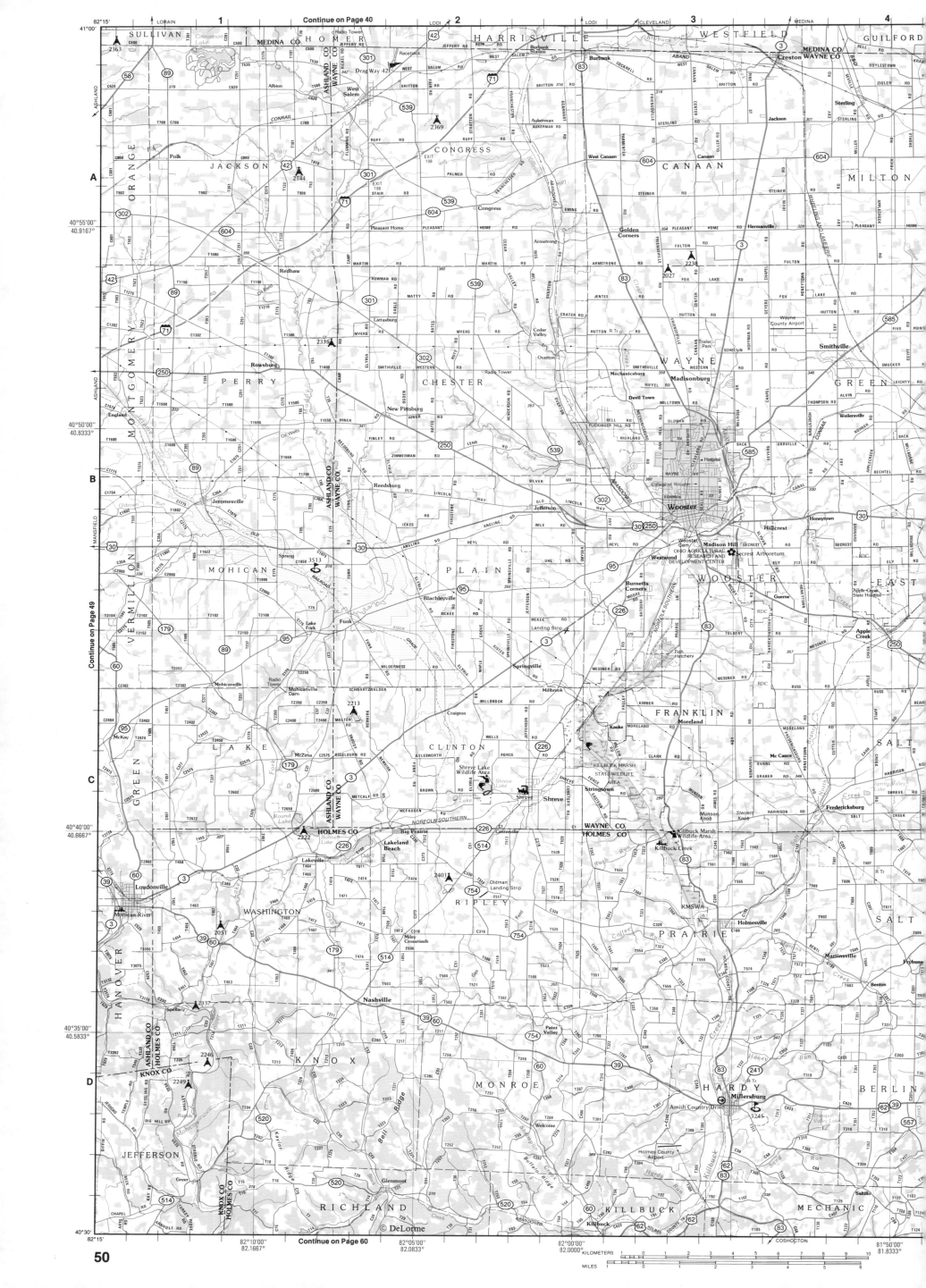

Continue on Page 49

© DeLorme

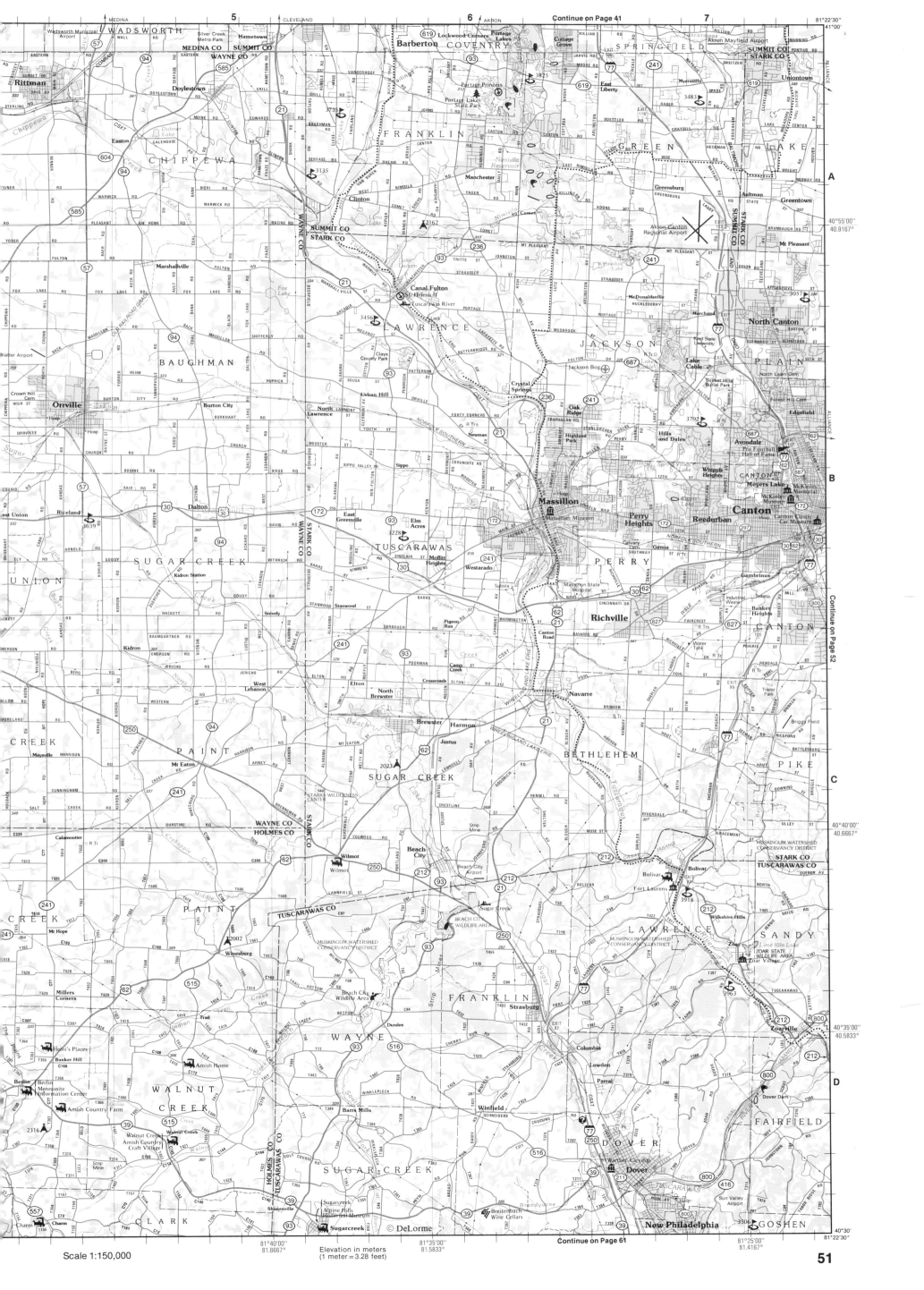

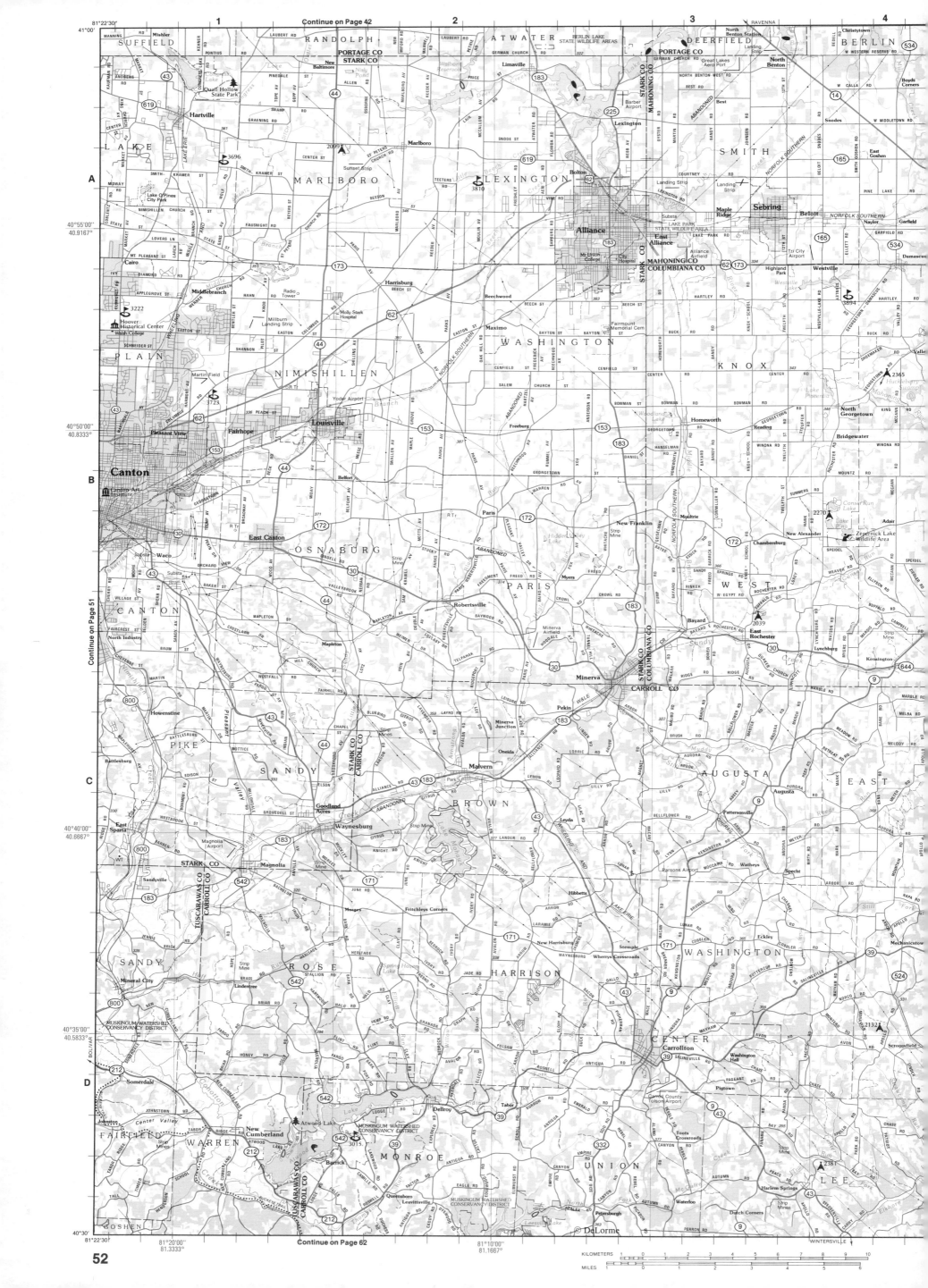

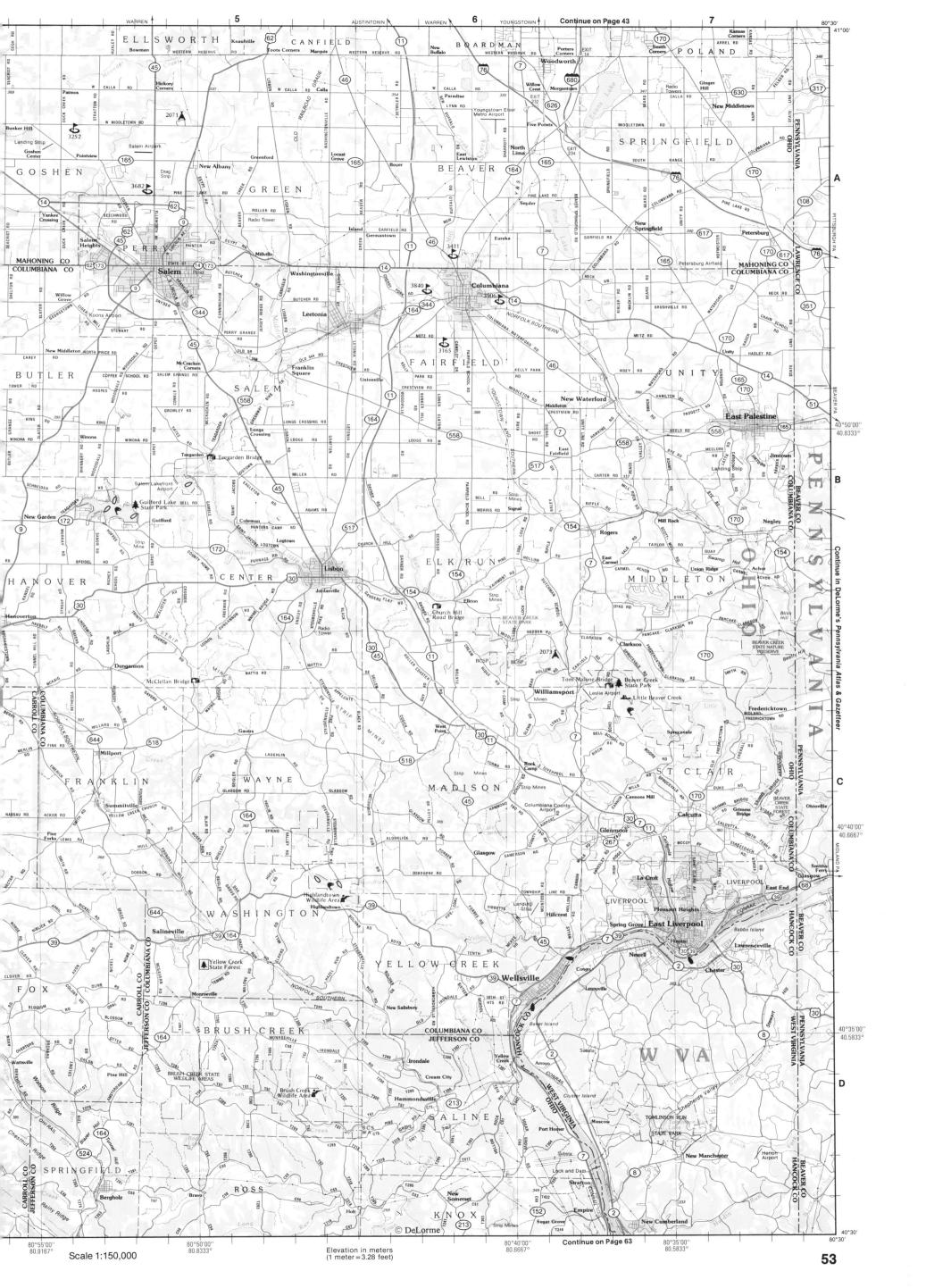

Continue in DeLorme's Pennsylvania Atlas & Gazetteer

Scale 1:150,000

Elevation in meters
(1 meter = 3.28 feet)

© DeLorme

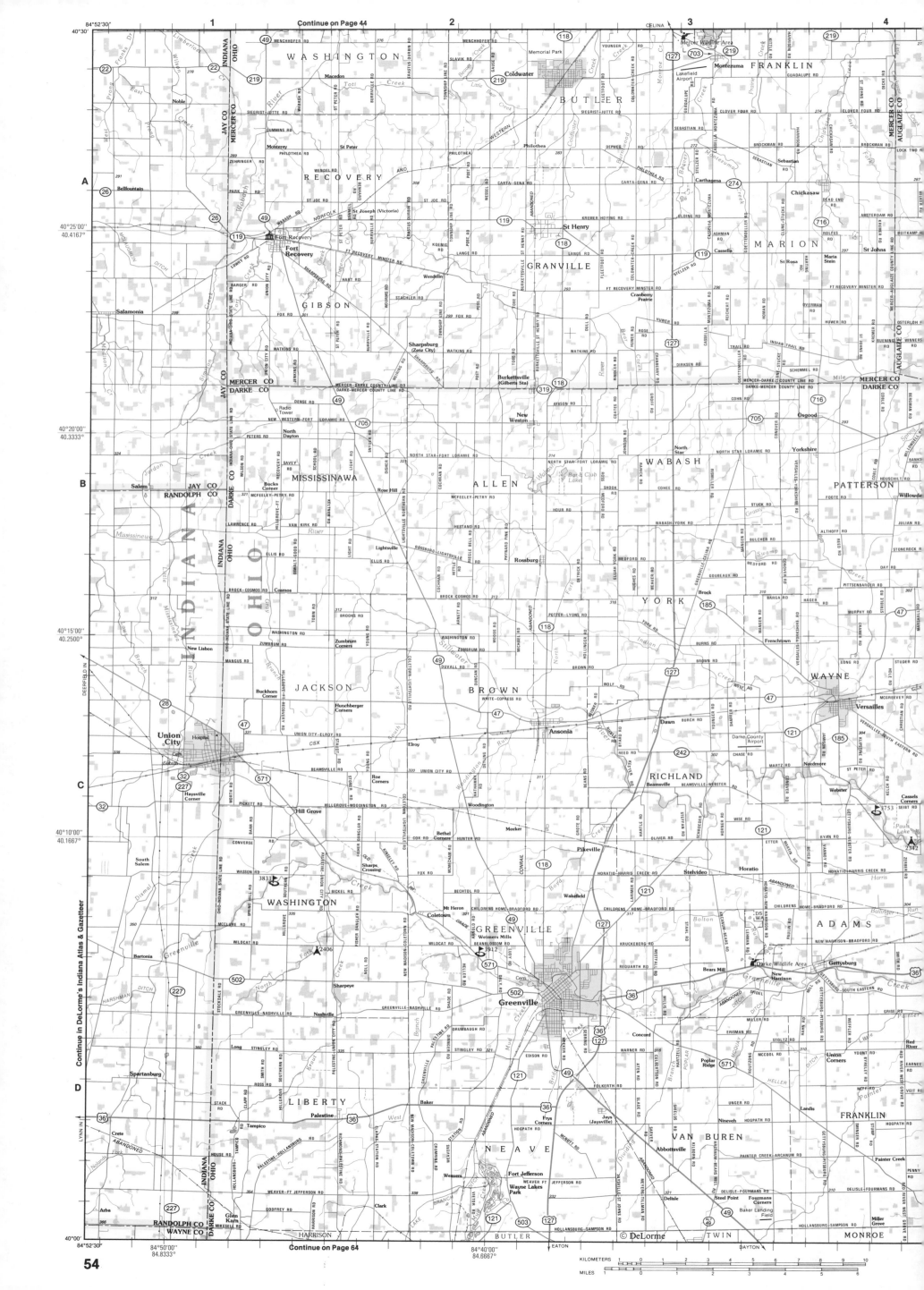

Continue in DeLorme's Indiana Atlas & Gazetteer

© DeLorme

KILOMETERS
MILES

Continue on Page 45
Continue on Page 56
Continue on Page 65

Scale 1:150,000

Elevation in meters
(1 meter = 3.28 feet)

© DeLorme

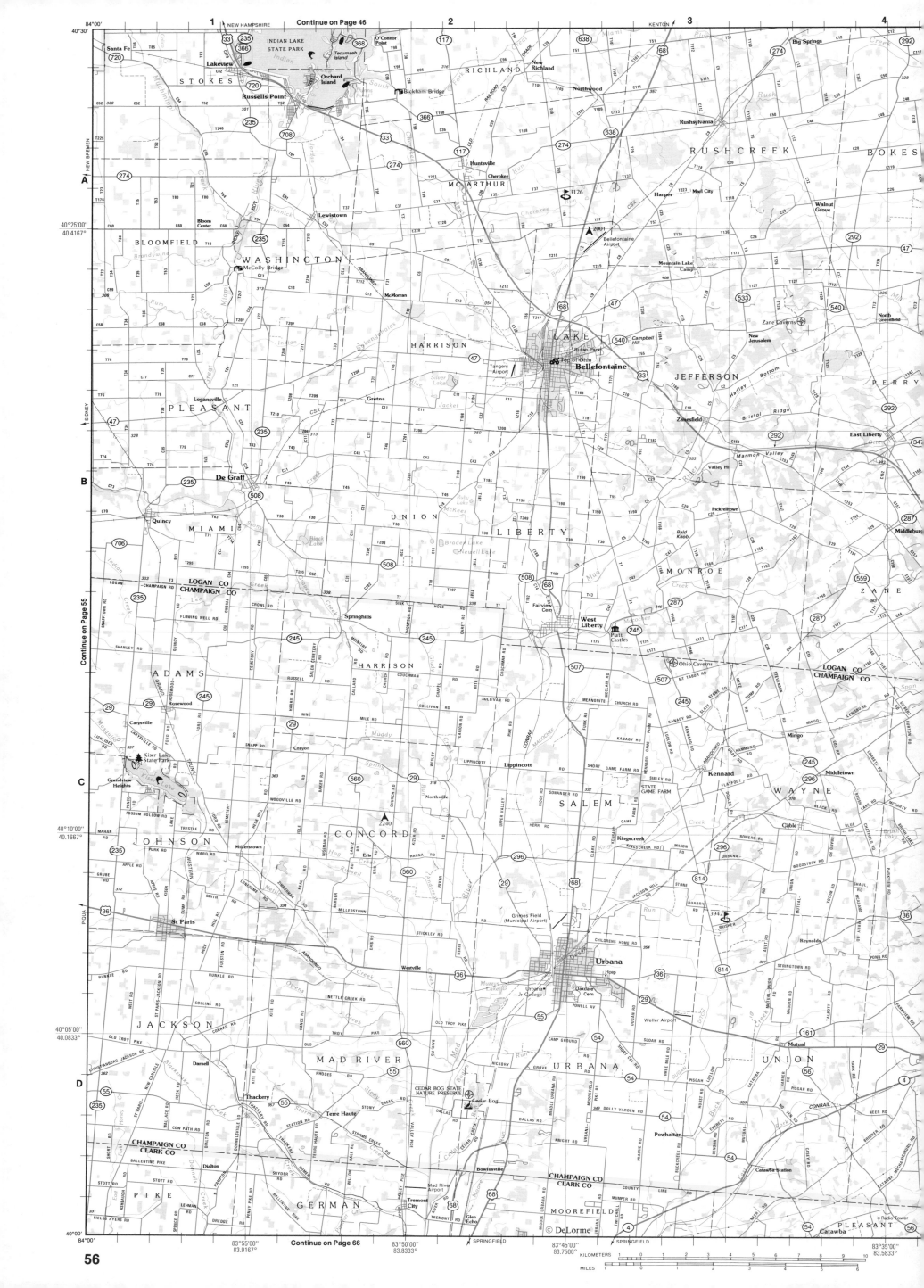

Continue on Page 46

Continue on Page 55

Continue on Page 66

Continue on Page 47

Scale 1:150,000

Elevation in meters
(1 meter = 3.28 feet)

© DeLorme

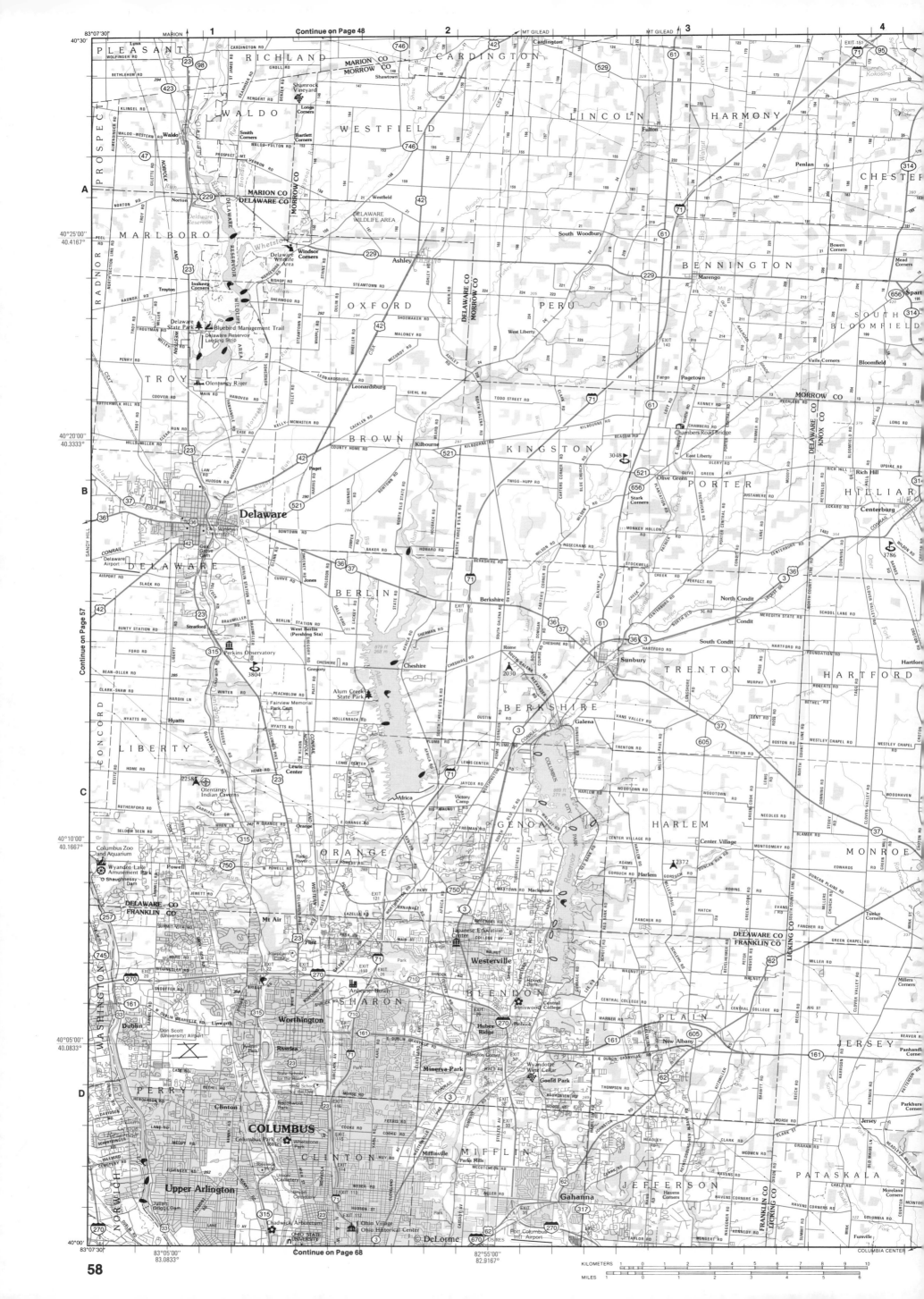

Continue on Page 48

Continue on Page 57

Continue on Page 68

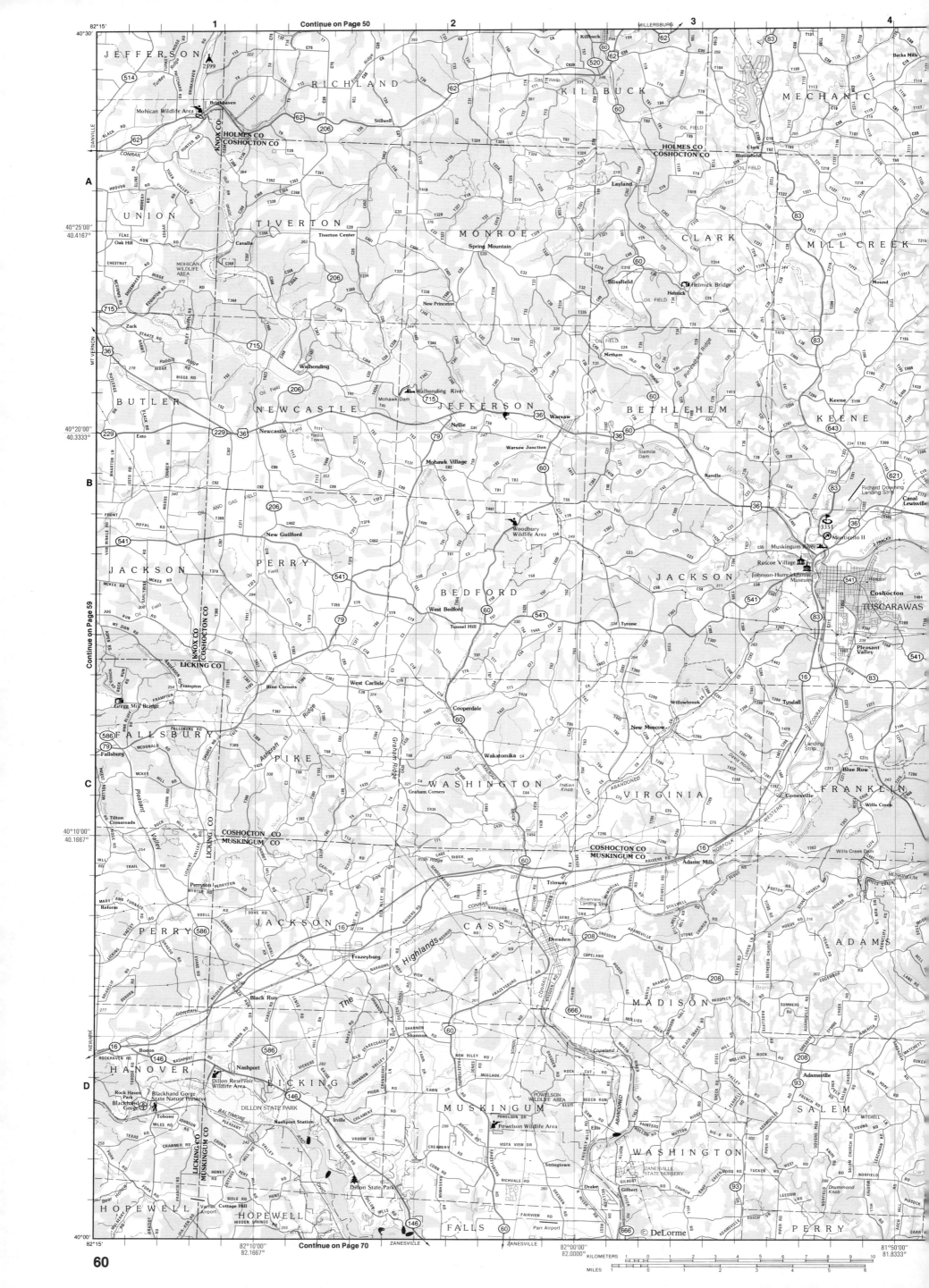

Continue on Page 62

Scale 1:150,000

Elevation in meters
(1 meter = 3.28 feet)

Continue on Page 71

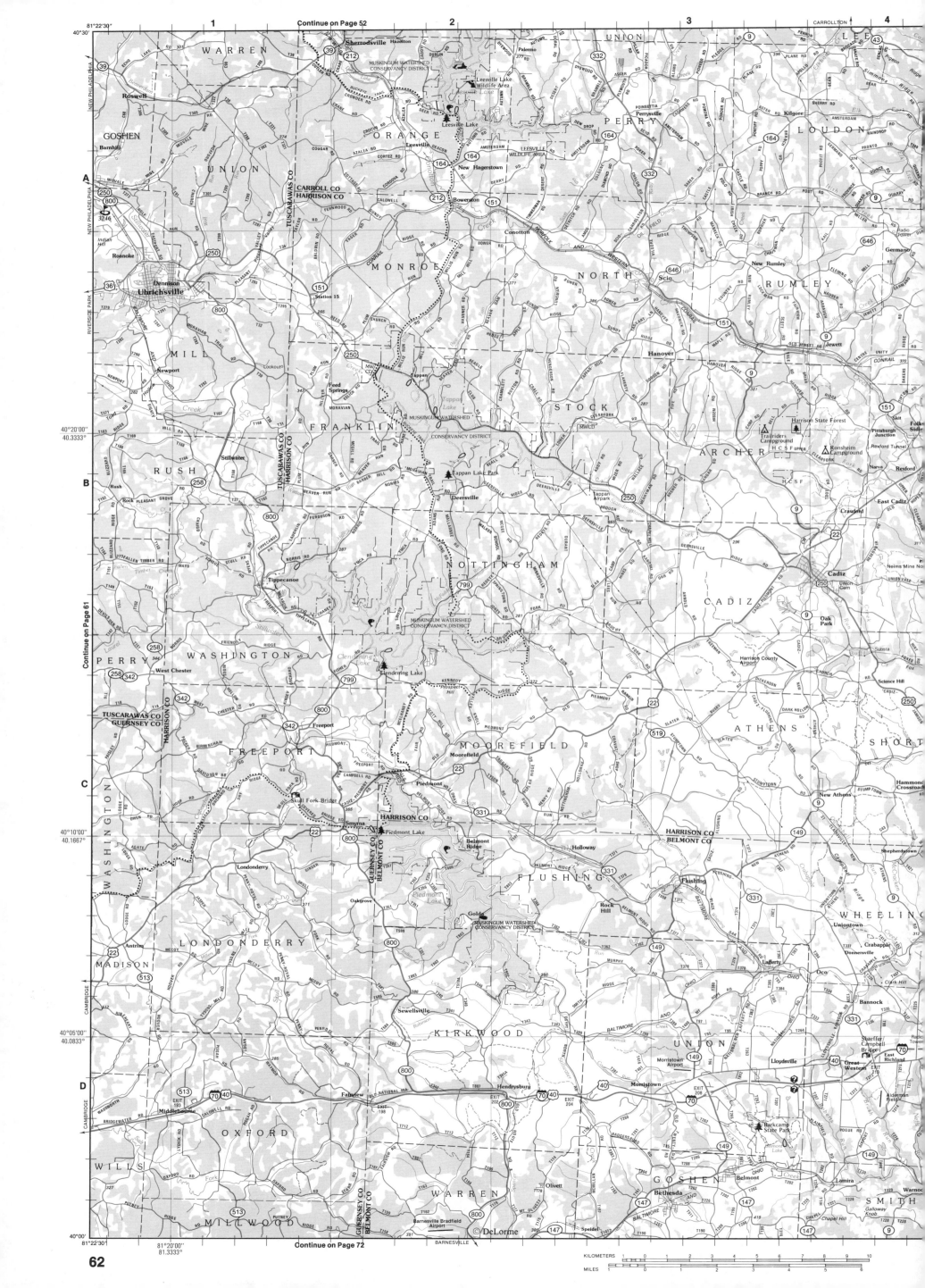

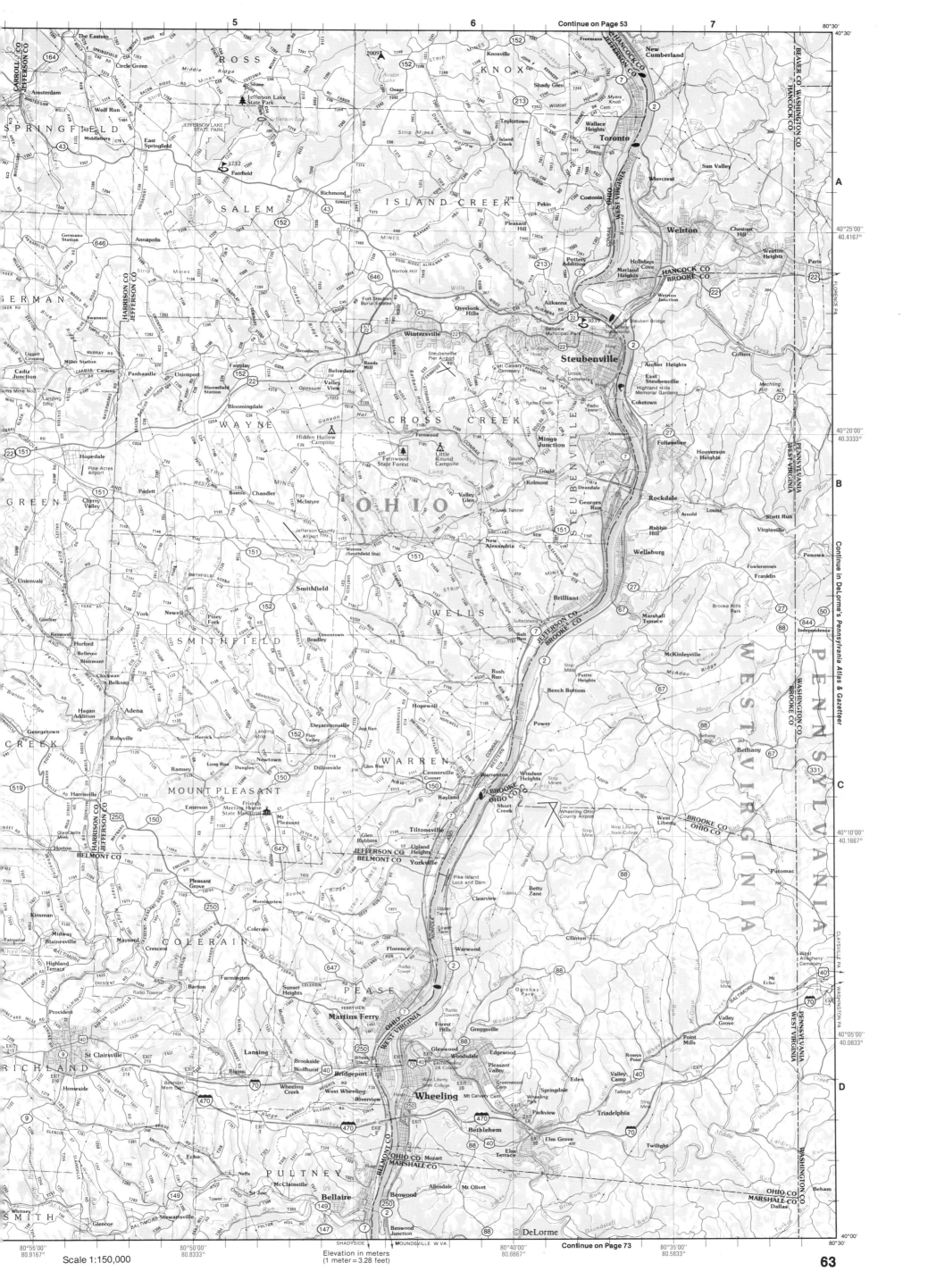

Continue in DeLorme's Pennsylvania Atlas & Gazetteer

Scale 1:150,000

Elevation in meters
(1 meter = 3.28 feet)

©DeLorme

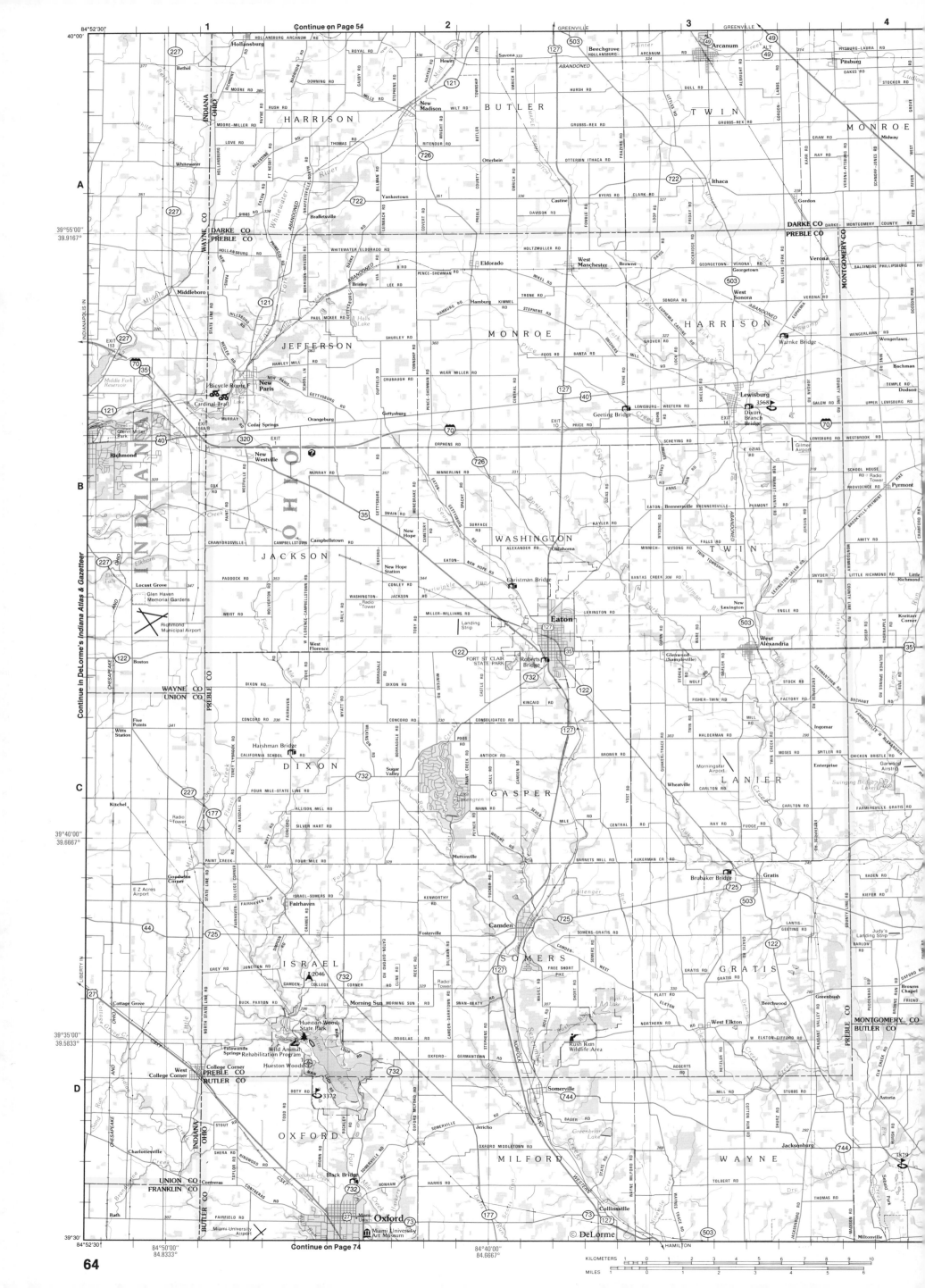

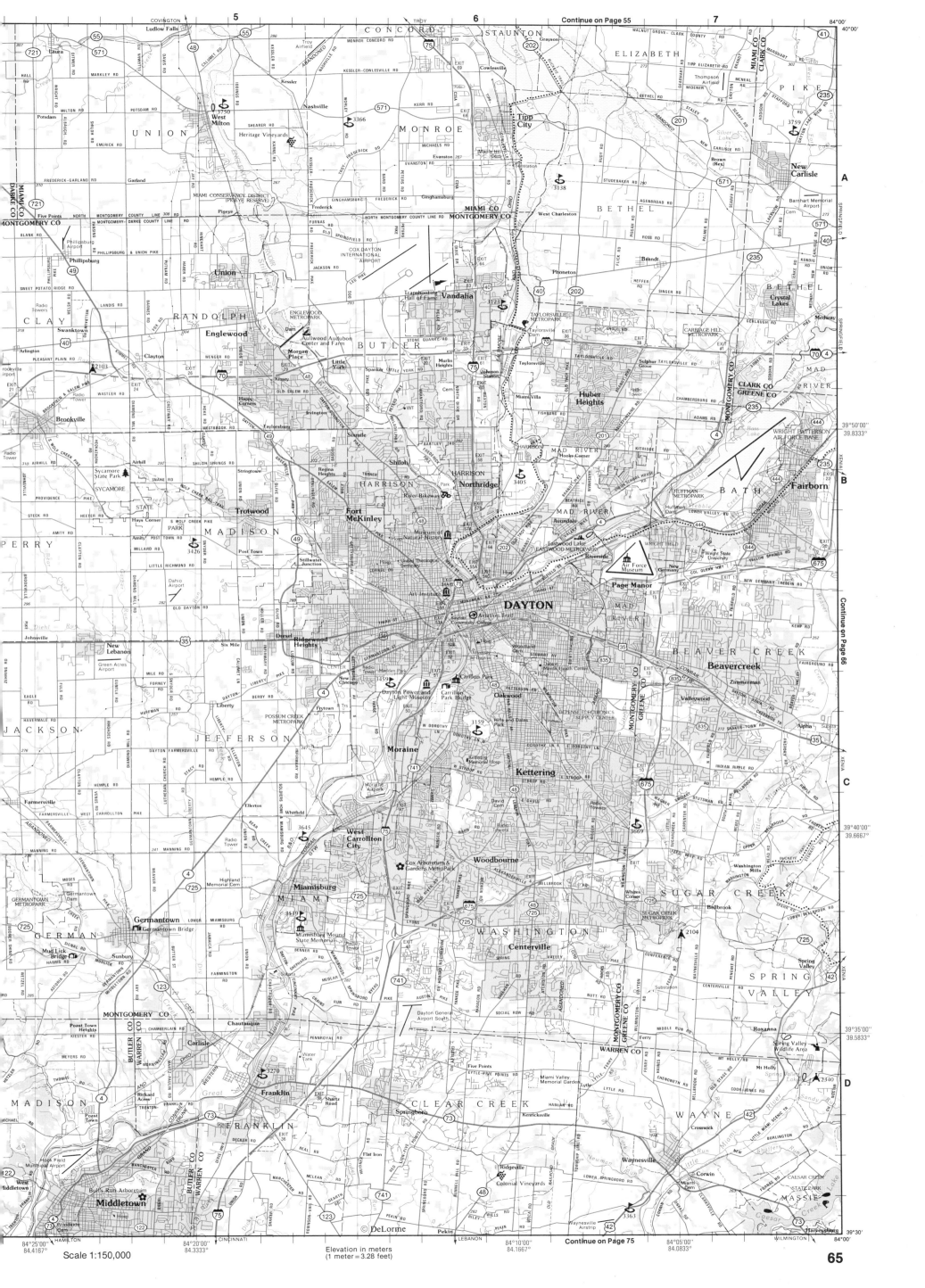

Scale 1:150,000

Elevation in meters
(1 meter = 3.28 feet)

© DeLorme

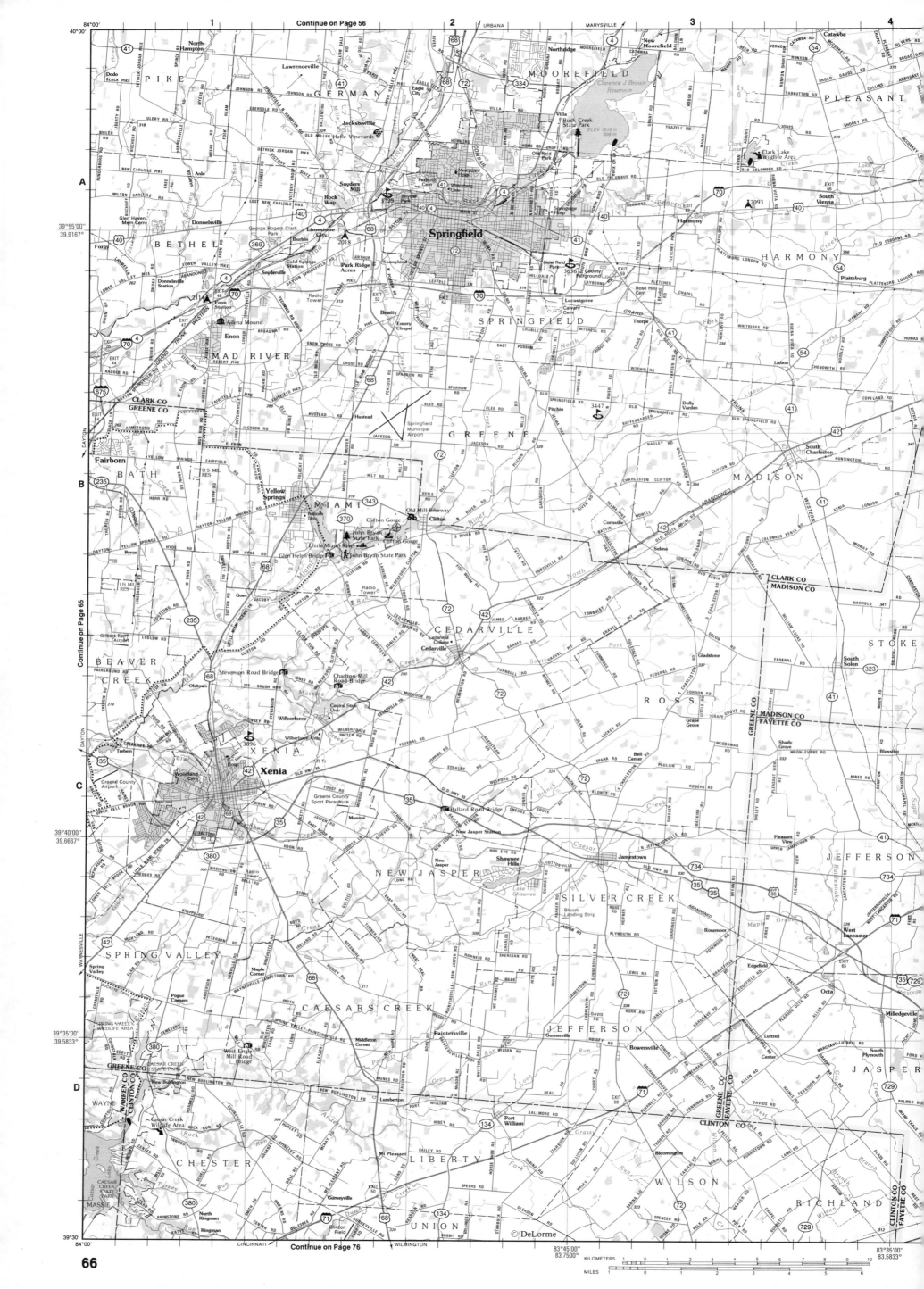

Continue on Page 65

©DeLorme

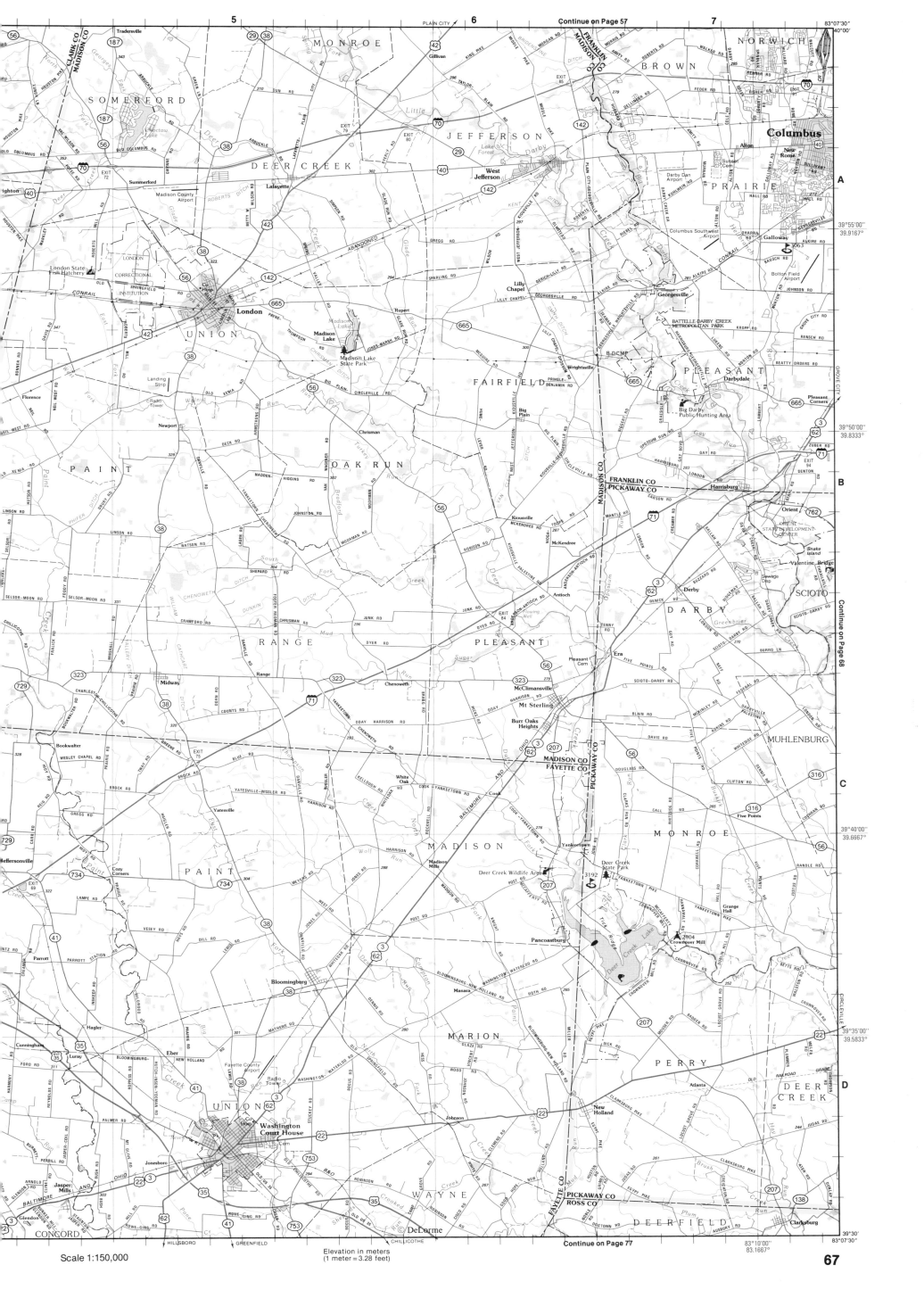

PLAIN CITY   Continue on Page 57

Scale 1:150,000

Elevation in meters
(1 meter = 3.28 feet)

© DeLorme

Continue on Page 68

Continue on Page 77

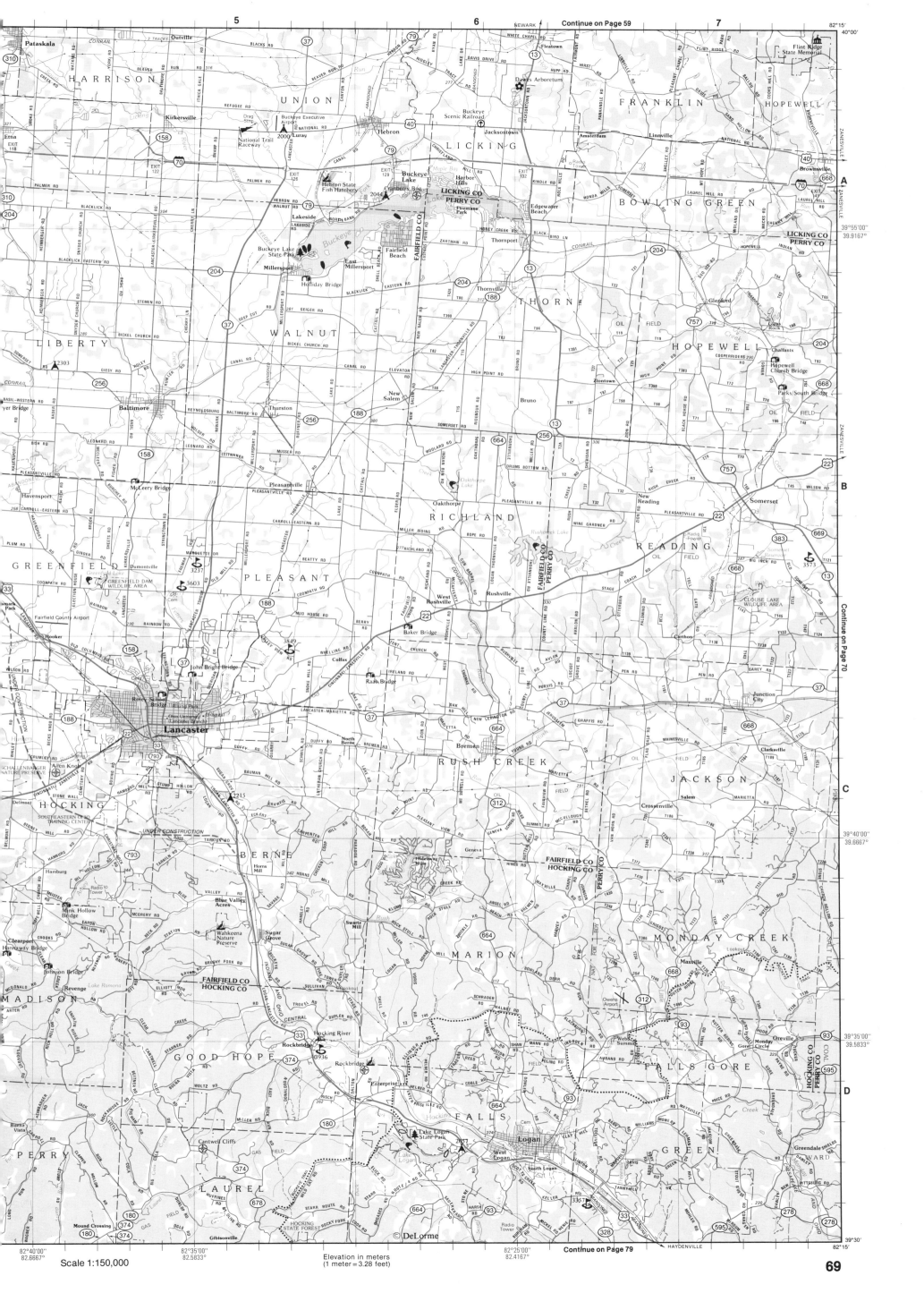

Continue on Page 59

Continue on Page 70

Continue on Page 79

Scale 1:150,000

Elevation in meters
(1 meter = 3.28 feet)

© DeLorme

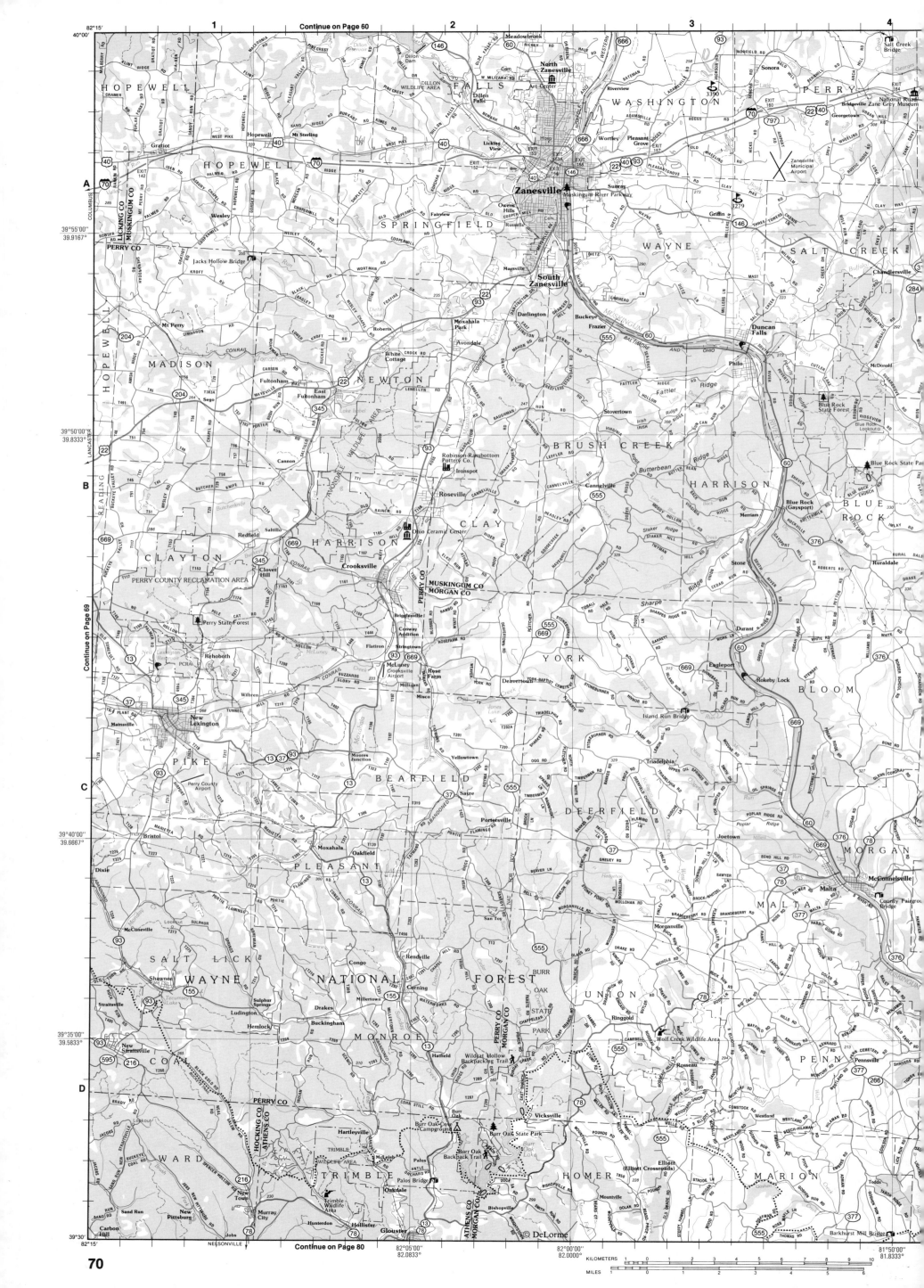

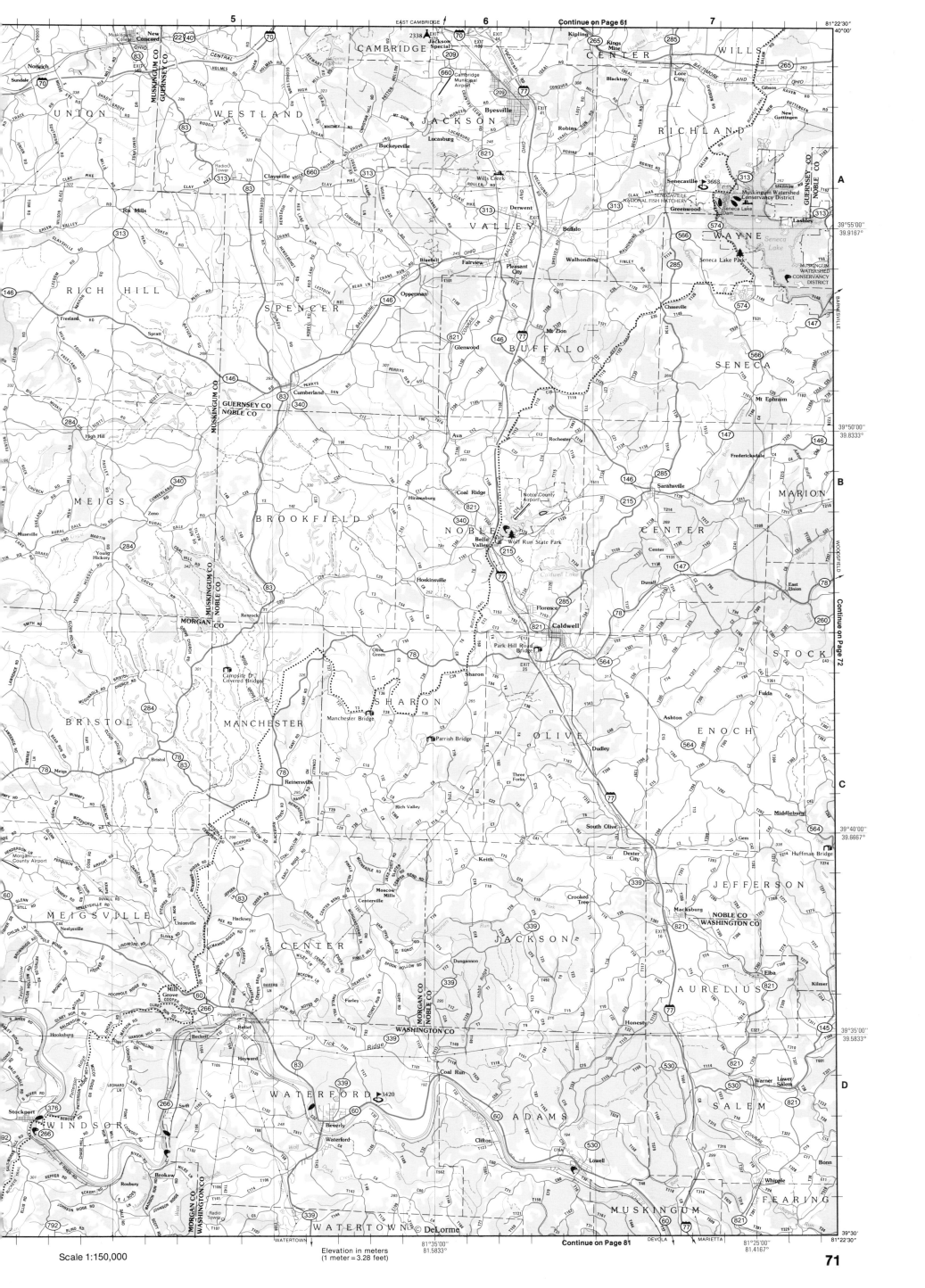

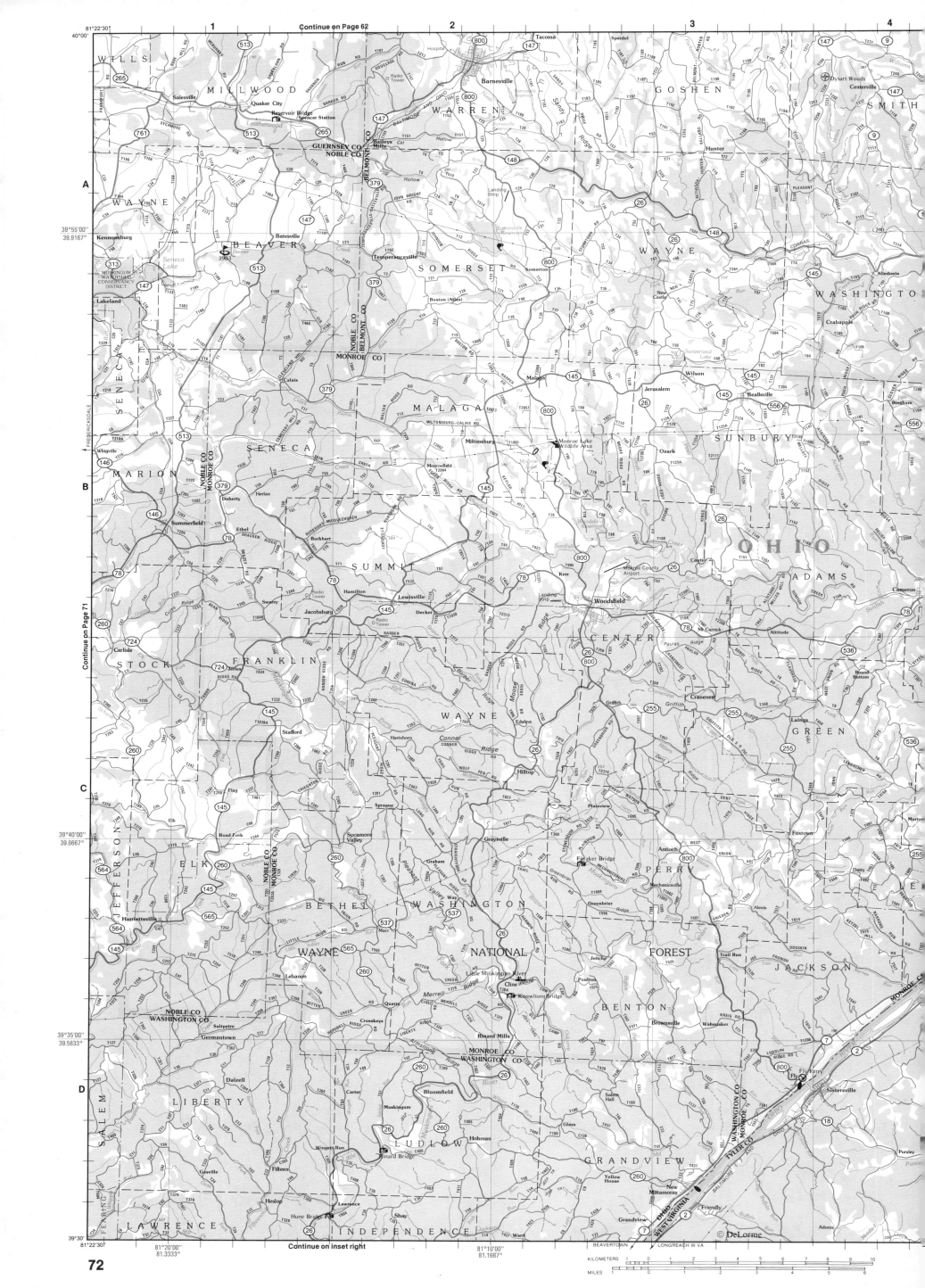

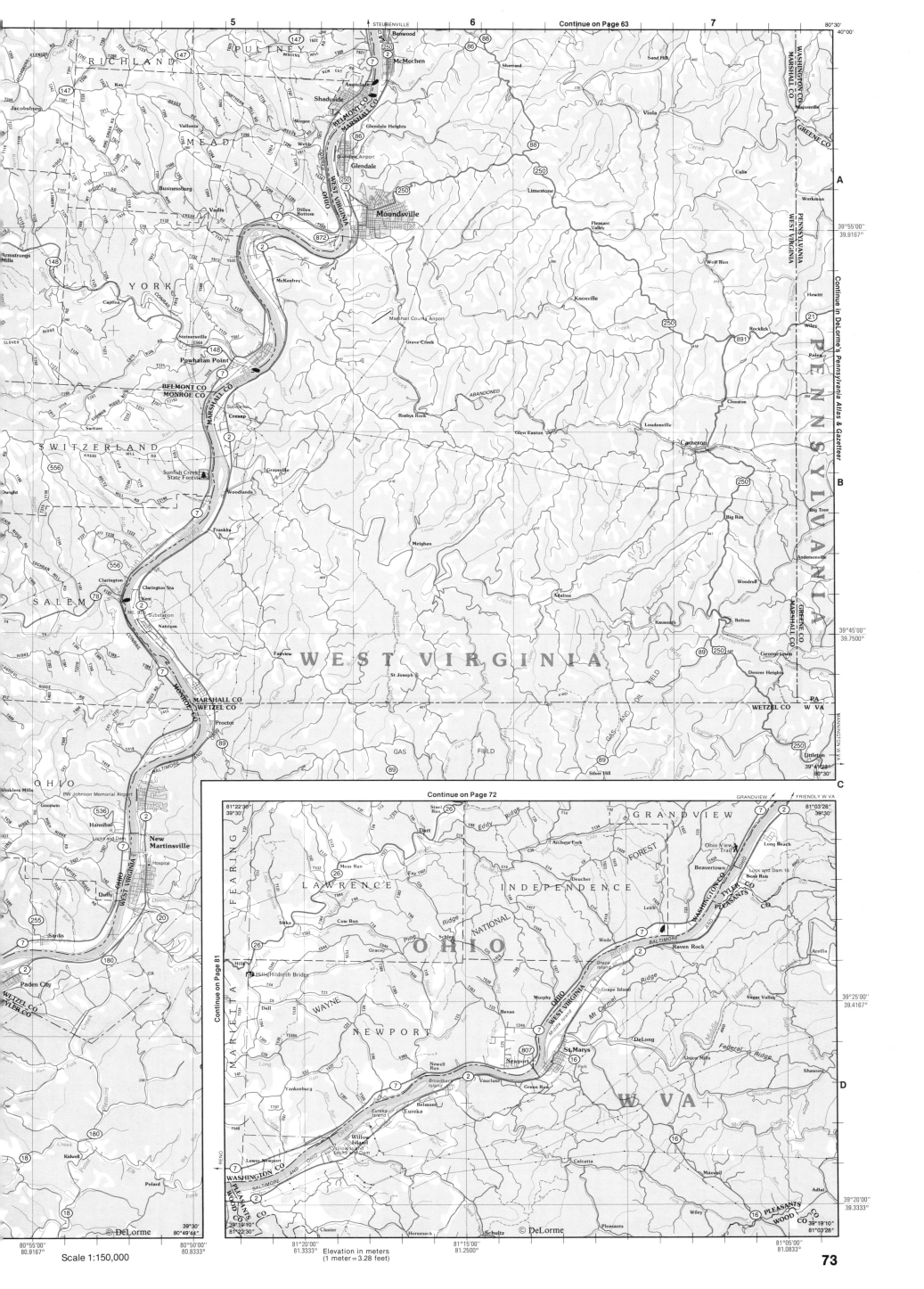

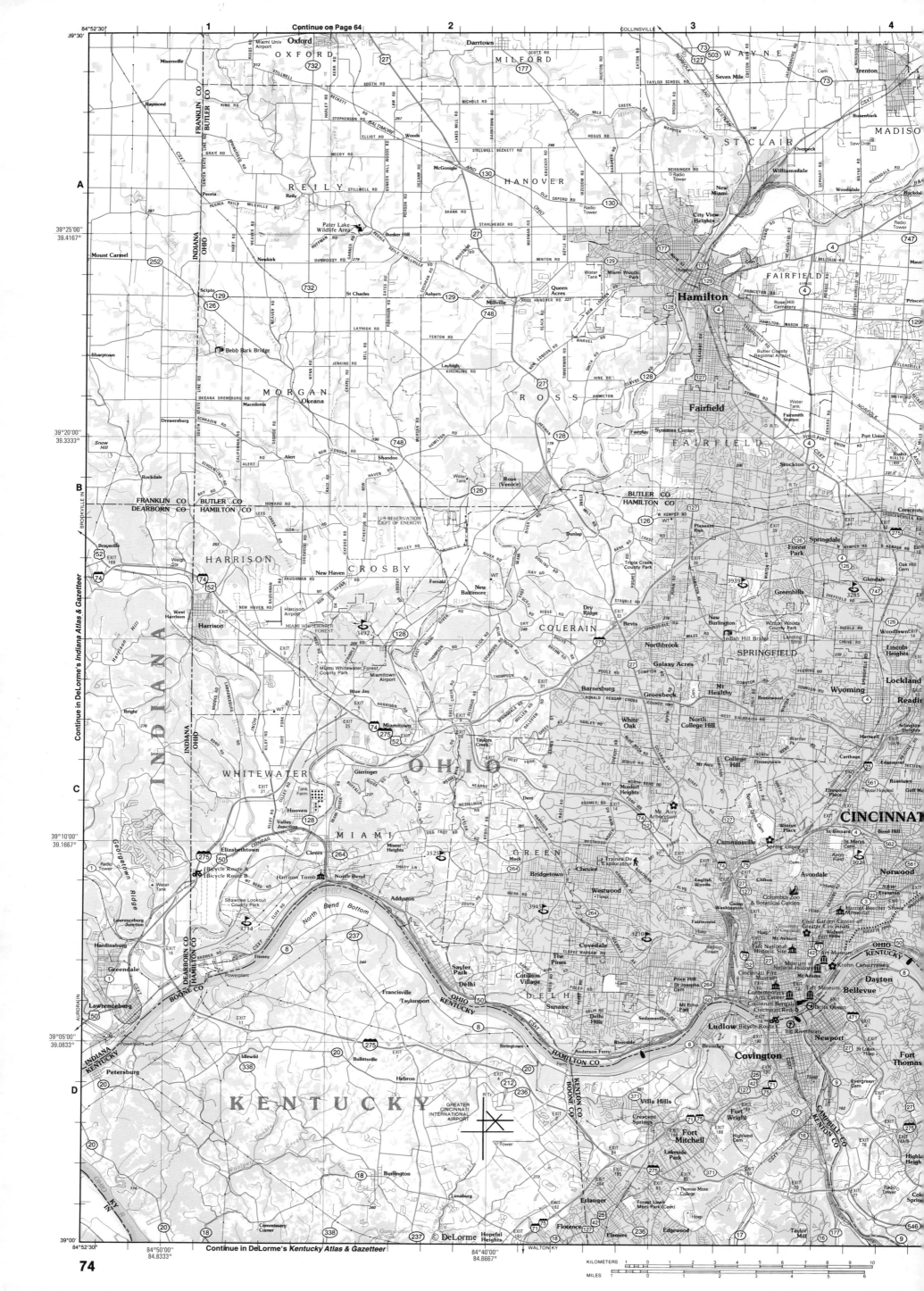

Continue in DeLorme's Indiana Atlas & Gazetteer

Continue in DeLorme's Kentucky Atlas & Gazetteer

© DeLorme

KILOMETERS
MILES

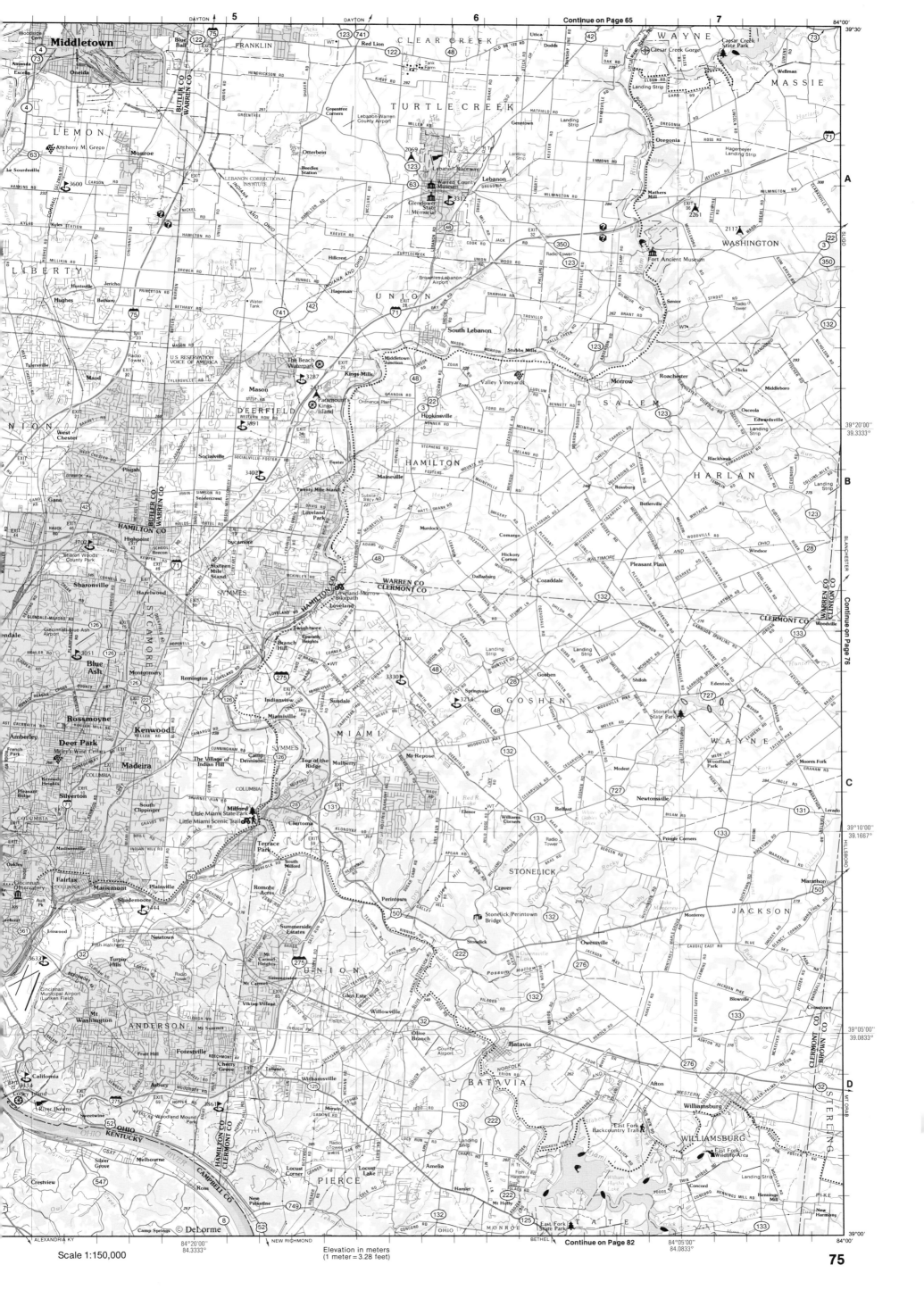

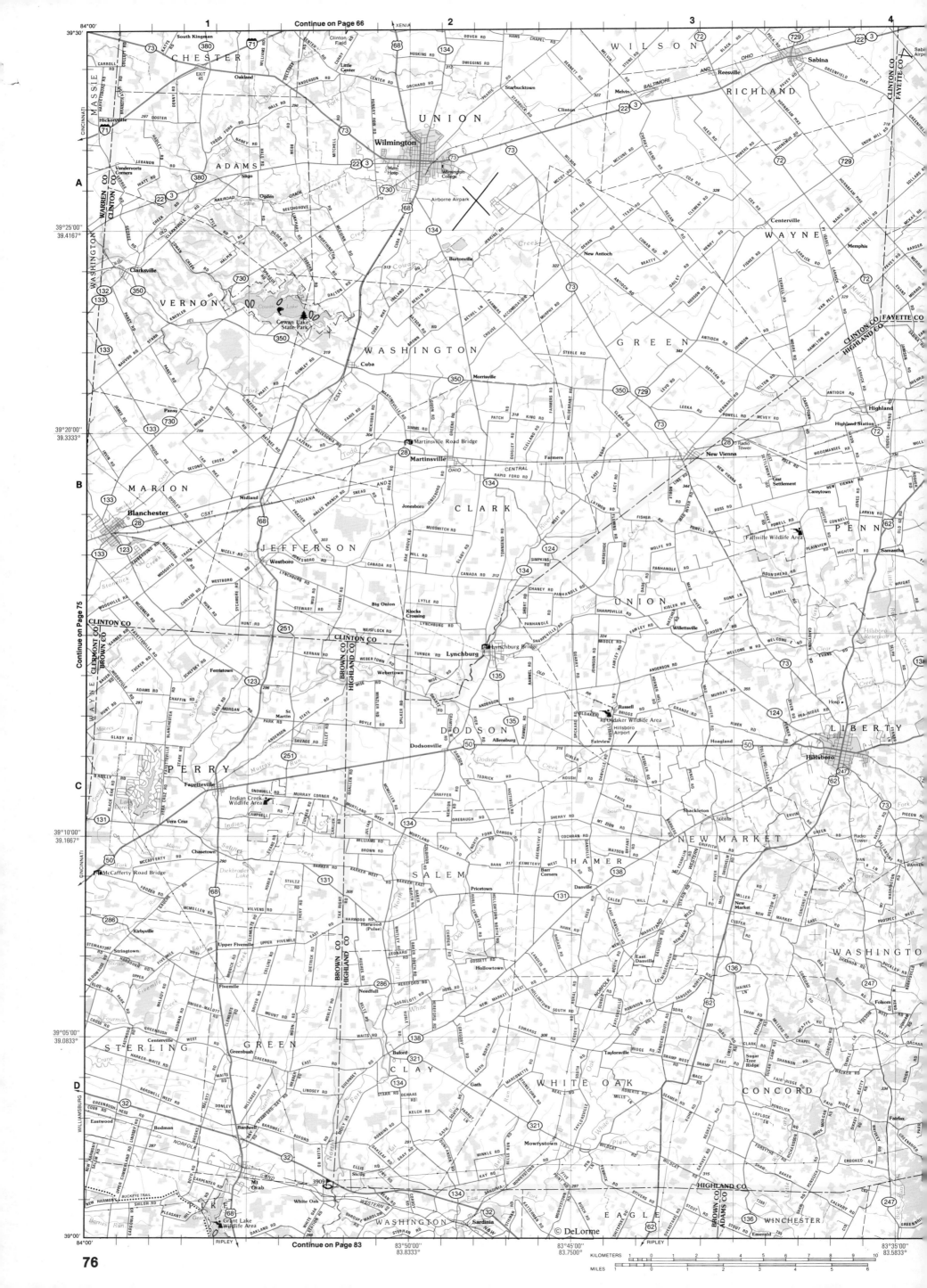

Continue on Page 67

Continue on Page 78

Continue on Page 84

Scale 1:150,000

Elevation in meters
(1 meter = 3.28 feet)

© DeLorme

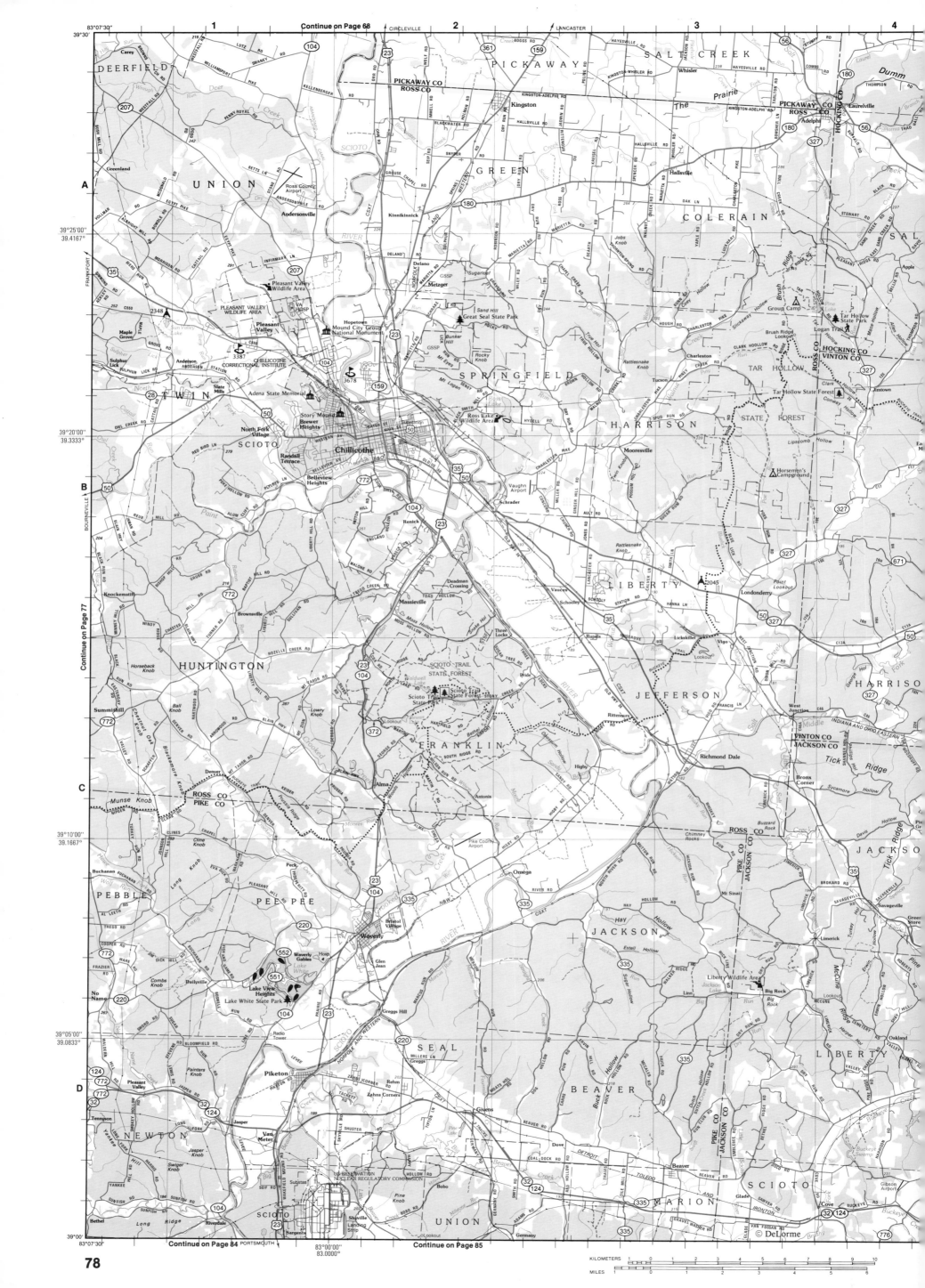

Continue on Page 68

Continue on Page 77

Continue on Page 84

Continue on Page 85

© DeLorme

Continue on Page 80

Continue on Page 86

Scale 1:150,000

Elevation in meters
(1 meter = 3.28 feet)

© DeLorme

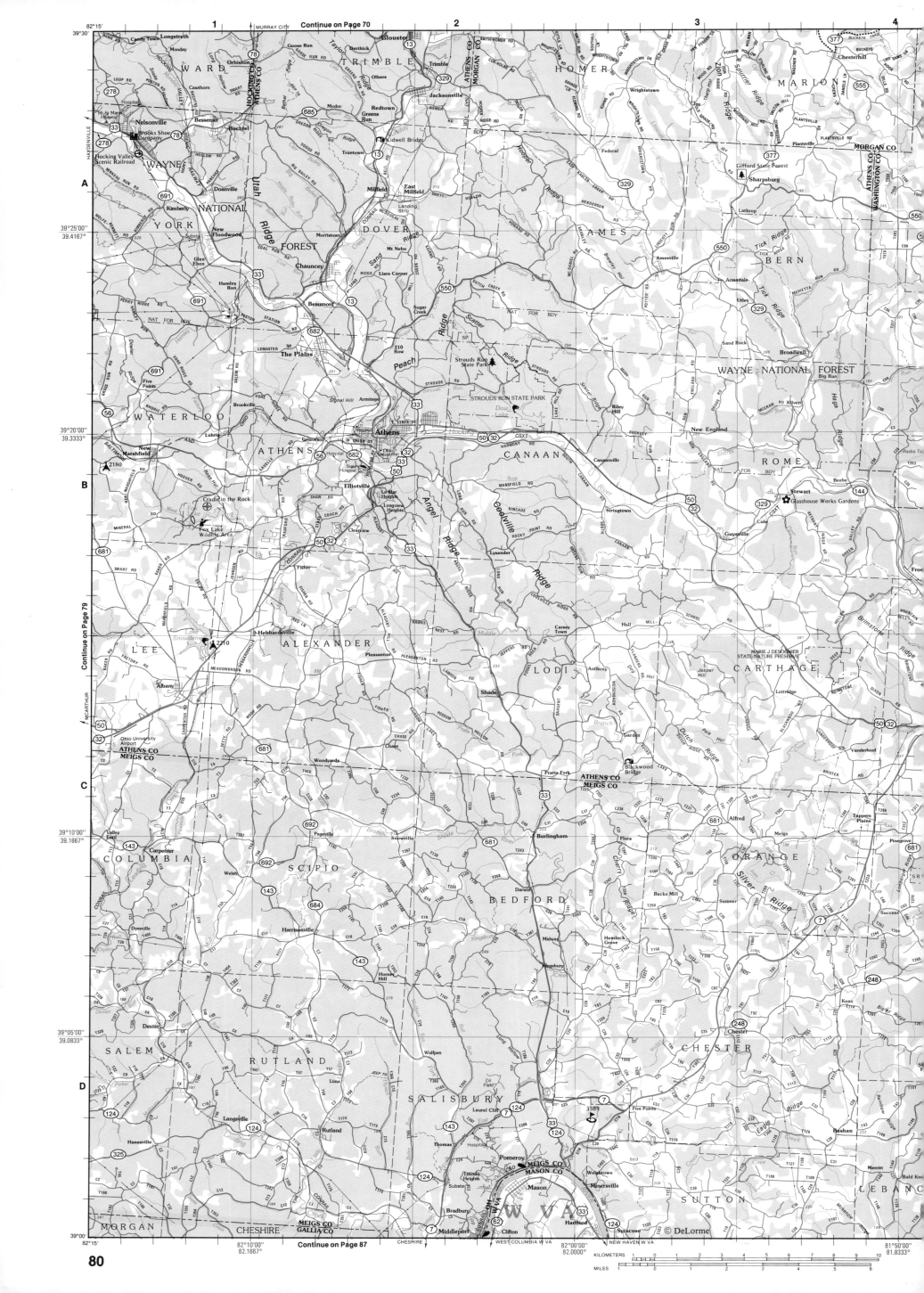

Continue on Page 79

© DeLorme

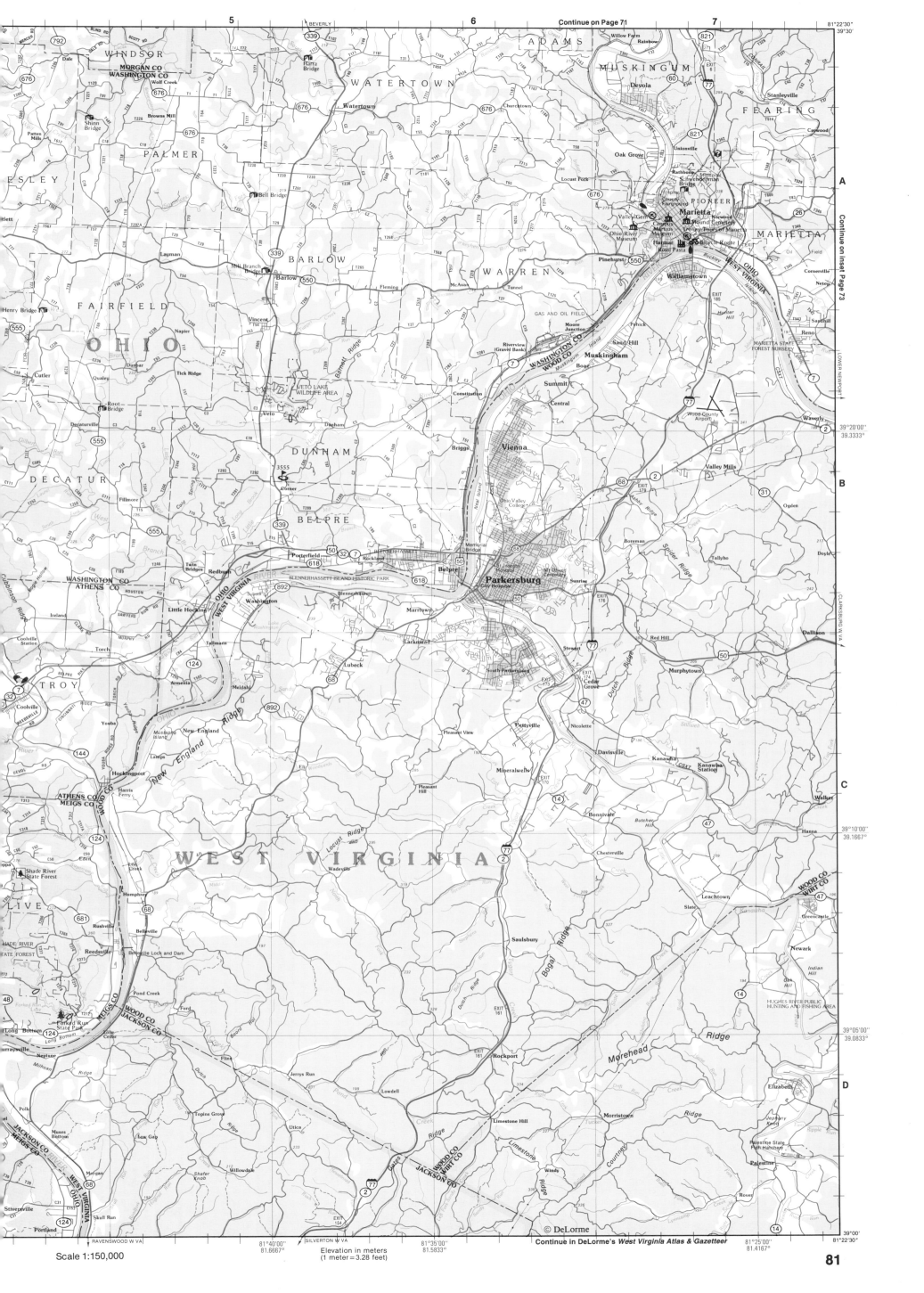

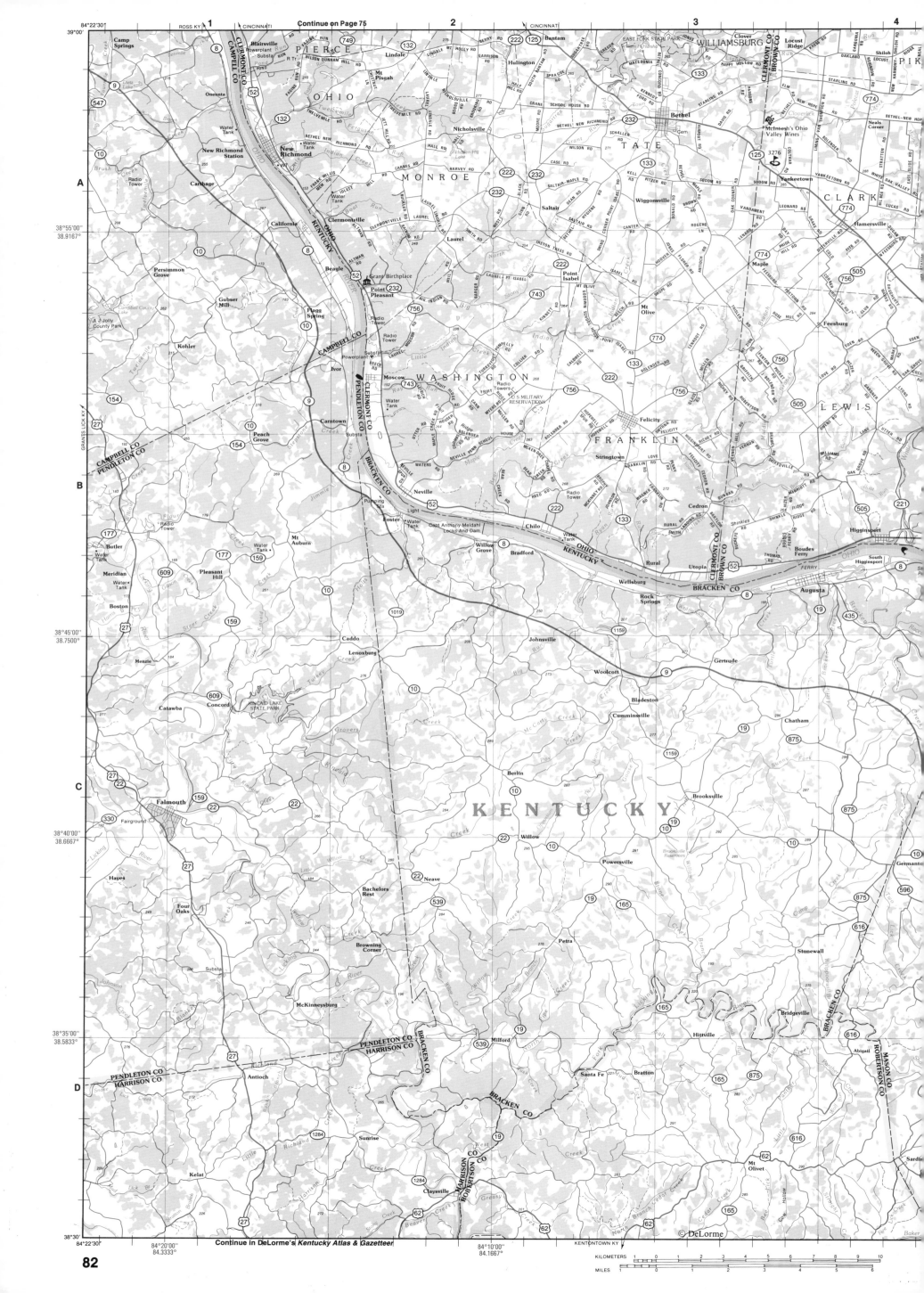

Continue in DeLorme's *Kentucky Atlas & Gazetteer*

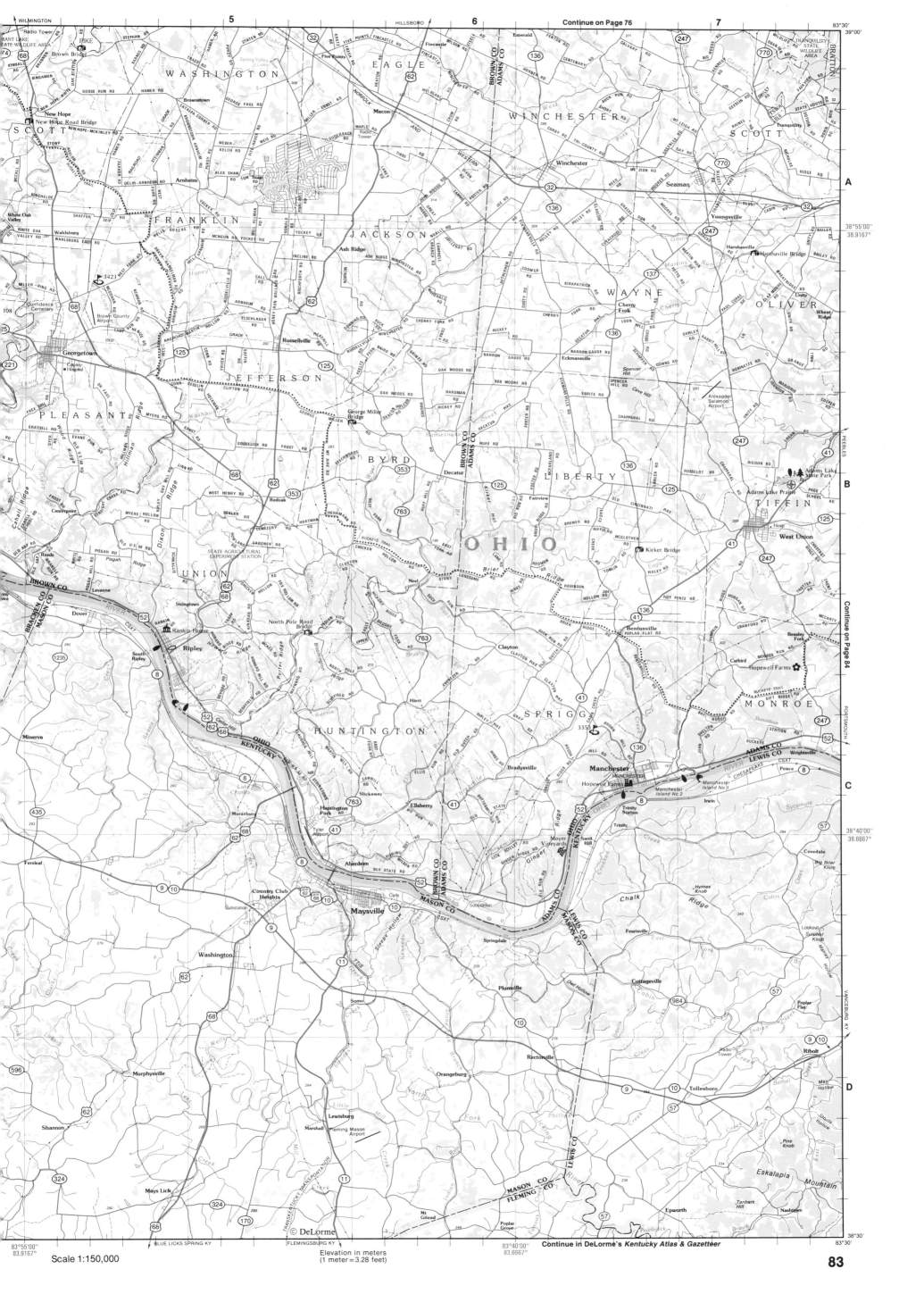

Scale 1:150,000

Elevation in meters
(1 meter = 3.28 feet)

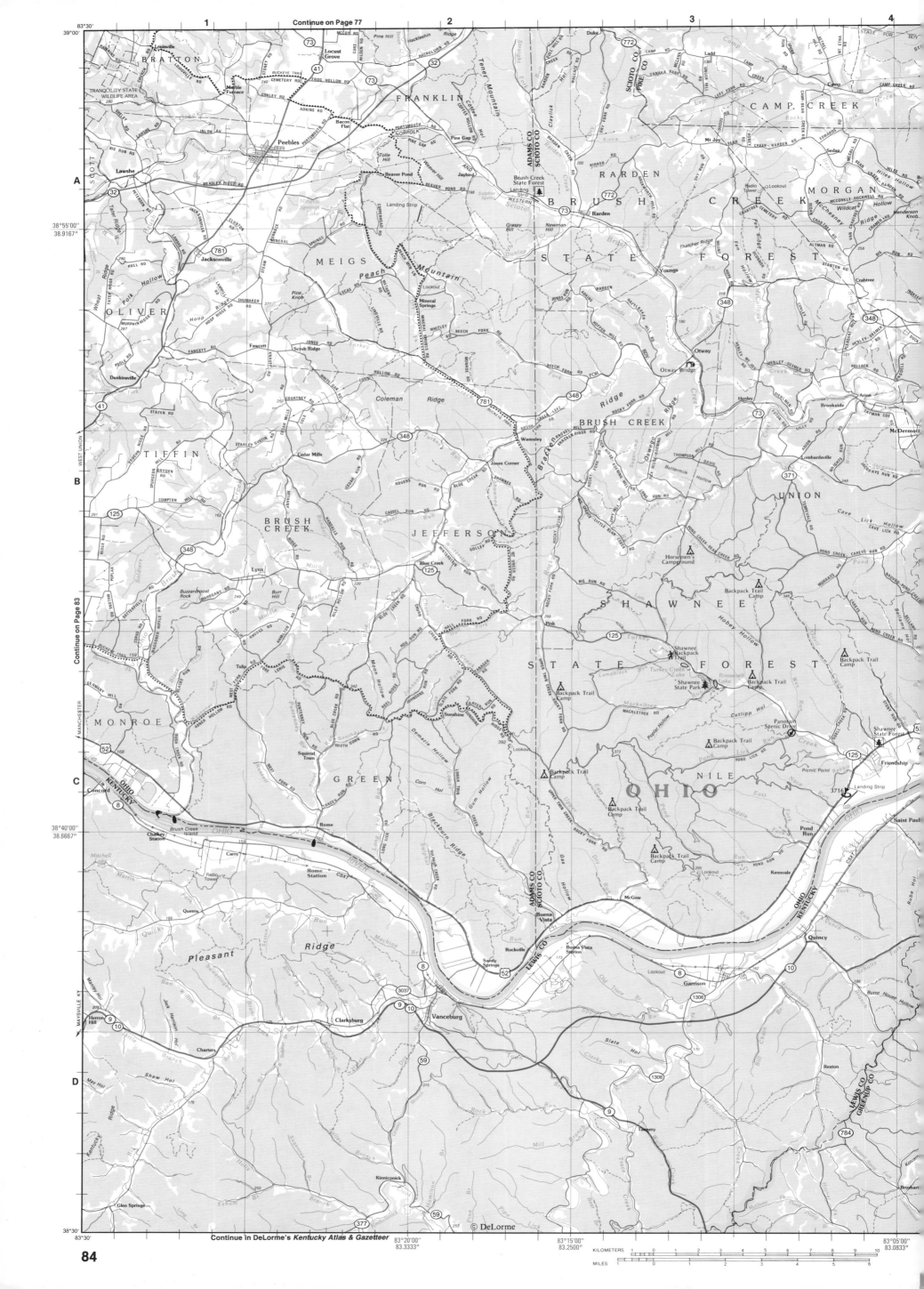

Continue on Page 83

Continue in DeLorme's *Kentucky Atlas & Gazetteer*

© DeLorme

Scale 1:150,000

Elevation in meters
(1 meter = 3.28 feet)

© DeLorme

ARGILLITE KY

82°55'00"
82.9167°

82°37'30"
38°30'

38°35'00"
38.5833°

38°40'00"
38.6667°

38°50'00"
38.8333°

38°55'00"
38.9167°

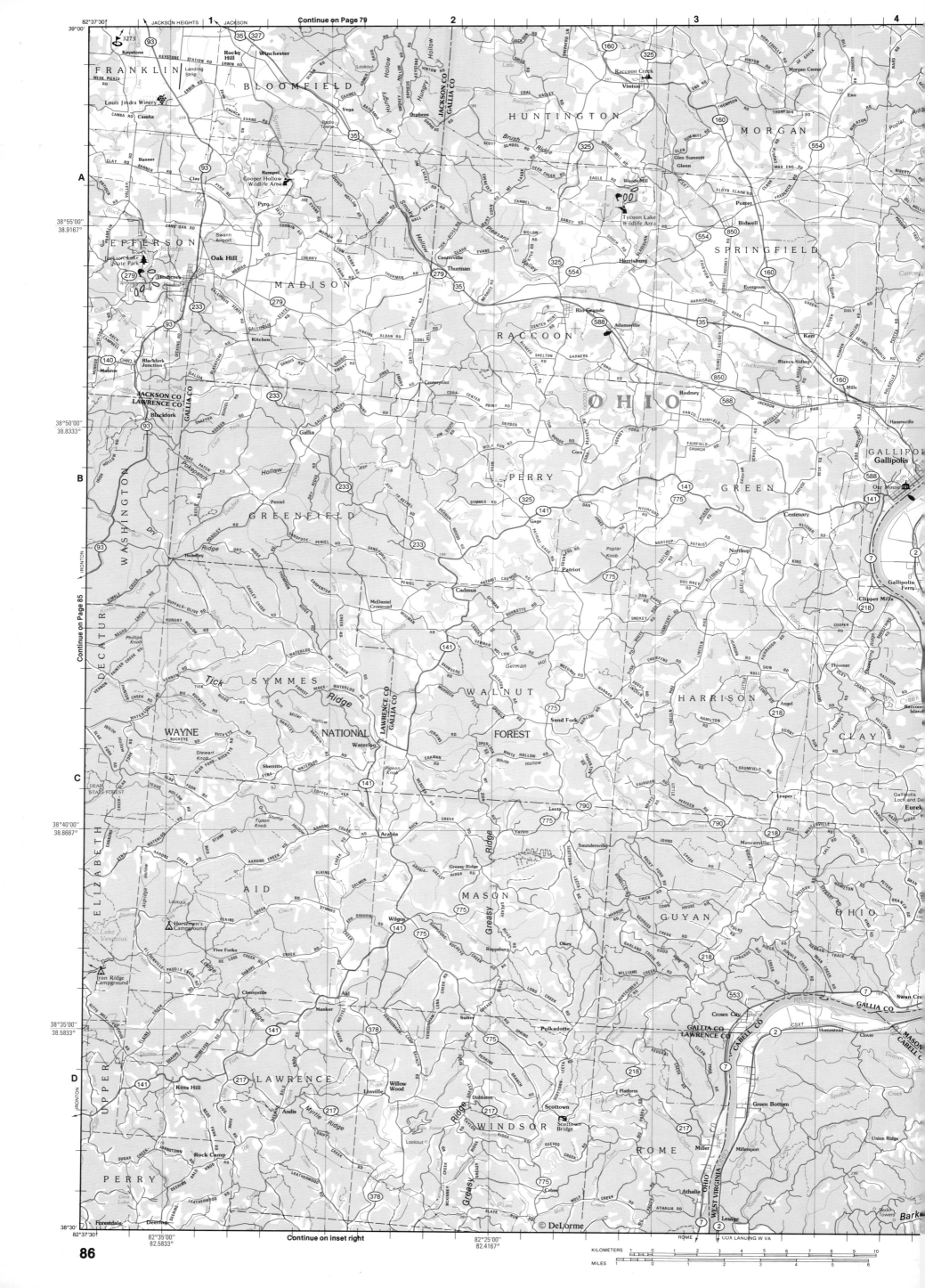

82°37'30"
39°00'

FRANKLIN

BLOOMFIELD

HUNTINGTON

MORGAN

Louis Jindra Winery

Rempel
Cooper Hollow
Wildlife Area

Tycoon Lake
Wildlife Area

A

38°55'00"
38.9167°

JEFFERSON

Jackson Lake
State Park

Oak Hill

MADISON

SPRINGFIELD

Rio Grande
Adamsville

RACCOON

OHIO

38°50'00"
38.8333°

JACKSON CO
LAWRENCE CO
GALLIA CO

Blackfork

Gallia

PERRY

GREEN

Gallipolis

B

Continue on Page 85

WASHINGTON

DECATUR

GREENFIELD

Peniel

Hoadley

Patriot

Cadmus

McDaniel
Crossroad

WALNUT

HARRISON

CLAY

C

Tick

SYMMES

Ridge

WAYNE

NATIONAL

FOREST

Waterloo

Sherritts

Arabia

Lecta

Yarico

Saundersville

Mercerville

Leaper

Eureka

38°40'00"
38.6667°

ELIZABETH

Lake
Vesuvius

AID

Horsemen's
Campground

MASON

GUYAN

OHIO

Iron Ridge
Campground

Cherryville

Five Forks

Manker

Suiter

Rappsburg

Okey

Polkadotte

Crown City

Swan Cre

GALLIA CO

38°35'00"
38.5833°

IRONTON

UPPER

LAWRENCE

Kitts Hill

Linville

Willow
Wood

Andis

Dobbston

Scottown

WINDSOR

Scottown
Bridge

Platform

Green Bottom

GALLIA CO
LAWRENCE CO

MASON
CABELL C

D

PERRY

Johnstown

Rock Camp

ROME

Miller

Millersport

Union Ridge

Cona
Lake

Forestdale

Deering

Athalia

WEST VIRGINIA

OHIO

Lesage

Bark

38°30'
82°37'30"

82°35'00"
82.5833°

© DeLorme

Continue on inset right

82°25'00"
82.4167°

ROME

COX LANDING W VA

KILOMETERS

MILES

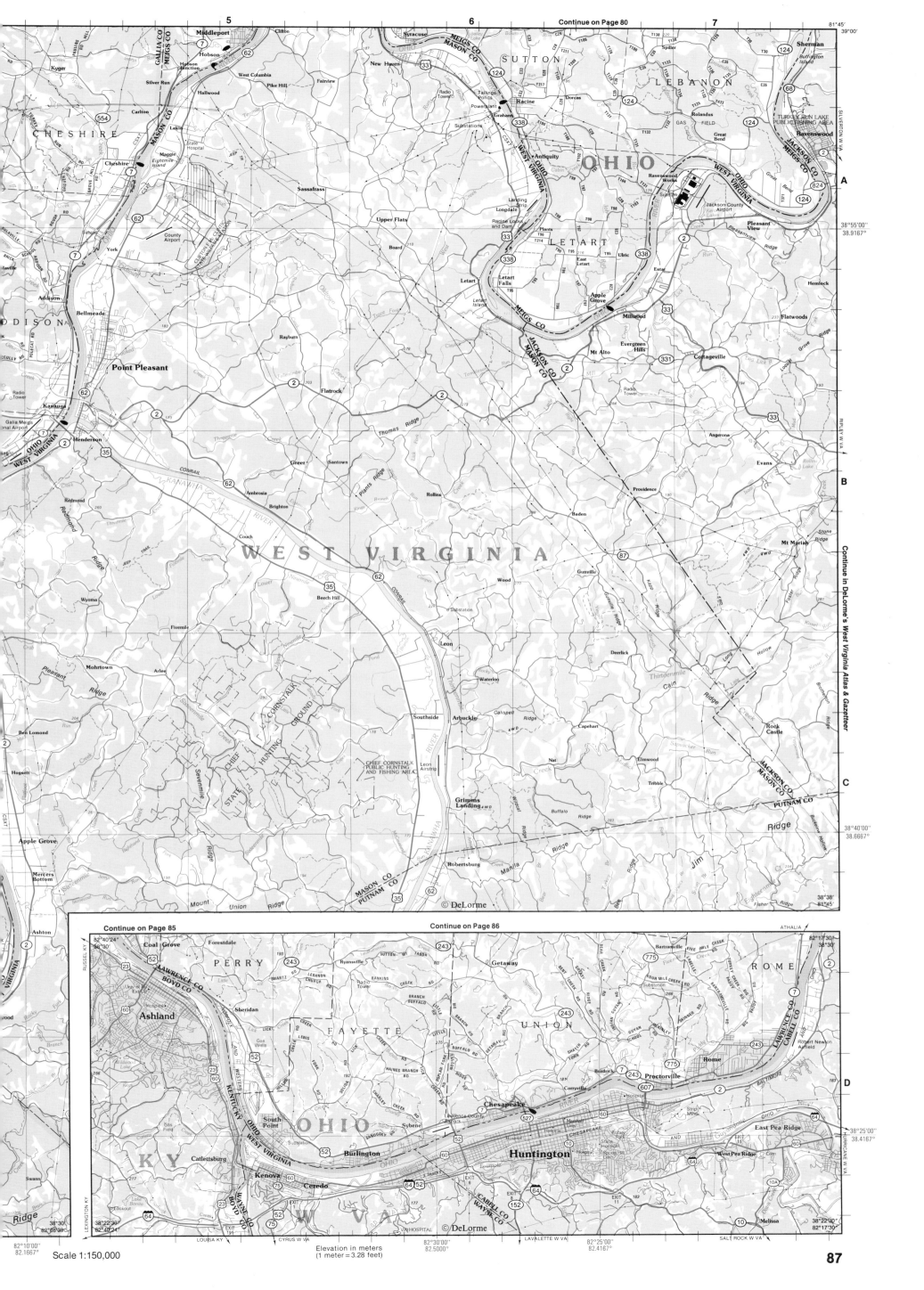

OHIO

WEST VIRGINIA

LEBANON

SUTTON

LETART

CHESHIRE

MEIGS CO
GALLIA CO
MASON CO

JACKSON CO
MEIGS CO

Middleport

Point Pleasant

MASON CO
JACKSON CO

MASON CO
PUTNAM CO

JACKSON CO
MASON CO

PUTNAM CO

Continue in DeLorme's *West Virginia Atlas & Gazetteer*

Continue on Page 85   Continue on Page 86

PERRY

FAYETTE

UNION

ROME

LAWRENCE CO
BOYD CO

Ashland

South Point

KY

OHIO

Huntington

Rome

Proctorville

Chesapeake

LAWRENCE CO
CABELL CO

CABELL CO
WAYNE CO

W VA

© DeLorme

Scale 1:150,000

Elevation in meters
(1 meter = 3.28 feet)

© DeLorme

87

⛳ Golf Courses

This Atlas locates almost 300 public golf courses. To find them, look on the appropriate map for the golf symbol and corresponding four-digit number.